South Asia:
A Short History
of the Subcontinent

WORKS BY MILTON W. MEYER

•

A Diplomatic History of the Philippine Republic
Asia: An Introductory Bibliography
Southeast Asia: A Brief History
Japan: A Concise History
India–Pakistan and the Border Lands
A History of the Far East
China: An Introductory History
South Asia: A Short History of the Subcontinent

To Fred and Dick

South Asia:
A Short History
of the Subcontinent

MILTON W. MEYER
Department of History,
California State University, Los Angeles

Second Edition

1976

LITTLEFIELD, ADAMS & CO.
TOTOWA, NEW JERSEY

Copyright © 1968, 1976

BY LITTLEFIELD ADAMS & CO.

First Edition, 1968

Second Edition, 1976

All rights reserved. No part of this book may be reproduced in any form without permission in writing from the publisher except by a reviewer who wishes to quote brief passages in connection with a review written for inclusion in a magazine, newspaper or broadcast.

Library of Congress Cataloging in Publication Data
Meyer, Milton Walter
  South Asia: A Short History of the Subcontinent

  (A Littlefield, Adams Quality Paperback No. 34)
  First ed. published in 1968 under title: *India-Pakistan and the Border Lands*.
  Bibliography: p.
  1. South Asia—History.
  [DS335.M39 1976] 954   75-28067
  ISBN 0-8226-0034-X

Printed in the United States of America

Contents

1. Introducing South Asia 1
   Setting 1
   India's Land and People 7
   Border Lands 16

2. Ancient India 25
   Dawn of History 25
   Religious Systems 32
   Early Empires 39

3. Hindu India 51
   Political Division 51
   Kingdoms North and South 59
   Traditional India 68

4. Muslim India 77
   Islam Introduced 77
   Turks 81
   Moguls 88

5. India and the West 105
   Early Europeans 105
   East India Company 115

6. Indian Nationalism and the British Crown 129
   Setting 129
   Incipient Nationalism (1858–1921) 140
   Militant Nationalism (1921–1941) 148
   Divided Nationalism (1941–1947) 160

7. Independent India 169
   Politics 169
   Economics and Society 183
   Foreign Affairs 195

8. Border Lands 209
    Pakistan and Bangladesh 209
    Sri Lanka 225
    Afghanistan 231
    Himalayan States 234

    Bibliography 247

    Index 257

Maps

South Asia: Physical Features viii
South Asia: Political Division 22
Ancient India 24
Hindu India 50
Muslim India 76
India and the West 104
Pakistan 240
Bangladesh 241
Sri Lanka 242
Afghanistan 243
Nepal 244
Bhutan 245

Tables

Countries of South Asia: Political Divisions 21
Growth of Indian Political Rights, 1861–1945 167
Republic of India
  I. Political Division, 1947–1956 207
  II. States Created Since 1956 208
South Asia: Political Leaders 255

South Asia:
A Short History
of the Subcontinent

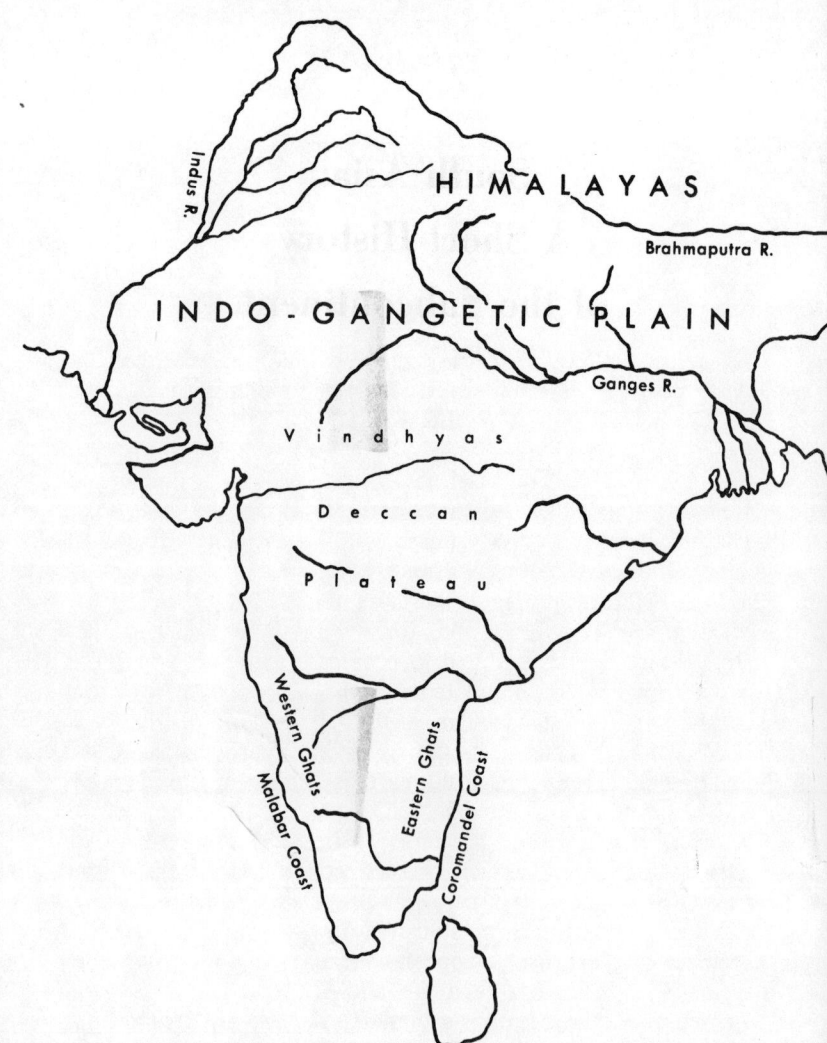

Chapter 1

Introducing South Asia

Setting

The history of South Asia, centered on the Indian subcontinent, is ancient and complex. It is one of the oldest, most continuous civilizations in the world. Long before the advent of the West, India produced a rich variety of religions and philosophies, a multitude of races and languages, and a succession of culturally brilliant empires. On these indigenous structures, western rule subsequently was imposed, which gave to India and its border lands additional historical variety. Among Asian countries, India was the first to receive concentrated European attention, for western advance in eastern kingdoms was closely related to occidental expansion in India. Europeans called the inhabitants of the subcontinent Indios or Indians, and the newcomers avidly sought Indian products. Neighboring kingdoms to the west had early used Indian items. King Solomon utilized various goods of India, while Greeks and Romans enjoyed Indian spices, cotton, and jewels. In a later era, but desiring similar items, Columbus sailed for India to confirm possession of such goods, but he discovered America instead.

Indian culture requires study in its own right because it is unique and because it appears puzzling to outsiders. Many aspects of traditional Indian life and geography seem strange to foreign observers. India's climate, its topography, and its involved customs require physical or psychological reorientation for their better appreciation and understanding. Many native religious practices are fundamentally different from those usually followed in the West. Traditional Indian values included an emphasis on a vegetarian diet and the observance of numerous fasts among certain high and ritualistically pure groups. Society, fashioned from prehistoric eras, consisted of a hierarchy of four major classes, or castes, and thousands of subcastes. In affairs of state, the theory of nonviolence was one main strand of political thought, though there were others that stressed force and the importance of force in politics. Among philosophic concepts, an idealistic interpretation of the nature of the world was advanced. While western ideas made limited inroads on some of these traditions, much of the old way of life has persisted into modern times.

In addition to inherent historic differences, any study of the Indian subcontinent must include considerations of its great geographic size, its growing population, and the important roles that its half-dozen countries play in power politics. The subcontinent includes not only India but also the border states of Pakistan, Bangladesh (initially East Pakistan), Sri Lanka (formerly Ceylon), Afghanistan, and the Himalayan kingdoms of Nepal, Bhutan, and formerly Sikkim. Within these boundaries, South Asia covers almost 2 million square miles of territory, or two-thirds that of the United States. India spreads over 1.2 million square miles, while Pakistan ranges a fourth of that. Demographically, the population of the subcontinent in the mid-1970's approximated 800 million. As the most populous country in the world next to China, India accounted for some 600 million, while that of the border states collectively neared 200 million. In the densely populated country of India alone lived one-sixth of the world's total estimated population, who occupied less than 3 per cent of the world's land area, excluding polar regions. Politically, the leaders of these populous lands of South Asia, such as the prime ministers of India and the presidents of Pakistan, commanded attention in the world's press. Yet, each political entity among the half-dozen states within the Indian subcontinent faced its own basic domestic problems. Each has had to adjust to intra-area issues and to impinging foreign interests as well. The proximity of a more populous, expansive, and revolutionary Communist Chinese regime to the north compounded policy considerations of all South Asian states.

India derives its name from the Indus river, which rises in Tibet and courses its way to the sea through arid Pakistan.

Ancient Indians called the river Sindhu, but the neighboring Persians, who had difficulty in pronouncing the initial *s*, termed it Hindu. From Persia, the word passed to Greece, where the whole of India became known by the name of its western river. Indians themselves designated their country by several appellations, though a commonly used name came to be known as the land of Bharata, a semi-legendary king and tribe in north India.

Both factual and fanciful sources abound on Indian history. Dating to approximately 2000 B.C. and written mainly in Sanskrit, a native literary tradition reconstructed some aspects of ancient life through the media of old hymns of worship and sacrifice, grand epics, royal genealogies, secular poetry, and prose works. Peoples of ancient India revealed an awareness of history, which they expressed in cyclic fashion, and in which they counseled man's resignation to nature's grand but inevitable patterns of rise and decline. Archeological finds, dating chiefly to the 1920's, uncover more facets of ancient times, particularly through excavations in the Indus river valley of old cities with advanced civilizations.

Complementing indigenous written and archeological records are early foreign accounts, either in the original or in copied contexts, which exist from the period when Alexander the Great invaded north India in the late fourth century B.C. The earliest precise date in Indian history was fixed by his invasion in 326 B.C. Chinese Buddhist pilgrims traveling to India between the fourth and eighth centuries AD. left impressions of contemporaneous sacred and secular events in the subcontinent. About the beginning of the Christian era, Hindus themselves commenced to reinterpret and to rewrite earlier works, but they added legends and a higher sense of aesthetics to previous literature. This trend continued until the Muslim advent in India around A.D. 1000.

With the imposition of foreign Islamic rule in India, Muslim historians emphasized the inviolability of the Koran, an unquestioned theological interpretation of history, and the finite, linear sequence of human events to which God gave meaning. Most historians of Islam were under royal patronage, or aspired to it. They portrayed their rulers as symbols of divine purpose, and they developed official histories to an extensive degree. These early and generalized histories of the

Muslim community were later supplemented by specialized and regional works of Muslims in India or in its peripheral areas. Later, European travelers added their accounts as well, for Marco Polo and other western writers and peregrinators wrote about India. Like the earlier Muslims, the Portuguese, as official chroniclers of the first national European interest in India, were theologically inspired, but their interpretation gave way to more politically motivated and self-centered accounts after the advent of other European national and secular interests. By the twentieth century, historical sources on India had become quite prolific, more complex, and decidedly disputatious. More westerners wrote with different interpretations, and more Indians composed with varying views. Schools of writers with particular points of emphasis arose, such as the native nationalists, the foreign missionaries, and the resident civil servants, to mention only a few groups. Interpretations of modern Indian history became controversial, particularly in the assessment of British colonial rule, initially advanced through the English East India Company and after 1858 through the British crown.

Controversies relating to the British colonial period constitute a problem in analyzing Indian history for that interim. English historians, having executed the most numerous and the most voluminous writing on India, contributed much to scholarship, but they tended to transfer to the record their biases relating to the "white man's burden." Generally apologists for the British rule, they stressed British rulers and policies, underemphasizing native institutions and behavior. Dependent in the main on official records, they wrote on subjects in which documentation was plentiful. On the other hand, Indian historians tended to glorify the alleged virtues of India's past civilization and to deprecate the British interregnum. With emotional national pride, Indians professed to see in ancient India an earthly paradise with democratic institutions, and they attacked the British administration, which lacked, they alleged, such attributes.

Besides debates over British rule, other problems (some not necessarily unique to India) exist in the study of the subcontinent. Periodization of recorded Indian history, covering some 4,000 years, is difficult. How is it to be "chopped up" for easier comprehension and for manageable form? An approach, similar to one used in survey courses that deal with western history, is to treat India in the light of the European experience, and to characterize ancient, medieval and modern periods, though the criteria in defining each of the three periods are arguable. An easier alternative, but as debatable, is to discuss broadly the subcontinent in terms of a native tradition before A.D. 1000, then under foreign domination of Islam and the West (1000–1947), and finally the period since independence and partition in 1947.

But, however Indian history is periodized, other problems remain. What levels of history are to be studied within the respective periods? What aspects of history are to be stressed, or even to be given appropriate study? Though some native records exist relating to politics, culture, economics, and society, much of Indian history dwells in the realm of metaphysics, philosophy, and intellectual thought. The sheer weight and presence of these types of documents favor an emphasis of these particular facets of Indian life. But, in analyzing these records, there exists a further problem in the levels of interpretations involved—whether to stress "high-brow" theological or "low-brow" popular attitudes, whether to emphasize the roles of the leaders or the lives of those led, for, while the latter group wrote nothing, they consituted probably 95 per cent of the populace. Another dilemma, more recent in origin, in the study of the Indian subcontinent, exists in assaying the varying effects of modernization on traditional life—what was superficial in nature, and what was more basic, revolutionary, and continuing in nature. How fundamentally were urban and village life and daily routines affected by western concepts and inroads? Was caste breaking down? Was religion becoming more secular in character? In South Asia much appeared to change, but much seemed unchanging.

In their historic relations with India, Americans adhered to certain images. These concepts, such as they were, were quite faint and less clear than stereotypes of the Chinese and the Japanese, since Indians were never in the United States in so great numbers as other Asians. Semantic confusion, moreover, existed in distinguishing between "Indian" Indians and American Indians. Nonetheless, some views persisted. American minds conjured up fabulous maharajahs with their ornate jewel collections and their ostentatious tiger hunts; the fasting, half-naked religionists with their epics, swamis, and vedas; and benighted heathen with evil and prolific sexual practices in life and religion. Symptomatic of the last interpretation was the book *Mother India*, published in 1927 by Katherine Mayo, a Boston spinster, who spent six months in India. Characterized by Gandhi as a "drainpipe study," the book was filled with biases, sweeping generalizations on lurid practices, and revealing photos. The volume went through twenty-seven editions in the United States, and it sold over 250,000 copies. Some dozen Indians returned the literary compliment on the more unsavory aspects of American life, but their products were hardly read. To conclude her part of the running dialogue, Miss Mayo reaffirmed her views in a book simply called *Volume II*.

While certain contradictory but popular American stereotypes of Indian life were dated, American professional interest in India was more recent. Prior to independence and to partition, there was little American study of India, which was a British colony. Few professors in American universities taught Indian history, and scarcely any Americans were trained in the Indian aspect of their disciplines. A few consular officers lived in India, and some traders and missionaries propounded their particular views. During the Second World War, many soldiers were stationed in India, but since they were there on an involuntary and temporary basis, sheer numbers and presence did not necessarily engender mutual understanding. Also stirring up the colonial waters, President Franklin D. Roosevelt made strong wartime democratic pronouncements relating to Asian politics and to possible Indian independence. The statements pleased Indians, but nettled Prime Minister Winston Churchill, then presiding over the British Empire.

After the Second World War, with independent countries established on the subcontinent, American interest grew. In the United States, the University of Pennsylvania established the first full-scale area program relating to the Indian subcontinent. Soon other academic centers, including the University of Chicago, the University of Wisconsin, and the University of California, also developed Indic studies. In 1947, diplomatic relations were established with independent India and Pakistan and in the following year with Ceylon, when that island colony achieved independence. Diplomatic relations had existed with Afghanistan since 1936. The American ambassador to India, resident in New Delhi, was also accredited as ambassador to Nepal until a separate embassy was established in 1959 in the capital of Katmandu. Bhutan and Sikkim, as Indian protectorates, did not merit separate diplomatic representation. Supplementing diplomatic missions and exchanges of official visits were the works of numerous popular authors, who wrote and traveled widely in both Orient and Occident. South Asian writers, including authoresses Mrs. Ruth Prawer Jhabvala and Santha Rama Rau, interpreted to the American public Indian life as they saw it from their particular viewpoints, and they added their private voices to public statements from regional or national Indian political leaders.

The newly established communication lines between South Asian countries and the West gave rise to both tension and accommodation. Among the more populous inhabitants of the subcontinent, Indians and Pakistanis attacked what they considered United States support of colonial rule in Asia and on other continents. They criticized domestic American attitudes condoning race discrimination. They were disappointed in United States unwillingness to supply as much capital as they desired for their industrial expansion and their over-all plans for economic development. They decried American reluctance to grant aid or extend credit to their state-supported projects. Some of them did not view the cold war between communism and democracies in the same light as Americans, and on this issue ideological differences in international relations resulted. Each country had its own issues with the United States, but some controversies spilled over national boundaries to affect neighbors. Clear-cut demarcations of what constituted domestic or foreign problems, and their possible resolutions, sometimes proved difficult for peoples of South Asia to unravel.

India's Land and People

Indian geography is complex and varied. It boasts of high mountains and flat plains, of snow and heat, of deserts and jungles. India extends north and south some 2,000 miles (a distance equivalent to that between Norway and Africa), and 1,000 miles east to west (a distance between England and Russia). Because of the long peninsula that juts out into the

Indian Ocean, the subcontinent all the easier could transmit to and receive ideas from neighboring lands. India exported Hinduism and Buddhism via sea channels to Southeast Asia, and it imported, also via ocean lanes, western concepts and colonizers from Europe. Though Himalayan mountains over 5 miles high helped to block northern land approaches, the ranges were not insurmountable. Over the millennia, from the north and the northwest, came waves of invasions that infused new peoples, ideas, and customs into India. In turn, Indian art and culture, again notably Buddhism, traveled cross mountain passes to China, and from there to Korea and Japan. Never completely isolated, the Indian subcontinent influenced and was influenced by neighbors east and west.

The simplest way to divide Indian geographic regions is into north and south, with the central east-west Vindhya range, some 3,000 to 5,000 feet high, as a geographic and cultural dividing line. India north of the Vindhyas consists of a mountain arc and river plains. The mountains commence in the west at the Persian Gulf, traverse Afghanistan, Kashmir, and the Himalayan border lands, and return to the sea in the east in Burma. Young in geologic time, the ranges give rise to all the major rivers that provide rich alluvial soil for the delta lands and riparian valleys. Of these, the most important is collectively known as the Indo-Gangetic plain, 80 to 200 miles in width, with its three main river systems. These three include the Indus, commencing in Tibet and joined by five main tributaries in the Punjab ("Five Rivers") in the northwest. The Ganges with its numerous branches flows through north India, a fertile area, the geographical, historical, and cultural heart of the nation, possessing two-fifths of the total population but only one-sixth of the total area. And lastly, the Brahmaputra in the east also originates in Tibet and twists in a horseshoe curve through Assam to join the Ganges and spill into the Bay of Bengal near Calcutta, the subcontinent's largest city.

South of the Vindhyas is the Deccan ("South") plateau, 1,000 to 2,500 feet high, much of it a rocky, impoverished, marginal area, never a main center of Indian civilization but geologically quite ancient and possibly connected at one time with Australia. The plateau, tilting west to east, has escarpments on both sides—the Western Ghats ("Stairs"), a steep range averaging 3,000 feet, with few passes; and the Eastern Ghats, less steep, averaging 1,000 feet. Bordering both Ghats are coastal plains. To the west is the Malabar coast, the first region reached by the westerners. To the east is the Coromandel or Carnatic coast, center of historic maritime kingdoms that extended into Southeast Asia.

India experiences every known climate except polar. Over all, however, the area is tropical. The months of October through January constitute winter, and they are relatively cool. From February to May, the heat builds up to the rainy season with its monsoons, which fall, if on schedule, from June through September. The monsoons, originally an Arabic word meaning "winds" but used in Asia in popular context as "rains," are the biggest climatic factor on the subcontinent. The most common word for "year" in the Hindi language simply means "rain." The Southwest monsoon originates in the Arabian Sea. It hits the western coast of India and Pakistan, but often dies out over the Deccan plateau. The Southeast monsoon sweeps in from the Sea of Bengal. It proceeds up the Gangetic plain to Delhi, but it loses force along the way. Part of it hits the Assam mountain areas, which "enjoy" an average of 454 inches of rain a year, though 800 inches a year are not uncommon. In one spot, 45 inches of rain, the annual rainfall for New York, fell in two hours. A lesser branch of the Northeast monsoon, which emanates in November and December from China, traverses the Bay of Bengal, where it picks up precipitation, which is dropped on the southeastern Indian coastal regions. Thunder and lightning accompany the monsoons, but these phenomena hold no terrors for Indians, who see life-giving processes in the rains. The uncontrollable vicissitudes of the monsoons help account, some aver, for the spirit of Indian "resignation" in accepting whatever fate comes along.

Indian resources are mainly in the soil and in the climate. Mineral deposits include bauxite, chromite, coal, copper, gold, manganese, mica, salt, and sulfur. Oil reserves are meager, but the northeastern iron belt is thought to be the largest in Asia, excepting the Soviet Union. Much of this is high-grade iron ore, not far from major coal fields, in Bihar province in northeast India. Much potential hydroelectric power exists, and dam building is included in Indian long-range economic plans. Fishing is not practiced widely. The main economic activity is centered, as in much of Asia, in agriculture, though only half of the land is utilized. The other half is marginal, wasteland, or forested. No important cultivable land has been left in reserve. In the cultivated and pastoral areas of India are produced most of the world's oil seeds, as peanuts and sesame, half of the world's rice and cattle, one-fourth of its sugar and flax, and one-fifth of its cotton, a crop ancient to India. Yet, with perennial deficits in production averaging 10 per cent, India must import food.

Agricultural problems abound, and many of them are similar in nature to those in other Asian countries. Too many people live on the land. More specifically and more importantly, too many people exist on too little available cultivated land. Low productivity results, not only from land deficiency but also from the uneconomic ways in which land is utilized. The small size of an average farm, usually between 2 and 7 acres, induces poverty. Fragmented holdings are wasteful, for these preclude the use of machinery. Time and energy are expended plowing various plots; ridges and dikes separating fields impinge on available land. In some areas, because fields cannot be left fallow, soil fertility is early exhausted. Where tenancy exists, 50 per cent or more of the yield is commonly paid for rent, an immutable economic factor which some again say helps to account for an Indian acceptance of fate in this instance in the guise of insatiable landlords. Credit facilities have been notorious. Interest of 100 per cent is not uncommon, and homes and clothing are used as collateral. Later generations try to pay off, but sometimes add to, the debts of their forefathers. Certain social behavioral patterns that favor great expenses on weddings and funerals, on which one year's income might be spent, plunge peasants even farther into debt. Agricultural marketing has hazards. With little means to stockpile food produce, usually rice, the farmers sell their crops during fall harvest months at low prices, which rise in the course of the agricultural cycle until the following harvest. Solutions to manifold agricultural problems seem evasive. Social patterns are difficult to change, sources of new arable land are limited, greater yields per acre might be realized. But with increased food supplies comes the usual corollary of increased population with more mouths to feed.

Population growth, with its resultant pressures on available land and food resources, is a most pressing issue. In the first half of the twentieth century, the increase registered about 54 per cent, or 153 million. In the decade of the 1930's, the rate of growth was predicated as approximately 15 per cent; in the 1940's as 12.3 per cent; in the 1950's as 23 per cent. For a country with low standards of living and with no rapidly expanding industrialization to absorb demographic surpluses, the percentages are ominous. Low standards of living are reflected in several indices. Estimates place the annual average per capita income of Indians as equivalent to $70 a year. Other estimates calculate an average daily wage at the equivalent of six cents a day. It is estimated that the peasant's annual harvest worth of crops is $100, of which $60 is consumed and $40 is sold. From the latter proceeds must be paid not only taxes but also the necessities of life. Marginal diets exist. Daily caloric intake averages 1,700 to 2,000 units, where a minimum of 2,500 is needed. Life expectancy averages thirty-seven years, and into this short period are crammed birth, early marriage, family life, and death. Why these human statistics, so baldly stated, are so adverse is a matter of debate. Some Indian nationalists ascribe them to shortcomings in British rule, which, they allege, discouraged industry, promoted excessive taxation, and neglected essential social services. Other sources find the answer in social and religious traditions and customs in Indian life that stress passive and conservative outlooks.

Life in India is basically rural. Four-fifths of Indians live in villages of some 100 to 200 families, who in the aggregate cultivate a few hundred acres. The traditional villages had no paved roads, no running water, and no modern sewage disposal systems. Inhabitants resided in mud and thatched huts with dirt floors, little furniture, and no windows. Cattle lived with the family, and mosquitoes in the rainy season spread malaria. Village life was dull. It consisted of routine crop planting and harvesting, with some handicraft and cottage industries practiced on the side by villagers. Urbanization came late, but superficial signs of westernization tended to conceal basic tragedies of city life, such as poor housing, long hours of labor, and inadequate pay. To improve their lot, rural folk trekked to urban areas, where they often found little surcease from troubles even in new environments. Where they could earn enough, they managed to supplement family income back in the village.

The Indian government propounded economic development schemes that paid attention to both rural and urban sectors of national life, yet disparity sometimes existed between planned goals and realized accomplishments. Indian insistence on neutralism in external policy was predicated in part on pressing domestic priorities. National leaders endeavored not only to pace their programs with growing populations and domestic issues, but also with developments in international affairs. Indians desired the luxury of time to solve internal problems, which were complicated because of foreign considerations, such as the Chinese Communist incursions into Indian-claimed territory and the perennial disputes with Pakistan over Kashmir and mutual borders. Impinging alien interests and factors such as these denied Indians the realization of plans formulated on preconceived schedules.

Reflecting their historical and cultural diversity, Indian races are heterogeneous. The earliest people were forest-dwelling negroids, related to the aborigines of Australia, Ceylon, and Sumatra in Indonesia. Their descendants—some 25 million—exist today as jungle and mountain tribes. Then, still in prehistoric times and probably from the west, came the Dravidians, the earliest large group of people, dark and small of stature. They settled in north India, until many of them were driven south by the Aryans, the first people to enter in historic times in a succession of immigrant waves also from the west around the second millennium B.C. Linguistically and racially related to ancient Persians, Greeks, and Latins, the Aryans were tall and fair, with dark eyes. They constituted a race and life apart from the Dravidians, though some intermarried with the earlier inhabitants of the land. Other varied but minor tribes enriched the Indian ethnic scene, such as the Turko-Iranians and the Scytho-Dravidians in the northwest and west, the Aryo-Dravidians in the north, Mongoloid strains in eastern Assam, and the Mongolo-Dravidians in the eastern provinces and border areas.

Linguistic diffusion, in addition to racial, also abounds in India. One estimate enumerates 179 languages and 544 dialects, though only a few of them are important. The Aryan language group, based on Sanskrit, is the most widely utilized. It embraces Hindustani, a spoken variety in north India that has two literary forms, of which one is Hindi, the official language of India, and Urdu, the national language of Pakistan. Other Aryan languages include Marathi and Gujarati in western India, Punjabi in the north, and Oriya, Bengali, and Assamese in the east. The Dravidian linguistic group in the south embraces some 100 million people speaking one of its four main languages—Telegu, Tamil, Malayalam, or Kanarese. Other minor languages, such as Sino-Tibetan and Munda, also exist. Loyalty to linguistic groupings has enhanced Indian regionalism, and in 1956 Indian provinces were realigned principally along linguistic boundaries. English is the lingua franca in the sense that it is spoken by a small minority of educated Indians spread through the cities and major towns of the country.

Religion again reveals complexity, though two main groups, Hindus and Muslims, exist. Prior to partition in 1947, Hindus constituted two-thirds of India's total population. Hinduism was more than a religion; it was a way of life. It was concerned not only with man's destiny and his after life, but also with the minutiae of daily life, social status, marriage, food, friends, and occupation. Birth decreed membership in a specific caste, an endogamous group with its own distinctive ritual practices, purity regulations, and relative position in the caste ladder or hierarchy. The four-tiered social and occupational arrangement that embraced the castes dated to the times of the early Aryan invasions, with Brahmans or priests at the top of the structure, followed by the Kshatriyas or nobles and warriors, the Vaisyas or traders and artisans, and finally the Sudras or serfs. Within these broad divisions subcastes evolved, but the untouchables—some 50 million of them —remained outside the traditional social arrangements. The Indian constitution of 1950 abolished untouchability and caste distinctions, though it appears to have been easier to formulate laws on the subject than to eradicate by legislative fiat longstanding social attitudes.

Similarly, Islam was a way of life. In pre-partition days, Muslims embraced one-fourth of the Indian populace, and even after partition they constituted a 10 per cent minority—a figure that made independent India then the third most populous

Islamic state in the world, after Pakistan and Indonesia. Islam was introduced into north India in the eleventh and twelfth centuries, and between the thirteenth and eighteenth centuries its rulers were dominant, in the Gangetic plain. Subsequent to the advent of the Westerners, a nominal Muslim emperor, tolerated by the English East India Company, ruled at Delhi until 1858. That year, when the British crown replaced Company rule in India, he was shorn of power and exiled to Burma. Many Muslims came from Hindu background. They accepted Islam partly to escape a low caste status, partly to avoid discriminatory taxes, or simply to make life more convenient. Fundamental theological and temporal differences between Muslims and Hindus were difficult to reconcile over the centuries, though there were tendencies from time to time toward some form of religious, as well as artistic and cultural, syncretism between the two faiths. But the cold reality of partition in 1947 supported the interpretation that basic Hindu-Muslim nonaccommodation was one logical result of historical processes. Hinduism, which possessed a tendency to absorb other ideas and peoples, could not assimilate hard-core Islam.

A half-dozen lesser but important religious groups exist in India. The Parsis, some 100,000 of them, live principally in the Bombay area. Intelligent and enterprising peoples, they are followers of Zoroaster. Their forebears left Persia in the eighth century to avoid the onslaughts of Islam. Six million Sikhs live in the Punjab. Their sect was founded in the fifteenth century by Guru ("Teacher") Nanak. He was one of several prophets of his day who tried to reconcile Hinduism and Islam by advancing a spiritual religion independent of outward ritual or form. He was succeeded by nine more gurus, who were regarded as leaders of the group. A militant and ascetic people, the Sikhs, universally using Singh as a surname, grew long hair, which was turbaned and never cut. Because of their physical prowess and tall stature, they were often used as policemen and bank guards in prewar British Asian colonies. More recently, the Sikhs have agitated for a separate state in northwest India.

Other religious entities include 1.5 million Jains, a sect founded in the fifth century B.C. as an offshoot of Hinduism. Though they are widely and thinly distributed, most Jains are concentrated in the west-central Rajputan area. Buddhism, founded at the same time as Jainism, originated in what is now Nepal and waxed strong in early India. It later died out, to leave only some half-million adherents today in India. About 6 million Christians of varying denominations and sects exist. "Doubting" Thomas, one of the twelve apostles, is considered to be the traditional founder of Christianity in India; he is reputedly buried near Madras in a church sepulcher. Finally, a scattering of Jews live in Indian cities.

The diversity of languages and peoples on the subcontinent was reflected in the traditional pre-British Indian divisive political patterns. Government was often a personal matter, and kingdoms north and south competed with each other in territorial expansion. More than once, Indian kingdoms did expand into proto-empires, but usually logistics, transport, and communications were too weak to permit them to continue if the ruling line weakened. Both Hindu kingdoms and Muslim empires had viable structures, but they were not readily adapted to rule over an extensive area. Where "national" rulers came and went, smaller political entities, as towns and villages, persisted in daily, uninterrupted routines, a trait that helped Indians to accept either native or alien rulers in far-away capitals.

British rule proved to be more omnipresent than that of earlier kingdoms. In the latter half of the eighteenth century, the English East India Company, after defeating other European powers and native princes, commenced comprehensive trading efforts on the subcontinent. With the expansion of commercial Company interests over a century came concurrent expansion of Company political and territorial influence, either by direct rule over Indian territory or by indirect rule through Indian potentates. After the crown replaced Company sovereignty, British colonial practice continued this division of direct and indirect rule. British India, roughly two-thirds of the total area, came to consist of a dozen provinces, including Burma, which were placed under direct British rule. The viceroy, as representative of the British government, was the highest officer in the land. Each province had its British governor, legislative and provincial officials, and each district had its district officers. An Indian civil service and army, earlier inaugurated by the Company, provided the continuing bureaucratic structure. The other third of India, excluding minuscle non-English colonies, constituted the princely states, some 562 of them, with 90 million inhabitants. The states varied in size from a few square miles to huge entities comparable in geographical scope to European countries. Exercising paramountcy, British advisers resided in state capitals, where the princes renounced to the British some of their sovereign attributes. After 1947, most of the states acceded to India and their rulers were pensioned off, though the contested and partitioned princely state of Kashmir, with its Hindu ruler but predominantly Muslim populace, remained a thorn in Indian-Pakistani relations. Partitions, separatism, and regionalism were some major political legacies of the complex Indian historical record.

Border Lands

Pakistan, sometimes translated as "land of the pure," was an acrostic coined to signify the provinces of British India that by Pakistani demand were to be incorporated into the new nation. Originally twice the size of pre-war Germany, it was equivalent to the combined land area of the states of Texas and New Mexico. As a new state created by the partition of India in 1947, Pakistan consisted of an eastern and a western wing with Muslim majorities. This unique national arrangement resulted principally from Islamic religious differences with Hinduism. The eastern half of Pakistan, though smaller in size than the western, edged its partner in population. The sections were studies in geographical contrast. West Pakistan was drier, produced wheat and cotton, exported food, and was comparatively underpopulated. East Pakistan was wetter, grew rice and jute, imported food, and was overpopulated.

West Pakistan, initially consisting of some eight political subdivisions after partition, became one province with the passage of the One Unit Bill in 1955, which created political and administrative equality with the one province of East Pakistan. Pakistan's national capital was initially located in the western wing at Karachi, a seaport near the Indus delta, until it was relocated in the northwest, after temporary residence at Rawalpindi, in the new city of Islamabad, designed by Greek architects. Three geographical areas existed in the then West Pakistan. Shared with India, the Punjab, which also constitutes a state of India, was the grain and cotton center of the west. Lahore, its most important town, was not only the provincial capital of West Pakistan but also a transportation and religious center. It is known as the "pink city" because of the widespread use of pink marble in its buildings. As a second geographical region, the Northwest Frontier, a military bastion under the British and still considered as such by Pakistanis, provides boundary and tribal disputes with the nearby Afghans. Lastly, Sind, the central and southern area, resembles the Nile valley with a narrow but fertile Indus river strip tapering off into desert lands.

Separated by a thousand miles of Indian territory, over which Pakistanis traversed when traveling by land or air, East Pakistan consisted mainly of delta area near the mouths of the Ganges-Brahmaputra river complex. As the Muslim part of the province of British Bengal, it was shorn in half, as was Punjab, from India. Its most important city and provincial capital was Dacca, which was hot, humid, and subject to recurrent floods. Population density in the eastern sector was great, with an estimated 850 persons per square mile of arable land. Despite national development schemes and attempts at political parity, East Pakistan, more economically underdeveloped than its western counterpart, considered itself the unfair recipient of less favorable economic and political treatment. Centrifugal regional pulls were noticeable, and local leaders, aided by Indian moral support and military intervention, declared in March, 1971, the independent state of Bangladesh (Bengal nation).

Pakistan's reserves of natural resources, as gas, oil, salt, and chromite, were located chiefly in the western part. But proven reserves constituted an insufficient base for a modern industrialized state, at least in a pre-atomic age (though Pakistan is developing an atoms-for-peace program, as are most Asian states). Besides deficiencies in raw materials, Pakistan began national life with great setbacks in administration and human resources as well. Upon partition, many qualified Hindus or Muslims stayed in or went to India. As a new state, Pakistan started fresh; on the other hand, India was considered to be the successor state to British India. Moreover, another Pakistani problem was chronic political instability in its few decades of existence. The country lacked direction despite a succession of leaders; and this resulted in a second partition of Pakistan itself.

Sri Lanka (an ancient designation for Ceylon readopted in May, 1972) lies south of India only 18 miles at the closest point. Physically connected to the subcontinent until A.D. 1480, the island is separated from India by shallow channels, some only 4 feet deep in parts and full of sandbars, known as Adam's Bridge. The pendant-shaped island has three main physical divisions. In the north are the lowlands. This area is marginal, and it receives moderate rainfall that drains off into a limestone base. Some rice is raised and coconuts are grown, but economic life centers chiefly in manufacturing, commerce, and processing of agricultural produce. The second division—or the maritime regions, consisting of the western, southern, and eastern coastal plains—is, on the contrary, rich and populous. The plains produce not only most of the rice and coconuts, but also tea, rubber, and spices such as cinnamon, in which Ceylon leads world production. Colombo, the largest city, seaport, and capital, is located on the west coast, and Trincomalee, a harbor on the opposite side of the island, was a huge British naval base. Finally, in the central part of the island lie the highlands, above 1,000 feet, which contain more plantations of rubber, rice, tea, and cacao, and produce various minerals.

Sri Lanka's population embraces about 14 million people in two main ethnic and religious groups. Comprising 70 per cent, the Sinhalese arrived from India around the sixth century B.C., and displaced the aboriginal Veddas, or primitive jungle races. The immigrants developed rice irrigation, and, in approximately the mid-third century B.C., they embraced Buddhism. Their capital in the northern lowlands of Anuradhapura, now in ruins, became a great center of Buddhist art and civilization. To this day, many Ceylonese still consider their country to be the home of "pure" Buddhism. In the eleventh century, the Tamils arrived from south India, and they pushed the Sinhalese farther south and west along the coastal plains. Predominantly Hindu, the Tamils constitute about 20 per cent of the population, but they are divided into two groups. The descendants of the early invaders are known as Ceylon Tamils, while the so-called Indian Tamils were brought in by the British in the nineteenth century to work on the plantations. Pursuing different languages, religions, occupations, and politics, the Tamils, collectively a significant minority, have clashed in bloody campaigns with the governing Sinhalese. Some Arabs live in Sri Lanka as well as some Europeans, who controlled the island, first through the Portuguese, then the Dutch, and finally the British, who took it over in 1802. From then on, it was administered as a crown colony, separately from India, until Ceylonese independence was declared on February 4, 1948.

Afghanistan, straddling the northwest frontier of Pakistan, has Kabul as its capital and chief city. As one of the few landlocked states of Asia, it has a population of some 15 million, and with 250,000 square miles, it is comparable in geographical size to Texas. In a strategic location, it provided in the past a relatively convenient gateway for invaders from the north and the west to enter India and what is now Pakistan. With an average altitude of 4,000 feet, Afghanistan has central valleys, plateaus, and numerous mountain ranges. The Hindu Kush in the north averages 20,000 feet in height. The Khyber Pass, when not closed by diplomatic disputes between Afghanistan and Pakistan, provides access between the two states. In the latter half of the nineteenth century, the buffer country, while maintaining its independence, provided a source of friction between imperialist Britain and Czarist Russia.

Predominantly Muslim, the inhabitants of Afghanistan adhere to Islamic precepts, including purdah, or the seclusion of women. In many ways it is a theocratic state, though some break with the past has been indicated by recent monarchs. Muslim law, society, and religious concepts are prevalent. Clan and tribal divisions are noticeable, but the dominant racial group is Pathan, who speak Pushtu, the official language. Afghanistan has had a long history of past invasions. These have included Alexander the Great and his troops; the Turks; the Arabs, who brought Islam as early as the seventh century; the Persians; and the Mongols under Genghis Khan and Tamerlane. Modern Afghanistan dates from 1747, at which time various principalities were consolidated into one kingdom. Modernization was slow. In 1929, a new ruling family ascended the throne. In 1932, a constitutional monarchy was formed which lasted until a name change in 1973 proclaimed a republic.

Independent Nepal, another landlocked state, is caught in its own cold war between India and China. The size of Arkansas, it is 55,000 square miles in area and has a population of about 12 million. Rectangular in shape, it is 500 miles in length east to west and 100 miles in width north to south. In the same latitude as Florida, it experiences a varied climate, ranging from tropical to alpine. The southernmost belt of Nepal constitutes part of the flat Ganges plain. Farther north, the terrain turns into hill country with valleys, including that of Katmandu, where lies the capital and chief city of the same name. Hills continue into the mountainous Himalayas, with towering peaks, such as Mount Everest, the world's highest mountain (over 29,000 feet), that mark the border with China. Though Nepal was the home of the historical Buddha, Hinduism, rather than Buddhism, is more prevalent. The country has received cultural, political, and racial impulses from Tibet, China, and India. In 1816, the British made Nepal a protectorate in effect through treaty, but, in the course of the nineteenth century, the state paid tribute to China, while between 1856 and 1953, in turn, it received tribute from Tibet. Between 1846 and 1951, the Rana family, though not on the throne, was the de facto ruler of Nepal, until a revolt in the latter year restored power to the king.

Nearby Bhutan, with a million inhabitants, is 19,500 square miles in area, the size of Costa Rica. Its capital is Punakha. First a British and then an Indian protectorate, it has had past close ties with Tibet in religion, race, and language. At least fourteen mountain passes lead from Bhutan into Tibet. Relatively homogeneous, most inhabitants are Bhutiyas of Tibetan stock. A Buddhist state, it contributes approximately 25 to 40 per cent of state revenues to support monasteries of the Tibetan type of lamaism.

Sikkim, a former Indian protectorate now incorporated into India, is wedged in the Himalayas. It is surrounded by Nepal, Tibet, Bhutan, and India. Its capital is Gangtok; its population approximates 200,000; its geographic area is 2,800 square miles, equivalent to that of the Canary Islands. It is a racial and cultural melting pot, for its native inhabitants are Lepchas, but Bhutiyas with Tibetan-Buddhist background and Nepalis with Indian-Hindu traditions also immigrated into the country. Its ruler was a maharajah. The monarch who ascended the throne in late 1963 had earlier that year married a young American girl. While Nepal's border has been demarcated with India and China, Bhutan's and Sikkim's borders were not clearly delineated to the satisfaction of the Chinese, who raised the issue from time to time. Janus-faced, the Himalayan lands were caught in historic stresses between Indians and Chinese. Though geographically small, Nepal, Bhutan, and Sikkim face political problems of international scope.

Countries of South Asia: Political Divisions

	Square Miles	*Est. Pop., 1974 (millions)*	*Capital*
Afghanistan	250,000	15	Kabul
Bangladesh	55,126	72	Dacca
Bhutan	18,000	1	Punakha
India	1,266,596	600	New Delhi
Nepal	55,000	12	Katmandu
Pakistan	310,404	65	Islamabad
Sri Lanka	25,332	14	Colombo

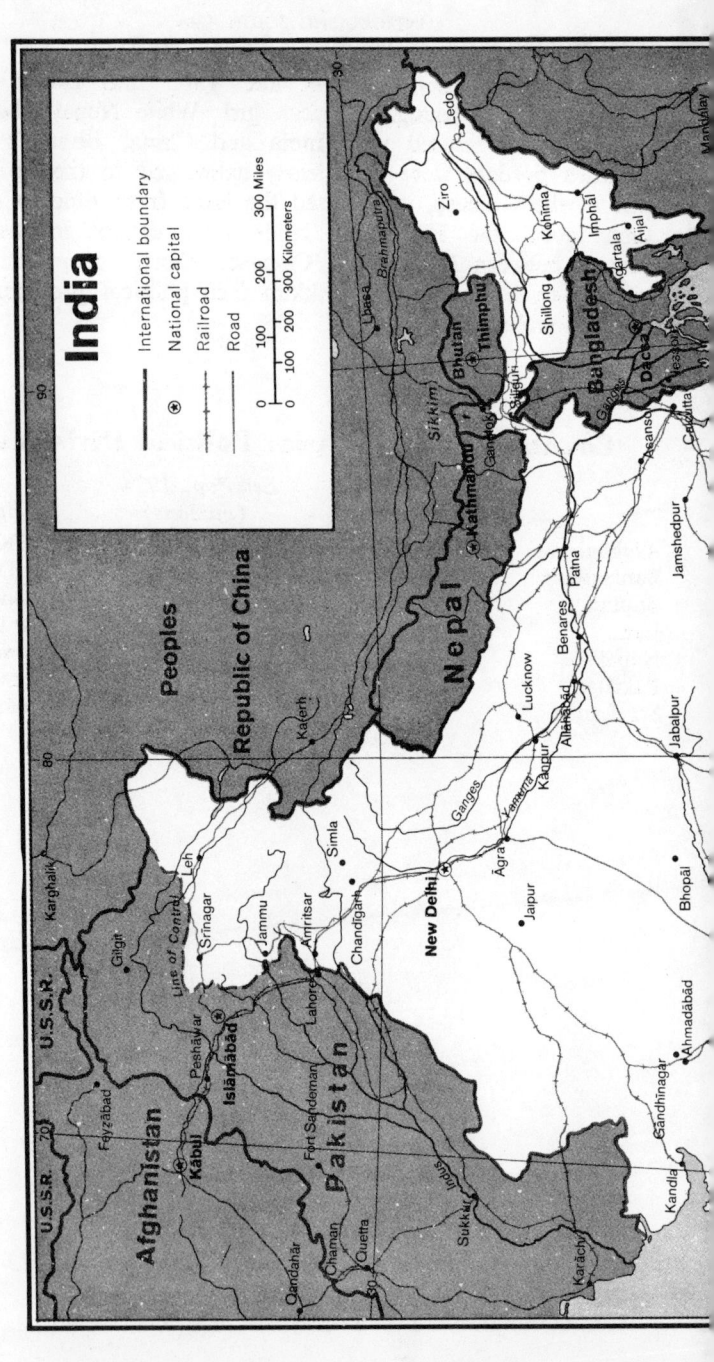

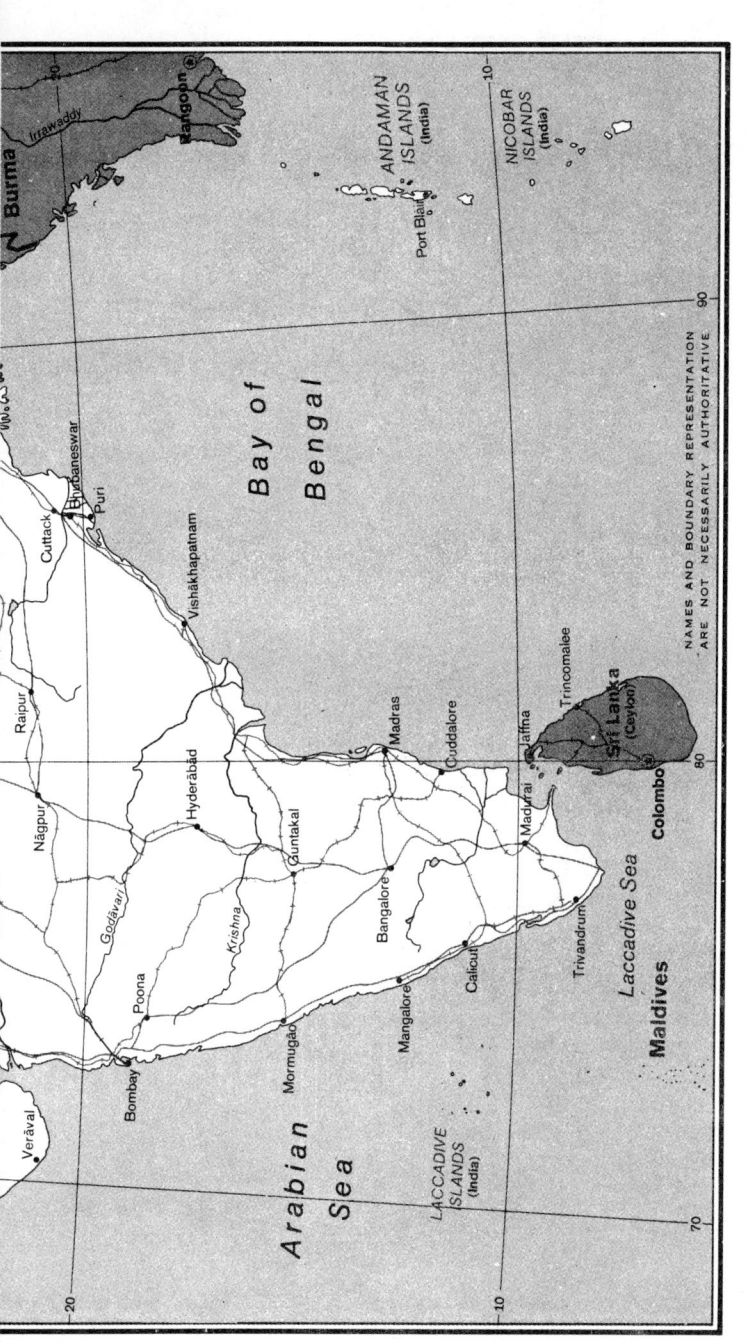

Chapter 2

Ancient India

Dawn of History

The human record on the Indian subcontinent can be traced back only imperfectly to its primitive state. The geographical area is extensive, and the archeological search is new and restricted in scope. Traces of man's existence date to the Paleolithic, or Old Stone, Age, which in India extended over some 300 millennia, between 400,000 and 100,000 B.C. This extensive period covered what has been designated as the pre-Soan, Soan, and evolved Soan cultures, derived from the river valley of the same name in northwest India. There, coarse pebble and flake tools, chiefly chopper-like instruments, have been discovered, but shaped cores, or molded artifacts, as pear-shaped hand axes, also have come to light. No human remains have yet been uncovered from this earliest stage of human life, which resembled that of ancient Europe, Africa, and China. Slightly more efficient and finished tools, possibly dating from the same age, have been excavated in Gujarat and in South India, which gave rise to the term Madras Industry for the latter. These primitive inhabitants in India hunted and gathered food. Semi-nomadic, existing in small groups in sparse and isolated communities, they lived in rock shelters or in huts roofed with thatch or skin.

Hints of the subsequent Mesolithic, or Middle Stone, Age appear in the Deccan, but the period cannot be dated accurately. In addition to stone implements, those of bone, flint, jasper, and other semi-precious stones have been uncovered. Polished stone axes and hand-made pottery were manufactured. A considerable variety of animal bones, including those of cattle and the pig, horse, dog, deer, and goat, have been found. Poultry appears to have existed. How far agriculture was practiced by these people of unknown race is unclear.

The Neolithic, or New Stone, Age, entered India between 10,000 and 6,000 B.C., when man began to domesticate animals, grow food crops, and settle down in communities. Neolithic sites have been discovered in the upper Sind, the lower Indus, and Baluchistan. The potter's wheel was utilized; painted pottery and clay figurines were produced, and, in the later times, copper tools. Neolithic man lived in more settled communities, where he practiced animistic religious rites. He buried his dead in cemeteries, and he used megaliths, or huge stone blocks, as tombs. Burial grounds were marked by stone circles. Earlier, bodies were interred in urns; later, they were cremated and the ashes placed in urns. Descendants of these early people survive in the more remote and inaccessible areas of India, where they speak mostly Munda, a group of languages apart from later Aryan and Dravidian tongues.

By the third millennium B.C., or possibly earlier, village life became a reasonably identifiable complex in Baluchistan and in the adjoining lower western areas of Sind, then a well-watered and forested area, in contrast to its geography of today. Life in these communities resembled their counterparts in adjacent Persia and the Middle East, with whose people they had some contact, probably by sea. The Baluchi people produced painted pottery, built mud brick homes, utilized some copper implements, and worshiped bull figurines, associated with a Mother Goddess. Specimens of such a goddess have been discovered in many sites. Village cultures varied one from the other, for the inhabitants produced pottery of different colors, and they practiced dissimilar burial patterns. Some cremated their dead, while others practiced inhumation of the bones after partial disintegration through burning or exposure to the elements. The racial admixture of these village settlers is unclear. Their communities are now merely mounds, formed by an accumulation of successive building and debris through time. They average about 2 acres in extent, and sometimes they range up to 100 feet in height. The size of the Baluchi mounds indicates a settled existence of considerable duration.

City life subsequently came to the Indian subcontinent, as manifested in the remarkable Indus valley culture. Archeological discoveries, commencing only in 1920, reveal a fully developed civilization extending over an area of 1,000 miles from north to south in that river valley, from the Himalayan foothills to the Arabian Sea. Widely spread out, encompassing about sixty discovered sites, the culture had two focal points, 400 miles apart: Harappa in north Punjab and Mohenjodaro ("Mound of the Dead") to the south. Provisionally dated as flourishing between 2500 and 1500 B.C., the Indus valley civilization, because of its uniformity (even to bricks of similar shape and size) implied, some historians theorize, a centralized state rather than a number of small communities of separate entities, as the earlier Baluchi hill settlements.

Similar to the contemporaneous urban centers of Mesopotamia and of the Nile, the two chief Indus cities, each several miles in circumference, with walls and towers, had neatly laid out blocks and straight streets, some of which were as wide as 30 feet. Each city had a citadel in the west, 200 by 400 yards in extent, 20 to 50 feet in height, with walls of both baked and unbaked brick. At Mohenjodaro, the citadel complex included a bath, a large residence, an assembly hall, and a granary. No stone buildings have been uncovered, for brick was the structural form. Houses of two or more stories were built, with bathrooms providing for a standing bath in which water was poured over the head, as is done in India today. Drainage systems with brick pipes led into street sewers. Rubbish chutes emptied their contents into the streets. People of more modest means lived in abodes of only a few rooms. At Mohenjodaro, possibly for ritual water purposes, a great public bath, 39 by 23 by 8 feet, was built, and bitumen sealed it water-tight. Public granaries existed, and what appear to be palaces, rather than temples, were erected.

From these city sites have come pottery remains, some of it painted, which was used for both practical and ceremonial purposes. Figurines of many types also have been uncovered, including that of a female, 4 to 6 inches in height, dressed in the Hindu style of girdled clothing and wearing a thick necklace and elaborate headdress. Children's clay toys include chairs and small wheeled carts, similar in nature to those used in the area today. Other discovered artifacts encompass some

2,000 seals, 1 inch square, possibly used as amulets. On these seals were engraved designs and symbols, some of which later became sacred to Hindus. Representations on the seals include those of a man squatting, yoga style, with hands down-pointing to earth and surrounded by animals; the pipal or bo (fig) tree, dear also to Buddhists because the founder of that faith reputedly found enlightenment under such a tree; the bull and the serpent; and the swastika, considered an emblem of well-being. The cow, so revered by later Hindus, is not pictured. As revealed by writing on the seals, the Indus peoples had developed a script of some 270 symbols, of possibly ideographic or syllabic content, but of which none has yet been deciphered. No remnants of written literature, painting, or monumental sculpture exist.

An agricultural folk, the Indus people produced wheat, barley, sesame, melons, and vegetables. They grew cotton, wove it, wore it, and exported it. They domesticated animals, and they utilized wheeled vehicles and boats. Men and women both wore ornaments of great variety and shape. They produced a number of tools in gold, silver, and copper, but their weapons were rarer and of more inferior quality. The absence of the sword is striking, though implements of war and of hunting were the hand sling, bow, spear, dagger, and ax. What is known of their religion is revealed, chiefly from the seals, as a preoccupation with fertility symbols, with the worship of certain animals, and with a Siva prototype as a god of destruction. Quite conservative in nature, the inhabitants rebuilt on identical sites rather than relocating after natural catastrophes. At least nine strata of homes and of city levels have been unearthed at Mohenjodaro. Skeletal remains indicate that inhabitants were of mixed races, with long-headed, narrow-nosed, slender Mediterranean types, as well as earlier Austroloids with flat noses and thick lips. A Mongolian-type skull also has been discovered.

After a millennium of maintaining a high, comfortable, but relatively stationary level of prosperity, the Indus civilization collapsed for reasons unclear, whether through geographical changes, internal decay, or external enemies, or a combination of factors. At any rate, the Indus cities lay athwart the path of the next invaders of India, the Aryans, who commenced to enter from the northwest about 1500 B.C. Over the centuries, the newcomers infiltrated in migratory groups and waves, to become successors to the culture that they in part destroyed and despised and in part appropriated. A militant people using chariots, horses, and bows, they fought each other as well as the earlier inhabitants they found residing in north and west India.

Aryan life was patterned on family and tribal lines. In the family the father had power, but women sometimes held high positions. Marriage was monogamous and for life; child marriages were not then practiced. Slavery existed, but it was not extensive. Patriarchal families were grouped into tribes, each with its chief or *raja*, a position that was usually hereditary. Tribal councils, generals, and priests constituted the other main positions. When the Aryans entered India, they already had tribal and class divisions. They perpetuated and ramified the system in their new surroundings, where they termed their opponents Dasyu, characterized as slave, black, and unintelligent. The word Aryan itself means kinsman, or, in derived form, noble. Previously nomadic and pastoral people, they settled down in villages and smaller towns. They prized cattle as a main source of wealth, but they also slaughtered it for food and sacrifice. They ate beef. They utilized horses and other domesticated animals. From the Indus, later tribes spread down the Ganges. By 500 B.C., the Aryan peoples, intermarrying with, imposing their rule on, or driving inhabitants farther south, had preempted the Gangetic plain. As they expanded, their life was transmuted from simple forms into more complex political ramifications that revealed greater kingdoms, rising royal pretensions, new sacrifices, and more emphasis on priestly power.

The traditional Aryan town, with double walls and an ordered pattern, was organized on compass points. The main road ran east to west, and houses of mud or brick were concentrated in four quadrants. In the town's center was a mound, a tree, or a platform that served as a focal point for tribal councils. The outside stockade had four gateways, each with a tower of bamboo or wood posts. Used for watching cattle or anticipating enemies, the towers, known as *gopuras*, became predominant in later Indian art and architectural forms. Though no works of art exist from Aryan times, some Aryan ideas and aspects of life helped shape traditional Hinduism.

In addition to raising cattle, the Aryans grew barley, wheat, and vegetables. In agricultural pursuits they used the ox-drawn plow. They drank beer brewed from grain, and they imbibed *soma*, an unidentifiable intoxicant connoting immortality and used in religious ceremonies. They gambled heavily. They were skilled artisans and craftsmen. They tanned leather, carpentered wood, and shaped bronze and copper utensils as well as those derived from iron, which was in use in India by the eighth century B.C. They continued the practice of cremation, but the body was cremated on a funeral pyre by relatives and the ashes scattered in a river. The departed soul was received by the king of the dead, who judged it and rewarded or punished it in the next world. The concept of rebirth was not yet subscribed to.

Religious concepts included reverence for nature and propitiation of spirits. Not practicing pessimistic religious rites, the Aryans believed in generally benevolent nature gods. Their universe was inhabited by numerous gods, demons, and ghosts. Their major gods, some apparently related to Greek and Roman types, were defined rather vaguely. The Aryans erected no temples and fashioned no images. The most important Aryan god was Indra, the ideal of the aristocratic Aryan warrior, who identified his hero as a strong drinker and liver of the active life. Sacrifices of cows and bulls were made to Indra for the successful pursuit and conclusion of war. Subscribing to fire cults, the Aryans also worshiped Agni, the fire god. Others in the pantheon included Rudra, the god of the whirlwind and dispenser of rain, and Dyaus (Zeus). As time went on, the sacrificial rites became more involved and their practitioners assumed more importance. The magic power inherent in the sacrificial prayers developed into spells called *brahman*, a term which was broadened to designate additionally the priestly class, or those related to prayer. As priests, the Brahmans advanced the view that they could influence or coerce the gods to the point of compulsion, if ritual were correctly performed. Brahmanical rites and formulas were expressed in the earliest Indian literature known as the Vedas ("Knowledge"). The first half of Aryan dominance is designated as Vedic India (1500 to 1000 B.C.).

The Vedas are four in number. Derived from oral tradition, they were anonymously composed over the centuries in Sanskrit, an Indo-European language related to Greek and Latin, that later became the classical language of India. The lower classes spoke Prakrit, a dialect. Hindus consider Vedic literature as divinely inspired. The oldest of the four texts is the *Rig* ("Rich") *Veda*. This is an anthology of over a thousand hymns of praise arranged in ten books, chanted by Brahmans to the various Aryan gods of nature. The *Sama Veda* rearranged the verses of the *Rig Veda* to aid the chanters, and the *Yayur Veda* added more prose prayers and spells. Last of the series, the *Atharva Veda*, included verse incantations under the apparent influence of Dravidian and pre-Aryan thought in the Gangetic plain.

In the course of time, other works, also considered of divine source, were added to the increasingly complex Vedic literature. The *Brahmanas* were prose ritualistic texts that helped to explain the Vedic hymns. "Forest texts" were incorporated into the *Brahmanas* as appendices by ascetics for further interpretation, elucidation, and mystic meaning. About 600 B.C., the *Upanishads*, numbering over a hundred, arose to propound more metaphysical, pessimistic, and monistic doctrines. Termed Vedanta ("End of the Veda"), the *Upanishads* and later elaborations of them carried the Vedic tradition into the modern world. Some Vedic ideas remained through time; others were added later. The earliest Vedas gave no indication of the doctrine of the transmigration of the soul, so important in classical Hinduism. They did not proscribe the slaughter of the cow, and they did not elaborate the caste system. Usually included in Vedic literature, but not considered of divine inspiration, are the *sutras,* or traditional learning relating to law, other rituals, and ceremonies. Such sacred laws of Hinduism, including that of the Law of Manu, dated between 200 B.C. and A.D. 200, further detailed the nature of man's secular and religious relations, enriched the literature of classical Hinduism, and defined the four classes.

The second half of Aryan India is characterized as the Epic Age, imprecisely dated between 1000 and 500 B.C. Most of the information for this period comes from two great epic poems, whose cores were composed at this time. These are the *Mahabharata* ("Descendants of Bharata"), and the *Ramayana*. The epics reflect the later and more settled but complicated life in the Gangetic valley. Outlines of classical

Hinduism were crystallizing. The *Mahabharata*, of much fable and some fact, is an anthology describing a succession dispute that resulted in a great civil war among families in a Gangetic kingdom. As the longest poem in the world, it grew from an original 9,000 couplets to 20,000, in time to swell farther to over 100,000. Inset into the sixth book is the *Bhagavad Gita* ("The Lord's Song"), a philosophical dialogue propounding a religion of moral duty. The *Ramayana*, attributed to one author, consists of seven books, of which five are considered original. It is a shorter poem of 24,000 couplets. It narrates the expulsion of Prince Rama and his wife Sita, the ideal couple in Indian literature, from a city in north India, their wanderings, Sita's abduction by the king of Lanka in Ceylon, and her eventual recapture with the aid of Hanuman, the king of the monkeys, a sacred Hindu animal. With no known historical foundation, the poem provides the basis for two popular Indian holidays, the Dasehra festival replete with firework displays that celebrates the seige of Lanka, and Diwali, the autumn festival of lights that commemorates the return of the royal couple to their northern home. Related to epic literature, the *Puranas*, eighteen in number in north India but more in south India, outline genealogies of families important in Hindu tradition.

Religious Systems

By about 500 B.C., after evolving through the pre-Aryan period and the Vedic and Epic Ages, the main outlines of Hinduism, the world's oldest religion, had emerged. It reigned supreme, despite challenges from heterodox Indian faiths, until the Muslims invaded India. Classical Hinduism claimed a multitude of religious leaders and saints, but it possessed no over-all unifying church structure and expounded no evangelical message to the world. It was a tolerant rather than a proselyting faith. Possessing some aspects akin to Protestantism, it consisted of many branches, yet it possessed no national authority or governing council.

Three general levels of Hindu thought prevailed, though their strands sometimes interwove. On the highest level, the theological approach was paramount, with the priestly Brahmans performing their rites, writing sacred works, and discussing learned treatises. The great mass of people, however, belonged to the sectarian type of Hinduism. At this level, any or all gods were worshiped, from which in time three main gods, unlike the earlier Aryan ones, emerged. These included Brahma, the creator; Vishnu, the preserver, with nine past incarnations, including those of Rama and the Buddha, and with one additional life to come; and Siva, the destroyer, with his spouse known variously as Kali, Devi, or Durga. Lastly, the most popular level of Hinduism embraced rites in which a plethora of animals were revered and beliefs in spirits of natural things were propounded. Yet, despite some disparity of outlooks, Hindu believers probably assumed, directly or tacitly, a certain core of basic and inspired literature that consisted of the Vedas, with particular emphasis on the *Rig Veda*. They would probably agree on a few basic religious tenets. These, for example, might include Brahman leadership and its interpretation of religious matters and the acceptance of one's position in his caste, into which he was foreordained by birth.

Orthodox Hindu further embraced several main concepts. The first was *varna* or color, loosely translated as class or order, and even more freely as caste, derived from the Portuguese *casta* and applied by early Europeans to that fundamental aspect of Indian life. Originally based on color and occupation, the sanction for class and one's position in it came to include moral considerations. Hindus believed that groups and individuals were of different moral worth, and consequently, because of this accepted and unquestioned fact, their positions varied on a fateful, predestined scale of good and evil. This basic moral code was *dharma*. Each of the thousands of subcastes or *jati* had its dharma, and all persons born into the jati were expected to obey and to maintain the dharmaic injunctions of their caste.

A second basic concept was that of *karma*, or the doctrine of moral consequences. It was a law of cause and effect, for one could not escape the consequences of one's actions, however good or evil they were. Lay or religious authority might extend temporary forgiveness for aberrations, but this absolution was not final. Associated with the concept of reincarnation, karma carried over from one life into another, for the character of one's previous life conditioned the content of the next. One's ultimate aim was to improve one's karma and through slow progress in an endless round of transmigrations move toward absolute good and release. A paradox, karma was deterministic in that the past determined the present, yet, through free will of choice of action in present life, one could help predestine future status.

Another fundamental doctrine was the concept of *maya*, or the illusion of the material world. This held that man and the universe were spiritual, and that the workaday world, on the contrary, was illusory. *Moksha*, or the release of the individual soul into the monistic world soul or ultimate unity of the universe, was the end of absolute reality and the termination of existence. According to the *Bhagavad Gita*, release could come in three ways: through knowledge, selfless action, or devotion to God. Through spiritual and physical exercises, yoga also promised release from physical perception. With doctrines of a type that revealed no particular urgency to take care of things in the present, for there was always another lifetime to adjust matters, orthodox Hinduism helped to nullify change and posed dilemmas for Indian adjustment to modern-day life at home and abroad.

By the time that classical Hinduism had crystallized, other and more heterodox doctrines had set in. These reformers were part of the ferment in intellectual, social, and political life around the sixth century B.C. Propounding doctrines chiefly in the peripheral lower Gangetic area, they were less affected by Aryan caste ideas. With the rise of cities and merchant classes, they preached in new milieus. With the development of organized states, small kingdoms, and the advance of material culture came new religious ideas, which also paradoxically expressed dissatisfaction with and insecurity in the changing times. Two main religions were founded, those of Jainism and Buddhism. Both were sects that grew out of Hinduism, the parent faith. They protested against some of the original doctrines but they accepted others, such as *maya*, rebirth, and *ahimsa* or the practice of nonviolence toward animal life. Both founders belonged to the Kshatriya class, whose leaders might have been desirous of counteracting growing Brahman influence.

Jainism never spread as Buddhism did; on the other hand, it never died out in India, as Buddhism did. Its founder was Vardhamana Mahavira ("Great Hero"), whose traditional dates are 540 to 468 B.C. Many legends grew up surrounding his life, though they were not so attractive as those concerning the Buddha. The traditional account is that Mahavira was the twenty-fourth in the line of prophets, all Kshatriyas, who appeared at intervals over billions of years. The twenty-third had appeared some 250 years previously. Of noble birth, Mahavira was born in what is now north Bihar, but he left home at the age of thirty to seek answers to salvation. After wandering for twelve years, he found enlightenment, gathered disciples, and propounded his doctrines for thirty years until he died at the age of seventy-two near modern-day Patna.

For a century or so after his death, Jains were not important, but they came to flourish later under the first great Indian empire, the Mauryan. While later schisms developed, Jains generally adhered to similar fundamental beliefs. Jains believed that all matter possessed souls even plants, stones, and the elements. The whole world was alive, and they grouped all things into five categories; the highest group possessed all five senses, and so down the scale. People were to free their souls from enclosed matter through varying patterns of fasting, penance, and asceticism. No one could escape the ceaseless rounds of birth and rebirth, but through careful actions one could build up merit and advance up the scale of life. Though their asceticism tended to be extreme, Jains, particularly their monks, left a legacy of great secular endeavor in such fields as literature, mathematics, astronomy, and linguistics.

Buddhism was more a middle way. It was not so ascetic as Jainism, nor was it so ritualistic as Hinduism. While it died out in the land of its birth, Buddhism had a profound effect in Asia. Its founder, whose traditional dates are given as 567 to 487 B.C., had several names, as the personal one of Siddhartha Gautama, and such appellations as Sakyamuni, or the Sage of the Sakya tribe, and the Buddha, or the Enlightened One. Born the son and heir of a rajah in Kapilavastu in Nepal, Gautama was brought up in luxury, given a good education, married, and fathered a son. A sensitive man, however, he brooded continually over the mysteries of human life and the problems of suffering, sickness, calamities, and death. According to tradition, he saw in rapid succession a sick man, a corpse, a cripple, and a monk. Profoundly affected, he renounced his riches and succession, and at the age of twenty-nine left home to become an ascetic. He submitted himself to six years of rigid self-discipline and penance, but mortification of the body brought no surcease to pain.

Finally, after meditation under a fig tree, he reached enlightenment. He concluded that formal rituals were not conducive to spiritual peace, which lay, rather, in the complete forgetfulness of self. According to tradition again, after enlightenment, he reappeared to his five disciples in a golden glow, subsequently the sacred Buddhist color. A later great Indian emperor, Asoka, who was converted to Buddhism, built a *stupa*, or memorial, on the spot of Gautama's enlightenment near Benares. From the date of his enlightenment at the age of thirty-five until his death forty-five years later at the age of eighty, the Buddha meditated and expounded his faith to disciples and followers. Upon his death, he was cremated and his ashes distributed as relics to some 84,000 stupas. Buddhist art portrays all aspects of the traditional account of the Buddha's life, and an appreciation of the former presumes a knowledge of the latter.

Buddha propounded a practical doctrine, rather than a philosophical one. Accepting the Hindu idea of rebirth and reincarnation, he promised, however, escape from the cycle in one lifetime. His great concern was in the source of sorrow and in the elimination of desire. He was not interested in metaphysics, in cosmology, in the nature of the soul, in a deity, or in the after-life. Since it lacked some of these aspects normally associated with a system of faith and worship, it is debatable whether Buddhism in its pristine form was even a religion. In its simplest doctrinal form, the Buddha enunciated four truths in syllogistic style. He posited that life equalled suffering, that suffering was caused by desire, that to rid oneself of suffering one had then to eliminate desire, and finally, that desire was to be eradicated through the eight-fold path. In turn, the eight-fold path, he declared, consisted of right views, resolve, speech, conduct, livelihood, effort, mindfulness, and concentration. For further guidance he also dictated to his disciples ten commandments, similar in nature to those found in the Old Testament. But each individual, he stated, had to seek for himself, through these precepts, the path to salvation, which he termed *nirvana*, or the annihilation of self.

Writing nothing, the Buddha bequeathed this doctrine orally

to a small, tightly knit group of disciples, chief of whom was Ananda. Over the years they worked together, and through a roving but rigorous life for most of the year, except for the rainy season when they retired to caves (and which, in time, gave rise to cave temples), they propagated the faith. To help preserve doctrinal unity, councils periodically were called. In 483 B.C., the first was convoked after the Buddha's death; the second convened in 376 B.C.; Asoka, the Buddhist emperor, called the third in 240 B.C. But by the fourth council, around A.D. 100, two basic branches of Buddhism had developed. The earlier and purer form was termed Hinayana, or Lesser Vehicle, because it rejected all later accretions. It is also known as Theravada, its main and only surviving sect. Drawing from the Buddha's sayings and doctrine, it emphasized self-salvation. Though monastic orders grew in this branch, emphasis was placed on the layman's activity to gain merit through the performance of ritual acts, as the building or taking care of stupas, offering flowers at the shrines, feeding monks, and engaging in pilgrimages. Hinayana is currently widespread in Ceylon and in the Buddhist Southeast Asian countries of Burma, Thailand, Cambodia, and Laos.

The later amended form was Mahayana, or the Greater Vehicle. First formulated in north India, it spread into China, to Korea, and then to Japan. It also gained hold in Vietnam. This branch posited fundamental differences from Hinayana Buddhism. Over the centuries, nebulously and anonymously, it developed the concept of salvation by faith in a plethora of buddhas, including the historical Buddha, who was venerated but as only one of many buddhas. Also revered were compassionate bodhisattvas, or beings of wisdom, who postponed salvation, though qualified for it, until they could save others. Moreover, to substitute for a "nothingness" nirvana, Mahayana advanced definite concepts of after-life. The idea of a western paradise arose, as well as a hierarchy of heavens and hells to reward the believer or unbeliever. Amida, as the buddha of the western paradise, commanded particular veneration. Another popular Mahayana figure, outside of India, was the female bodhisattva called Kuan-yin in China and Kannon in Japan, or the Goddess of Mercy, who evolved from a male Hindu deity, Avalokitesvara. What might be considered a third but minor stream of Buddhism was Tantrism, or the vehicle of the thunderbolt. The term derives from the tantras or scripts that emphasized spells, formulas, magical practices, and signs. This form existed mainly in Tibet.

Differing in basic respects, both major streams of Buddhism adopted the canonical categories of the *Tripitaka* ("Three Baskets"), that for conduct, or rules for monks and nuns; that for discourses, which consists of the Buddha's sayings, known also as sutras; and that for supplementary doctrines, which are works of Buddhist psychology and metaphysics. With nothing comparable to one book considered holy as the Bible or the Koran, the *Tripitaka* was elastic in content and scope, not only between Hinayana and Mahayana, but also among the Mahayana sects themselves. While the Lotus sutra was especially venerated by some Mahayana sects, as to what specifically constituted the orthodox canon in the *Tripitaka* was never crystallized, and country and regional variations remained great.

The Buddhist legacy in India embraced the doctrine of individualism, at least in its incipient form. This discouraged the pretensions of divine kings, and it implied, rather, that through a contract theory kings were the chosen leaders of the people. Monasteries developed. Congregational in nature, their monks settled their own questions. Buddhism buttressed Hinduism and Jainism in the ideas of nonviolence, for it invoked the use of moral suasion rather than that of force. Buddhist art motifs and forms were mixed into Indian culture. Some 600 *jatakas* (birth stories) recounted episodes from the Buddha's life prior to enlightenment. Because the Buddha had been initially revered, for the first five centuries he was depicted not in sculptural or pictorial form, but rather through suggestive associations. The three "jewels" of Buddhism were similarly and indirectly represented: a wheel represented the Buddha, footprints his doctrines, and an empty throne his order. The rounded stupas, themselves developing out of early Hindu mound forms, were symbolic of the Buddha's cranium. Not until Greek cultural influence was manifested in northwest India around the time of Christ was the Buddha represented in plastic and pictorial forms.

After an initial expansion and millennium of persistence, Buddhism began a decline around A.D. 500 to die out in India. There had been some persecution of Buddhism, but traditional

India remained remarkably free from holy wars. While earlier emperors had espoused that faith, later monarchs did not subscribe to it. This tended to undercut the religion, which was, however, rarely proscribed. But, over the centuries, Buddhism appeared to have become more watered-down in doctrine. It came to incorporate more and more popular beliefs, so that Hinduism, as the older, the more persistent, and the more inclusive religion, assimilated the newer faith. Emerging in India from Hinduism, Buddhism returned to it.

Early Empires

With the spread of Buddhism and Jainism, as well as with fresh invasions from the West, more sources of information, indigenous and foreign, come to light in early India. Persian and Greek works are definitive in dating western events, but the Puranas and the native and Ceylonese religious chronicles give rise to discrepancies in establishing domestic regnal eras. Out of conflicting records, the story emerges of the existence of several Gangetic kingdoms in north India in the seventh century B.C. Of these, the most important was Magadha, located in what is now south Bihar. About 650 B.C., the Saisunagas of the Khastriya class assumed the throne of that kingdom. Of its ten dynastic rulers, the only monarch of note was Bimbisara, the fifth one, a contemporary of the Buddha and Mahavira. Reputed to be a Jain, Bimbisara administered his compact and strategically located land in an energetic, ruthless manner. Mountains and rivers helped to protect his domains, and the trade route along the Ganges contributed to its wealth. He enlarged his kingdom by annexing east Bihar and by marriage alliances with neighboring kings. He met an untimely end in 494 B.C., when he was deposed, imprisoned, and murdered by his son. The line progressively weakened in the following century until it was replaced by the Nandas, a low-caste dynasty, whose founder was a sudra. For forty years, between 362 and 322 B.C., the nine Nandas, which consisted of the founder and his eight sons, ruled Magadha. In the latter year they were overthrown by Chandragupta Maurya, possibly also of Nanda extraction, who established the Maurya dynasty, the greatest in ancient India.

As the political complexion changed in the Gangetic plain,

the Persians and the Greeks penetrated the Indus river valley. In the mid-sixth century B.C., Cyrus the Great founded in Persia the Achaemenian dynasty, which presided over the world's first great empire. Held in respect by the Jews, who were permitted by him to return from Babylon to their homeland, Cyrus expanded his conquests into Indian territory west of the Indus. About the time that the Buddha was living, between 517 and 509 B.C., Darius I of Persia extended his predecessor's conquests by annexing west Punjab. Darius claimed possession of what he termed in inscriptions as Gandhara, which consisted of the Peshawar and the Rawalpindi districts, as well as a province he called Hindush, or India. He pushed Persian territorial limits not only into north India but also to the east of the Indus into the Rajputan desert. He dispatched Scylax, a Greek mercenary, to explore the Indus from Gandhara to the sea. Voyaging for two and half years, the admiral sailed down to the Indus delta, and then probably coasted along the south Arabian coast and up the Red Sea to the isthmus of Suez. In 480 B.C., in the Persian invasions of Greece, Xerxes, son of Darius, used Punjabi troops as infantry and cavalry. Serving under a Persian general, the Indians, clad in cotton, used bows and arrows in the campaigns and utilized chariots drawn by wild asses.

According to Herodotus, those conquered portions of the Punjab and Sind were organized into a satrapy, or province, of the Achaemenian Empire. They remained subject to Persian rule for one and a half centuries. During this interim, contact between Persia and India gave rise to a considerable amount of shared information. Arabic and Phoenician merchants traded with the Punjab, west and south India, and a form of Persian alphabet formed the basis of one of two early Indian alphabets. The exotic Indian peacock was introduced into Greece. Plato's *Republic* reiterated Hindu doctrines of reincarnation and of karma. The Greek philosopher's division of the ideal political orders into the three classes of guardians, auxiliaries, and laborers paralleled the three Indian varnas of Brahmans, Kshatriyas, and Vaisyas. Though these similarities in thought could have been coincidental, the relatively free movement of men and of ideas between India and its western neighbors might posit a thesis of cultural borrowings.

A Greek empire replaced that of the Persian when, in 330 B.C., Alexander of Macedonia defeated the last of the Achaemenids. Three of the Macedonian's thirteen years of rule were related to the consolidation and expansion of the Indian portion of his empire. Pushing out from Persia, Alexander conquered Bactria, a country south of the Oxus river, that today forms part of the boundary between Afghanistan and Russia. In May of 327 B.C., his army crossed the Hindu Kush mountains and remained in the vicinity of Kabul for the rest of the year. Proceeding, then, into northwest India by the Kabul river pass, in February of 326 B.C. his troops crossed the Indus over a bridge of boats. Alexander advanced to Taxila, a chief city and center of Hindu learning in Gandhara. Local rivalries made foreign conquest the easier, a repeated story in Indian history. The ruler, who was fighting neighboring chiefs, welcomed him. According to Greek sources, the Taxila king slaughtered cattle to feed his guests, an indication that the proscription on the eating of beef had not yet become an accepted part of classical Hindu doctrine. The Greeks witnessed a marriage market, where the poor, who could not marry off their daughters, exposed them for sale. The Greeks also recorded *suttee*, or the self-immolation of widows on the deceased husband's pyre.

Consolidating his gains in Taxila, Alexander continued his eastward march across the Punjab until he met Porus, the warlike ruler of a kingdom that lay between the Jhelum and the Beas tributaries of the Indus. Porus put up stiff resistance and gave battle with an army that included 30,000 foot soldiers, 4,000 horses, 300 chariots, and 200 elephants, but the proud, courageous king and his valiant army were defeated by the more mobile cavalry and troops of Alexander. The Macedonian pardoned the Indian, who was confirmed as ruler of his previous domain. Probably inspired by reports of rich eastern Indian kingdoms, Alexander pushed on to the Beas river. There his troops, in September of 326 B.C., by that time eight years away from home, mutinied and refused to proceed any farther. Alexander marked the limits of his advance by the erection of twelve stone altars on the north bank of the Beas. Because of subsequent changes in the course of the river, the markers have long since disappeared.

Alexander returned to the Indus river, which he sailed down

to the mouth. Before leaving the delta, he divided those portions of India he had conquered into three parts. Greek viceroys remained to govern Gandhara and the Sind, but Porus continued to administer his own kingdom. Toward the end of 325 B.C., Alexander and his army proceeded on the last lap of the homeward journey in three columns. The first group, carrying the sick and the heavy baggage, crossed Baluchistan from central Sind. Alexander himself marched along the coast through the desolate Makran desert, while his admiral Nearchos sailed with the remaining forces across the Persian gulf. Alexander had taken pains to ensure an empire behind him, but, within a few years after his death in 323 B.C. in Babylon, his empire fell apart and the Indians went into rebellion against foreign rule.

Alexander's conquests were not directly successful in the political field in India, and he himself left little impression there. No references are made to Alexander in surviving ancient Indian literature. But Greek colonies established by the conqueror in central Asia came later to influence Indian art, and, more immediately but more indirectly, local political forces were realigned in north India. The existing balance of power in the Gangetic plain was changed by the Macedonian advance, and it was possible for new states to arise or existing ones to be reshaped. One such strengthened kingdom was Magadha. Its young ruler, Chandragupta Maurya, was the first historical person who might be designated as emperor of India. After reputedly serving in Alexander's court, he put himself on the throne of Magadha and established the Mauryan dynasty, 322 to 184 B.C. Sources of Mauryan history include accounts by Megasthenes, a Greek ambassador, and passages from the *Arthasastra,* a manual of political conduct attributed to Kautilya, the Brahman minister of the new king. Discovered in a library in south India in the early part of this century, the handbook advanced Machiavellian-like policies to achieve and to retain power.

According to accounts such as these, Chandragupta Maurya's capital was sizable. Located on the banks of the Ganges, it was in the shape of a parallelogram, some nine by two miles. It was surrounded by moats and timber palisades, with 64 gates and 570 towers. Today, only some ruins of the emplacements remain. Located in the center of the city amid a park, the royal palace was built also of timber with elaborately gilded pillars. The king dwelt in great luxury, but also in great uneasiness. Having ascended to the throne through the use of force, he was aware that he might also be deposed in a similar manner. Fearful of his security, he never slept in the same room for two nights in succession. The palace was riddled with underground passages, hollow pillars, collapsible floors. For added protection, the king maintained a bodyguard of armed Amazons. He seldom left the palace, except for festive occasions and on rare hunts. When he essayed forth, he rode on the usual elephant or was carried on a palanquin. But he worked hard and conscientiously. Every morning he held audiences, heard reports, and received his ministers. Keeping a close grip on the administration of his empire, he appointed all important officers and issued codes and rescripts.

In his reign of twenty-four years, Chandragupta Maurya extended Magadha might into Afghanistan, the Punjab, Kathiawar, and probably Bengal. As he expanded his empire westward, he came into conflict with the Alexandrian general, Seleucus Nicator, headquartered at Baghdad, who had succeeded to part of the Middle Eastern portions of Alexander's divided empire. About 305 B.C., the two rulers met in battle. The Indian monarch, who used 500 elephants as part of his military equipment, came out the better in the encounter. In the treaty settlement, he received Greek cities in Afghanistan and northwest India. He married the Greek's daughter as well.

Seleucus stationed Megasthenes as his representative at the Indian court. Through this diplomat's writings, which have been lost but which are incorporated into works of later Greek and Latin historians, such as Pliny, much can be learned of life in India at the time. Megasthenes pictured an idyllic life in north India. He noted the absence of slavery, the chastity of women, and the bravery of men. He wrote about unlocked doors and honest people. He characterized the inhabitants of the empire as sober, industrious, diligent farmers, with litigation rare and life peaceful. He outlined seven rather than the traditional four classes of society: philosophers, peasants, shepherds and hunters, artisans and merchants, soldiers, spies or inspectors, and officials. Caste system existed, but it was not yet apparently rigid.

The emperor divided his realm into three provinces, each

under a viceroy. For a reputedly peaceful kingdom, a large paid, standing military structure was maintained. Chandragupta Maurya continued the traditional four-part Indian military components in a force that included an infantry of 600,000 men, a cavalry of 30,000, elephant detachments that utilized the services of 36,000 men, and chariot contingents of 24,000. Ground troops consisted of squads of ten men, companies of a hundred, and battalions of a thousand. Infantry used swords, javelins, and bows and arrows. Each elephant carried a driver and at least three archers. Chariots, each with a driver and usually two men, were most often four-horsed, but two-horse chariots also were used. An ambulance service existed in field operations. From the capital, a war office of thirty members and six boards coordinated military plans and action.

In a similar fashion, civil bureaucracy was highly organized. Another commission of thirty, also consisting of six boards, centralized administrative functions at the capital. The first board regulated industrial arts The second controlled affairs of foreigners in the country, their lives, their residences, and their estates in case of death. The third board concerned itself with census statistics, as registration of births and deaths. The fourth, fifth, and sixth boards regulated commercial matters that included retail trade, manufactures, and tax collections. Civil and criminal courts existed, and cases were heard by panels of three judges. An extensive secret service operated throughout the empire. In many guises and disguises, state spies maintained a constant espionage system. Daily, their reports filtered through to the emperor. Torture was condoned as a means to extract confessions, and the *Arthasastra* lists at least eighteen types of approved methods.

Mauryan economic life centered on agriculture. In theory, the emperor owned all land, and taxes on the gross produce, usually rice, were extracted. As stipulated in the books, the accepted ratio of tax proceeds to actual production was one-sixth, but collections usually approximated a ratio of one-fourth. Extra imposts sometimes were added. Irrigation systems were expanded, and a good road system linked key areas of the empire. Commercial life, though strictly regulated, was active. Trade channels extended into south India, China, Mesopotamia, and the Greek city-states. In spite of the presence of some Indian coinage, foreign rather than native currency was preferred.

Over this personalized, centralized, despotic, peaceful kingdom, Chandragupta Maurya reigned. According to Jain tradition, the monarch abdicated in later life, became a monk, and practiced ritual suicide through fasting, a method approved for Jain saints. His son, Bindusara, after assuming the throne in 298 B.C., was also an able and capable ruler. He is credited with adding to the kingdom that portion of the Deccan as far as Mysore. He received envoys from Egypt, and he corresponded with the king of Syria, who was the son of Seleucus Nicator. Bindusara requested his colleague to dispatch figs, wines, and a philosopher. The Syrian king sent the commodities, but replied that no philosophers were then available for export. In 273 B.C., after a quarter-century of rule, Bindusara was succeeded by one of his many children, Asoka, who had been viceroy of one of the three provinces. As the most famous of the Mauryan line, and possibly the greatest of all Indian emperors, Asoka ruled until his death in 232 B.C.

Asoka expanded the Mauryan empire beyond the limits of those established by his father and grandfather. It ranged from Mysore to the Himalayas, and from Assam to the Hindu Kush. In 261 B.C., he extended the boundaries to include Kalinga, or the present-day Orissa, on the east coast. This campaign was successful, but it turned Asoka to Buddhism. According to the king's own account, remorseful after all the bloodshed experienced in a war that recorded the death of over 100,000 persons, he underwent a change of heart. He abandoned stern and militant measures and devoted the rest of his life to furthering Buddhism. Termed the Constantine of India, he established Buddhism as the state church, and furthered the faith through several ways. He convoked the third general Buddhist council to settle doctrinal differences. He authorized a collection of sacred Buddhist books. He established a department of religion at his capital. He dispatched missionaries throughout India to convert peacefully others to the cause. Upon the invitation of the king of Ceylon, he sent his brother (or son) Mahendra to convert that country. Asoka's sister became a Buddhist nun.

Asoka further erected stupas as memorials to the Buddha, and he carved Buddhist edicts on rocks and pillars that exhorted his people to be good Buddhists and to turn from Hinduism. The inscriptions were for the purpose of inducing morality according to the Buddhist law of piety, or *dhamma*. Asoka particularly stressed the three themes of pursuing filial piety, practicing ahimsa, and telling the truth. Scattered through north and central India, the Asoka pillars, fourteen of them, are architectural wonders. Consisting of a single stone, they range from 40 to 60 feet high, with sculptural forms as capitals. Animals resembling Persian types were carved on top of the columns. Derived from the sculptural top of the column at Sarnath, the quadrapartite lion heads are the symbol of the Indian state. The sandstone columns and figures were so highly polished that from a distance travelers took them to be wrought of metal.

In this era, before sculptural representation of the Buddha, four animals with symbolic Buddhist meanings were portrayed in Mauryan art. The lion represented the Buddha himself; the elephant connoted the majesty of the Buddha; the horse, derived from Brahman concepts, portrayed a world ruler; the bull was the sign of the zodiac under which the Buddha was born. A common Buddhist emblem portrayed in Mauryan (and later) art forms was the wheel, also derived from the Aryan symbol of the wheel of the law. It appears as an emblem on the Indian national flag. No actual building stands from Mauryan times, though the great stone stupa at Sanchi, 56 feet high and 121 feet in diameter, encases an earlier but not visible stupa dating to Asoka's reign. A portion of the stupa railing, with relief sculpture, at Barhut is said to date to the Mauryan era.

Ostensibly a devout man, Asoka supported 64,000 Buddhist priests. He founded religious houses and he appointed censors to enforce the law of piety. But he also emphasized secular social services, as the digging of wells, the planting of trees along roads, and the promotion of medical aid. Though religious, Asoka might have had as well a political motive in supporting Buddhism. By focusing on a unified, casteless society, the emperor, through moral prescript and good example, sought to transcend religious differences and divisive ideologies. To this end he did not succeed. After his death, the Maurya dynasty went into decline, and in 184 B.C. it ended when another, but less extended, dynasty rose to replace it.

Comparatively brief in duration but brilliant in nature, Maurya India opened wide, but fleetingly, an early era in Indian history.

By the time of the demise of the dynasty in the second century B.C., some fundamental aspects of Indian life and culture had been cast. These in part dated back to the remarkable prehistoric Indus river valley civilization and in part to the Aryan invasions that overtook it, borrowed from it, and modified it. After evolving through the Vedic and Epic Ages, in the sixth century B.C. life in the historic Gangetic and Indus river plains came into clearer historical focus. Some basic aspects of classical Hinduism had now emerged in its literature, its social and occupational stratifications, it main gods, and its metaphysics. Concurrently, Jainism and Buddhism enriched the philosophic and religious systems. Subsequent Persian and Greek invasions added cultural dimensions to India at a time when early historic Indian kingdoms were taking shape in the Gangetic area. Drawing inspiration and strength from East and from West, the Mauryan empire was a fitting concluding era for ancient India.

Chronology

B.C.
400,000–100,000	Paleolithic Age: Soan cultures, Madras Industry
10,000–6000	Neolithic Age
3000	Baluchi hill settlements
2500–1500	Indus valley civilization; Mohenjodaro and Harappa
1500–1000	Aryan invasions; Vedic India
1000–500	Epic India: *Mahabharata* and *Ramayana*; Gangetic life established
650	Magadha state arises—Saisunaga Dynasty
600	*Upanishads* appear
6th century	Classical Hinduism emerges; Sinhalese arrive in Ceylon
567–487	Traditional dates for life of Buddha
540–468	Traditional dates for Vardhamana Mahavira, founder of Janinism
mid-6th century	Cyrus the Great incorporates into Achaemenian empire Indian territory west of Indus

517–509	Darius I extends empire into west Punjab (Gandhara)
483, 376, 240	First, Second, and Third general Buddhist councils
480	Xerxes utilizes Punjabi troops in invasions of Greece
362–322	Nanda rule in Magadha
326–325	Alexander the Great in north and west India; Greek colonies established
322–184	Mauryan empire established by Chandragupta Maurya; Kautilya's *Arthasastra*
273–232	Asoka's rule; Buddhism into Ceylon
200–A.D. 200	Laws of Manu formulated
c. 100	Fourth general Buddhist council; Hinayana (Theravada) and Mahayana strains emerge

Hindu India

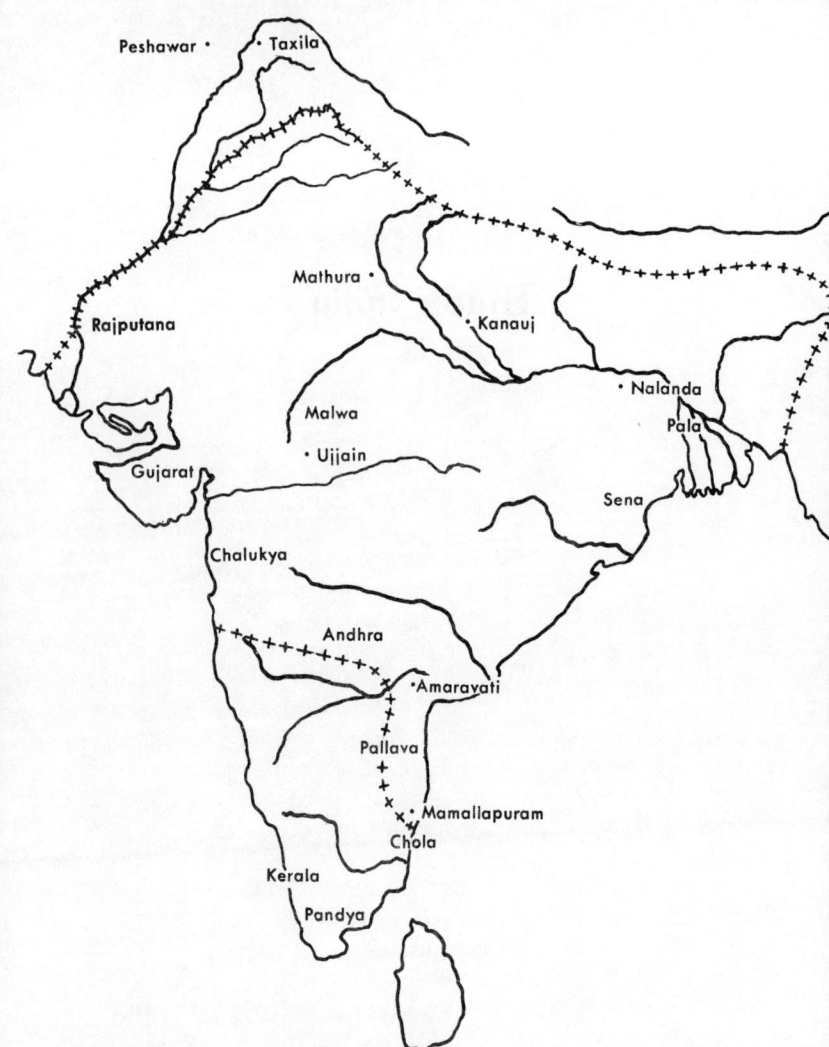

Chapter 3

Hindu India

Political Division

Five centuries of disunity followed the collapse of the Mauryan empire. Political disintegration and diversification resulted from fresh foreign invasions, more alien conquerors, and new states arising in the Deccan and in south India. In the struggle of one dynasty against another to attain dominant position, political unity was lost. Historical materials are not in abundance to document these centuries, and it is sometimes difficult to ascertain with any precision either dates or events. The main sources are limited to often contradictory and confusing traditional dynastic lists, some inscriptions and coins. Numismatics assumes a role of importance in shedding light on particularly the half-dozen or so foreign dynasties established in west and north India at this time.

Soon after Asoka's death, two of the three Mauryan provinces broke away from centralized rule. In the northwest, Taxila regained independence; in the south, Kalinga, which Asoka had wrested only after a bloody campaign that converted him to Buddhism, followed a similar pattern. In 185 B.C., the bulk of the Gangetic plain previously held by the Mauryan line was transferred to the authority of Pushymitra, who founded the Sunga dynasty. According to the Puranas, the founder was a general of Brahman family, who overthrew his Mauryan overlord. Pataliputra continued as his capital, but he set into motion a reaction against Buddhism. He restored the official cult of Brahmanism and reinstituted the ritual, dating to Aryan times, of the horse sacrifice.

After a thirty-six-year reign, Pushymitra was succeeded by a son, subsequent to which the dynasty lapsed into relative obscurity. The Sunga appeared not so much a closely knit centralized empire as one of much looser organization, which was a normal pattern in the political life of Hindu India. In the course of time, small independent states arose in the Ganges basin that were ruled by the Kshatriya class. In 73 B.C., a Brahman minister killed the last of the Sungas and established the Kanva line. The Kanvas permitted the Sungas to continue to rule a portion of their previous domain, but not much is known about the Brahman Kanvas. Four kings ruled for forty-five years in the short, turbulent era. In 28 B.C., the last one was killed by a monarch of the Andhra line, a rising power in the Deccan, which, for the first time, began to play an appreciable role in Indian political life.

The dynasty that ended the Sungas and Kanvas was one that presided over Telegu-speaking Dravidian-type peoples, who at one time had been the vassals of Asoka. The Andhras dated to approximately 225 B.C., when they established themselves as a power in the east central portion of the Deccan, between the mouths of the Godaviri and the Kistna rivers. The early rulers allied themselves with other chiefs in west Deccan. By the end of the second century B.C., the Andhras had appreciably expanded from coast to coast, to round out their kingdom east to west, where Bombay is now located. They assumed the honorific of "Lords of the Deccan." In the course of another century, they conquered some of the Gangetic kingdoms, including the two successor states to the Mauryan empire. Ruling for three centuries over an extended empire, from 28 B.C. to A.D. 225, the Andhras divided their state into three provinces, each of which was ruled by semi-independent hereditary chieftains, and then again into districts, each of which was presided over by an officer. Some village self-government prevailed at local levels. Commerce was extensive, and autonomous merchant guilds existed.

The Andhras were of orthodox Hindu faith, but they were tolerant of Buddhism. The religion flourished, and the dynasty is renowned for several outstanding examples of Buddhist art and architecture. About 30 miles from the west central coast, a cave monastery at Karli was cut into the Western Ghats as a religious retreat. Its main hall, in the shape of a basilica, is of sizeable proportions 125 feet long and 27 feet high. Pillars line the hall, and, reminiscent of Asoka's columns, they are inscribed with edicts advocating pious acts. The rows of columns lead to a stupa, at the end of the hall, carved in relief. Another edifice from the Andhra period is the great marble stupa at Sanchi in the central Deccan. Its gateways are elaborately carved with Buddhist motifs, Jataka stories, and other episodes from the life of the Buddha, who himself is portrayed only in symbols. Near the eastern central coast at Amaravati, on the Kistna river about 80 miles inland, another stupa complex existed. Now gone, the Amaravati remains, executed over many decades, are contained in the British Museum in London and in the Madras museum. On the railings and stupa remnants is portrayed, with great artistic skill, lavish design, and vivid patterns, the Buddha, in earlier representations through symbolic means and in later times in human form. In these Buddhist shrines, Hindu motifs are also intermixed, as well as secular scenes depicting palaces, houses, court life, street scenes, and dancing girls.

The Andhras were crushed by the Pallava dynasty, who had set up an independent state. The new line had been founded in the central Deccan around a nucleus of predatory tribes who, under the leadership of the Pallava kings, were formed into a militant power that lasted for some seven centuries. The state was primarily Hindu, but Dravidian influences were present. As an outpost of Hinduism in its gradual advance in historic times toward the south, the Pallavas were of tolerant persuasion, like the Andhras whom they had overcome. They permitted Jains and Buddhists to follow their respective religions. They were also commercially active, and they dispatched, from east-coast ports of their kingdom, traders and missionaries across the Bay of Bengal to Southeast Asia.

The Pallava kingdom abutted newly rising states farther to the south in Tamil land. By the early centuries of the Christian era, three Tamil states had risen in power and in stature, those of Chola on the eastern Coromandel coast, Chera or Kerala on the west Malabar coast, and Pandya at the southern tip of the peninsula, with its capital at Madura. Each state was governed by its courts and its kings, who engaged in incessant warfare with each other. Dravidians had inhabited these lands from prehistoric times, and they spoke Dravidian languages, principally Tamil. They modified some aspects of Hinduism that had emanated from farther north. The Tamils, for instance, maintained a caste system to include Brahmans, Sudras, and untouchables, but they failed to adopt, in large measure, the Kshatriya and Vaisya classifications. Despite a warlike and warring tradition, the Tamils developed a rich literary heritage, and Madura became the literary capital of south India. The first centuries A.D. gave rise to the compilation of the *Eight Anthologies*, which were, in the main, secular poems revealing little Aryan influence. About AD. 200, the *Kural*, a religious work attributed to a poor weaver and termed the Bible of the South, was composed. The volume consisted of short poems relating to religious and moral precepts.

Possessing extended coastlines jutting toward the Indian Ocean, the Tamil kingdoms turned seaward for many commercial and territorial enterprises. To the south, the three states continually struggled for control over Ceylon, which was frequently invaded until the second century A.D., when the invasions were at last successfully repulsed by the Ceylonese. Tamil expansion and contacts to the west and the east were also noteworthy.

Leading toward the Roman Empire and its outposts to the west, two main sea routes existed from the peninsula, one via the Persian Gulf to the mouth of the Euphrates, and the more open and unprotected route across the Arabian Sea and up the Red Sea to the isthmus of Suez. The Tamils used and benefited from these routes. Tradition credits the discovery in A.D. 45 by the Alexandrian sailor Hippalus of the monsoons, on which winds he sailed in a time-saving itinerary directly from Arabia across the sea to the mouth of the Indus. Utilizing the monsoons, Indians, but principally Arabs and other foreigners in this trade to the west of India, plied the seas between Indian ports and the Middle East, where, processed by middlemen, goods were dispersed throughout the Roman Empire. In the halcyon centuries of Pax Romana, up to 120 ships a year sailed from Egypt to India. As early as 20 B.C., the Pandyas dispatched an embassy to Augustus in Rome. In this trade, India gave more than it received, a pattern that persisted into modern times. The Romans, paying in bullion, imported such Indian items as cotton, teak, ebony, sandalwood, spices, rice, rare animals, and precious stones. Roman gold coins have been discovered in south India, where the Romans also established permanent trading agencies.

The Tamils faced eastward as well. From early times, Indians had coasted along or sailed across the Bay of Bengal to Southeast Asian lands. The Jatakas refer to such voyages, and the earlier *Rig Veda* contains accounts of sea travel. In contrast to the western trade that utilized foreigners to a great extent, it was Indian ships and Indian crews (from Gujarat as well as from south India) that brought Indian merchandise and ideas to Southeast Asian countries. In a long-drawn-out process, colonies, commerce, and conversions to Hinduism and Buddhism proceeded in lands across the sea. As early as the third and fourth centuries B.C., Kalinga, Andhra, and Pallava had contact with inhabitants of Southeast Asia, who also, in a two-way exchange, came in some numbers to India. Later travelers and migrants departed from the Tamil kingdoms, mainly Chola. They went eastward, and they or their descendants governed some of the early Southeast Asian states, which possessed rudimentary social, economic, and political patterns. By the fifth century A.D., Hinduism and Buddhism, which coexisted in Southeast Asia as they had earlier coexisted in India, had been accepted by ruling houses in the delta and coastal areas of Burma, Thailand, south Indochina, Malaya, and Indonesia. The faiths were propagated peacefully in the eastern lands, where the political elite voluntarily adopted the new ideas.

As Deccan and Tamil states waxed and waned, new power alignments shaped up in north India, which fell in large part to foreign conquerors. Of these, the first were the Greeks, with an Alexandrian heritage, from the central Asian kingdom of Bactria. In the mid-third century B.C., their ruler, as well as that of neighboring Parthia in present-day Iran, revolted against the Seleucids and formed their own independent kingdoms. Demetrius, the successor to the founder of the new Bactrian line, experienced pressures from other tribes to the north. He turned south to conquer Afghanistan. About 184 B.C., he crossed the Hindu Kush and took Gandhara. Menander, or Milinda, an able lieutenant of his, pursued raids farther into the Gangetic plain. His troops clashed with those of the Sungas, and his cavalry almost took Pataliputra, which withstood a siege. In 167 B.C., while Demetrius and Menander were in India, the Greeks in Bactria revolted and the land passed into other hands. The Greeks in India did not acknowledge the new overlord, who also pressed his campaigns into north India. Two Greek dynasties were established in India. Menander ruled Gandhara and Mathura, while his rival presided over lands west of the Jhelum river and Afghanistan.

The Greeks, termed Yavanas by the Indians, ruled over Indian kingdoms. They utilized both Indian and Greek cultural forms in some media, for numismatic evidence reveals coins of fine quality that included nickel, portraying rulers, with bilingual Greek and Prakrit scripts. Some of the Greek kings became Hindus or Buddhists. Embodying a cultural synthesis of Alexander and Asoka, the Greek Menander espoused the Buddhist faith. He is noted as the subject of a Buddhist work, *The Questions of Milinda*, which presented in dialogue form the conversion to the faith of the ruler by a Buddhist monk. The Greek heritage to India from this period included art and sculptural forms, as well as word loans to Indian astrology and Hindu medicine. But western impact was not decisive, and the Greeks in India, far from home and arriving a century and a half after Alexander's departure, made little impact on the complex Indian mind. By the first century B.C., Greek rule seems to have disappeared. The only surviving monument of the Indo-Greek dynasties is a pillar with inscriptions, discovered in 1909 in Gwalior state, and which once was surmounted by Garuda, a mythical bird and vehicle of Vishnu.

The Greeks were replaced by three other groups of foreigners, the Scythians or Sakas, the Parthians or Pahlavas (no relation to the Deccan Pallavas), and the Kushan or Yüeh-chih, as Chinese annals term them. The successive waves into India reflected previous migration patterns from China by way of central Asia. In a type of falling domino sequence over the centuries, the Greeks in Bactria were conquered by the Sakas, who had been driven out of their home in west China by the Yüeh-chih. These, in turn, moved out of northwest China as a result of pressures generated by the Huns or Mongols from Mongolia. This course of movement and migration westward from Chinese border areas for one reason or another into central

Asia and then into north India was to be repeated again in later centuries.

According to Chinese sources, the Sakas withdrew from west China into central Asia. There they conquered the divided Greeks. From Bactria, after 135 B.C. they entered and gradually extended their sway into the Indus valley and over western India, in association with the Parthians to their south. In the northern campaign, the Sakas moved by way of Baluchistan up the Indus to south Punjab. Around 75 B.C., Gandhara fell; within another half-century all Greek resistance in northwest India and the west Gangetic plain had ended. While some of their tribe moved north, a second Saka movement thrust south into Gujarat and east to Malwa in the Deccan. There the Sakas established their capital at the ancient city of Ujjain, a center of Hindu learning and one of the seven sacred Hindu cities. In Malwa they came into conflict with Andhra expansion westward, but they survived in spite of long struggles with the enemy. The Saka line in Malwa lasted, but those in other areas of India were absorbed by Hindus. About A.D. 150, a ruler of the Sakas in Malwa left the earliest important inscription, recording his martial exploits, in correct Sanskrit.

The Pahlavas or Parthians were closely related to Saka expansion up the Indus. Toward the end of the first century B.C., a line of kings with Persian names gained temporary suzerainty over northwest India. According to the apocryphal *Acts of Thomas*, St. Thomas is said to have brought India's first knowledge of Christianity to Gondophernes, one of their rulers. One tradition maintains that the apostle traveled from Alexandria to the mouth of the Indus. He moved up the river valley and preached in Gandhara and Taxila, its capital. Subsequently, he returned to the mouth of the Indus. He sailed down the Malabar coast, where he remained for a time, and then proceeded up the Coromandel coast on the other side of the peninsula. There he was martyred by Brahmans. Other traditions advance other versions, and the story of the introduction of Christianity into India remains a matter of debate.

In the last of a series of invasions from the Chinese borders, the Kushans pushed into north India by way of central Asia. They had originated as nomadic tribes, collectively known as Yüeh-chih, in the northwestern Chinese province of Kansu. In

174 B.C., they were forced out of their homes by Mongolian hordes. Half a million of them migrated to the Tarim basin in west China, driving the Sakas before them. They followed the Sakas into the Oxus valley, where they established five principalities. Kadphises I, chief of the Kushan section, consolidated the divided tribes into a powerful monarchy. He proceeded to attack the neighboring Parthians to the south, took Kabul, and moved into Indian border lands. His son, Kadphises II, pushed farther into India, but the kingdom, which straddled the area between the Ganges and the Tarim basin, was centered in Bactria. The monarch became a Saivite, and like his father, issued fine gold coins that resembled Roman *denarii*.

The greatest of the Kushans was Kanishka, usually regarded as the third of the line. Because of conflicting sources, his accession dates vary widely, between 58 B.C. and A.D. 288, but they have been narrowed down to a period between A.D. 78 and 144. A reign period of A.D. 78 to 96 is one of several advanced. One system of Indian reckoning, known as the Saka era, harks to an accession date of A.D. 78, and, with this as the base year, the chronology was continued by later Kushans for several generations. Ruling over a wide territorial expanse that included Kashmir, Malwa, and much of the Indus and Ganges valleys, Kanishka established his capital first at Peshawar and then at Mathura. Like Asoka and Menander before him, he became a convert to Buddhism. Also like them, he propagated the faith peacefully, for he was not a bigot. At Peshawar he built a great Buddhist monastery. He convoked the fourth general council of 500 scholars, who, in meetings that lasted six months, tried to reconcile Hinayana and Mahayana doctrines. Because of a renewed religious impetus, Buddhist sculpture flourished in Kushan. Reflecting earlier human Greek art forms, the Buddha now appears in the so-called Gandhara style which portrays him in smooth lines and wearing carefully delineated but diaphanous drapery.

Because of its geographical location, Kanishka's kingdom was a cultural melting pot. Kushan coins reveal Greek; Indian, and Persian deities. Greek-inspired statuary, as Hercules and the Lion, have been discovered. A headless statue of Kanishka himself has been uncovered; he is dressed in martial robes and wears big boots. Buddhism in both forms flourished; Mahayana doctrines percolated into China from north India.

Indian writing penetrated central Asia. The Kushans exported Indian spices and re-exported Chinese silks to Rome, from which city they received gold, wines, and luxury items in return. In A.D. 99, ambassadors from India presented their credentials to Trajan, the Roman emperor, who gave them senatorial seats in the arena. The Peshawar mint struck gold coins similar in design to those of Rome. Through their multi-directional outlooks to the Hellenistic and the Chinese worlds, the Kushans by land channels were adding dimensions to Indian international relations, as the Tamils similarly were doing by sea.

Kingdoms North and South

After the Kushan, the next main empire to rise in north India was that of the Guptas ("Protected"), which lasted from A.D. 320 to 480. Sources on the period are abundant, and they are quite definite as to general outlines and particular details. Information derives from coins, inscriptions, temples, sculpture, wall paintings, literature, and accounts both native and foreign, including those of Chinese travelers. Arts and the sciences flourished. The Guptas recorded, in a second outburst of cultural achievement after the Mauryas, a golden age of India. The era was one of culmination and completion of effort, and one of rounding off of accomplishment. The founder of the line was Chandragupta I, who ruled for a decade, from A.D. 320 to 330. He married expeditiously, and, building on the ancient Mauryan state center at Pataliputra, extended his sway over much of the Ganges valley.

Under the near half-century of rule of his son, Samudragupta, 330 to 375, the Gupta empire became the paramount power in India of the time. The second of the dynasty expanded his control over all of the Gangetic valley and north India. He marched south into the Deccan and came into conflict with the Pallavas near Madras. The limits of the greatest empire since Asoka's time ranged from the Brahmaputra river in the east to the Narbada river in the south to the Jumna in the west. Tribes on the peripheral areas acknowledged Gupta supremacy, and five frontier kingdoms paid tribute. Kashmir was not conquered, but the Kushan kings in the northwest respected Gupta might. Beyond the Indian border, Samudragupta enjoyed friendly relations with the rulers in Afghanistan and with those of Ceylon. The Gupta monarch was an able, gifted, and versatile man. He was skilled in music, and medals portray him playing the Indian lute. A poet and writer, he enjoyed the company of intellectuals. A devout Hindu, he especially worshiped Vishnu. His most competent son, Chandragupta II, was next enthroned. Ruling between 375 and 413, he adopted the title of Vikramaditya, or "Sun of Valor." He added the domains of the prosperous Saka states to the west and more of Bengal to the east. From a new capital in Oudh in north central India, he ruled over a prosperous empire that ranged across the north from sea to sea. He was a strong and vigorous king, and coins issued during his reign show him doing battle with lions. His son, Kumaragupta, who reigned from 413 to 455, continued the strong, autocratic, centralized Gupta rule.

Sources on Gupta rule are varied, but those on Chandragupta II's reign include an account entitled *A Record of the Buddhist Countries*. This was written by a Chinese Buddhist pilgrim, Fa Hsien, who traveled in India between 404 and 410 to study sacred texts and to visit holy places. With several companions, he embarked from north China on a long, hazardous journey. He traversed central Asia and Himalayan northwest passes on a three-year trip to India. After seven years' residence in India, which included three years in the capital and extensive visits throughout the country, he returned home via Ceylon and Southeast Asian sea routes. Though the Gupta period was a brilliant era in Indian art and culture, Fa Hsien, more interested in Buddhistic matters, did not observe or inform himself on secular affairs as extensively as Megasthenes had done earlier. He never mentioned the monarch by name, but he declared him to be a devout Buddhist—probably an exaggerated report, because the author himself was a Buddhist and the emperor was tolerant of varying faiths.

Fa Hsien's account showed an India changed from Mauryan times, some seven hundred years earlier. The pilgrim recorded the peacefulness of India, the rarity of serious crime, and the mildness of administration. Revenue was derived mainly from rent of crown lands. Royal guards and officials were paid salaries. Offenses generally were paid by fines. With the ethics of Buddhism and of Jainism helping to leaven Indian society and make it more gentle and humane, Fa Hsien declared that it was possible to travel from one end of the country to the other without molestation and without need of passports. He noted that all respectable people were now vegetarians and eschewed wine. Meat eating was confined to the low castes and to the untouchables, in regard to whom he gave us the earliest clear reference to the concept of pollution on approach. These were great changes from Mauryan times, for Asoka had not definitely forbidden the slaughter of horned animals, and the *Arthasastra* provided for the licensing and the control of the liquor trade. The pilgrim found Buddhism in both its main forms, flourishing and intermixed, but the faith was strongest in Bengal and in the northwest, or the geographical fringes of north India. Hinduism was quite widespread and entrenched in what he called mid-India, or the Gangetic plain.

Where Fa Hsien recorded the state of Buddhism in Gupta India, native Gupta art and literature noted the high state of Indian culture. In a peaceful and prosperous realm, the Guptas indicated great religiosity, subjectivity, and idealism in their artistic forms. It was in this period that the *Mahabharata* was fashioned into its present shape, and the *Puranas*, old genealogical studies that developed from the epics, were finalized. Secular literature abounded. The greatest Indian poet and playwright, Kalidasa, a native of Malwa who wrote between 400 and 455, enjoyed the patronage of the Guptas. His lyrical nature poem, *Cloud Messenger*, deals with a banished official in central India who sent a cloud as his messenger to his wife who lived in the Himalayan foothills. The poem is essentially an evocative description of the countryside over which the cloud is to pass in the course of its journey to his wife and home. Drama also flourished. Kalidasa's play, *Shakuntala*, which Goethe so highly praised in a later day, related the story of the love, separation, and reunion of a king with his lover, who is the title of the play, and their son. Another drama, *Little Clay Cart*, attributed to a contemporary, is a type of mystery play in which the protagonist is saved at the last moment from execution. Gupta dramas were performed in the courtyards of private houses with plain stages and little scenery. Actors were all male; boys played women's parts. The main themes, developing little action and much verbiage, dealt with love rather than tragedy. They were written in a mixture of Sanskrit and Prakrit. Other authors composed fables and stories about animals that eventually, in modified form, found their way into the Arabian and western worlds.

In sculpture, fine but stereotyped Buddha and Hindu images emerged. Building on the Gandhara style, the Gupta Buddha, generally in a sitting posture, appears with full cheeks, a full mouth, long earlobes, arched eyebrows, a long nose, an elaborate halo, and a smooth rounded body, pneumatic in character. In architecture, though later invading Muslims and Mongols destroyed much, Gupta secular structures were erected of wood as well as of brick. Buddhist-inspired religious buildings, later incorporated also into Hindu styles, became stereotyped. The stupa or shrine, rounded in north India, towered in the south; monasteries, with their cells, were planned around a quadrangle. Both shrines and monasteries, principally in west India, were also hewn out of solid rock. The famous rock caves at Ajanta, with both Buddhist and Hindu pictorial and sculptural representations, reflected Gupta life and times. Executed over a period of some five centuries, the Ajanta caves with their frescoes reveal traditional aspects of the life of the Buddha as well as scenes from royal and ordinary Indian life.

The sciences noted progress. In medicine, dissection was practiced; medical students cut and cleansed wounds, and applied ointments. In mathematics, Indians worked with equations and established the value of *pi*. By AD. 600, they had derived the decimal system, with a special cipher for zero. In astronomy, they noted the law of gravity, observed the daily rotation of the earth on its axis, and propounded causes for the eclipse of the sun. In metallurgy, they cast copper statues of the Buddha and other deities. Dating to the reign of Kumaragupta, near Delhi the 23-foot-high solid iron pillar, which has never rusted, records some of the accomplishments of the monarch's father, Chandragupta II.

What were the reasons for all this activity during the Gupta dynasty? Foreign contacts possibly stimulated Indian creativity; political leaders, through patronage, encouraged the arts; with peace and prosperity came no basic problems. Then, in the mid-fifth century, the Guptas came to their inevitable decline, and the empire broke up. This time the aggressors were the Huns, who simultaneously were overrunning Europe from central Asia. From Bactria, a branch, the White Huns, after extending their power into Afghanistan, entered India by way of the usual strategic passes in the northwest. In 455, after an initial encounter with the Guptas, they were defeated, but only temporarily, for they continued their raids with increasing severity until they made themselves masters of much of the northwest and of the Indus basin. Intolerant peoples, they destroyed Buddhist temples and monastic orders, and they imposed harsh rule. The Guptas, surviving in a contracted kingdom, paid tribute to them.

Once again, India was fragmented into small empires and kingdoms. The political history of sixth-century India is almost a blank. In central Asia, the Hun empire was eventually broken up by the Turks, but in India the invaders were absorbed into society. From one of their accompanying tribes descended some of the Rajputs, from another the Gujars. Both peoples have bequeathed to modern India the names of the areas in which they settled, Rajputan and Gujarat. The Rajputs ("king's sons") played an important part in north and west Indian history from the eighth to the twelfth centuries. Nearly all clans in these extensive regions were associated with Rajputs. They were warlike tribes who claimed aristocratic rank. They achieved Kshatriya status by virtue of their mode of life, which they adapted to the style expected of that class. The Brahmans treated them as such and so validated their claim to be Kshatriyas.

Post-Gupta India saw political divisions in north and south. But in the north only one short meteoric dynasty approximated the boundaries of the early Gupta empire. In 606, at the age of sixteen Harsha Siladetya came to power in the east Punjab. He inherited only a small kingdom, but through systematic campaigns within six years he built up an empire. His armies were large; they included 5,000 elephants, 20,000 cavalry, and 50,000 infantry. Chariots were no longer utilized. The king established his headquarters at Kanauj, near present-day Lucknow. An old city on the Ganges, the capital was 4 miles long and 1 mile wide, with gardens and parks. More than a hundred Buddhist monasteries and an even greater number of Hindu temples were contained within its limits. Because the city was destroyed in the sixteenth century, no building in Kanauj, or elsewhere, is identified from his reign.

Reflecting an expansive career, Harsha established diplomatic relations with Tibet, and married his daughter to the Tibetan monarch. He sent an emissary to the brilliant T'ang dynasty capital in north China and received two Chinese embassies in return. In later life, he turned to religion and philanthropy and to the support of cultural movements and literary ventures. In 647, his empire died with him. The subsequent usurper on his throne attacked a Chinese diplomatic mission, whose leader escaped to Tibet, then a powerful kingdom. He returned with troops to defeat the usurper, who was carried off to the Chinese capital. This was the first recorded instance of a strong Chinese aggressive campaign into India, and it was not to be the last.

As with Chandragupta II, so with Harsha we have a Chinese Buddhist pilgrim source on the nature of the Kanauj kingdom. Away from China from 630 to 644, Hsüan Tsang traveled to and from India via the central Asian silk routes to visit, as did his predecessor, holy Buddhist shrines and to bring home Buddhist canon. Not only was he received by Harsha, he also visited nearly every province of India. Absent for sixteen years from his home country, upon his return to the T'ang capital he translated Buddhist works in quantity twenty-five times the size of the Bible. According to Hsüan Tsang, Harsha heard complaints of all his subjects with great patience, not in an audience hall, but in a small traveling pavilion erected by the roadside. The king liked pomp and circumstance; he took along tremendous trains of attendants, officials, and monks. The administration was similar to that of the Mauryas and the Guptas, but officials were paid in land grants rather than in money. It was a well-organized kingdom, but it appeared to be a collection of subordinate provinces governed by tributary *rajas* or rulers. Each province kept special records. Taxes were the usual one-sixth of gross production. The penal code was light.

Harsha was a loyal, generous, and warm friend. He loved philosophy and literature; he composed three Sanskrit dramas. Every five years he disposed of all the wealth of the treasury to the needy. Hsüan Tsang noted that the higher castes led a simple, frugal life, which emphasized ceremonial cleanliness. City walls were constructed of brick, but houses were built of wood. In religious affairs, the pilgrim recorded a court devoted to the worship of Siva, but the eclectic Harsha additionally gave homage to the sun and to the Buddha. Mahayana forms, creating tensions with Hinayana, were spreading. The pilgrim studied Mahayana doctrines at Nalanda, a great Buddhist center of learning in the east. There, in 643, the king sponsored a great debate between the schools. Three thousand monks attended, as well as several thousands of Brahmans and Jains. But, over all, Buddhism appeared to have declined, as India generally also seemed to be on a cultural decline. Feminine divinities were worshiped, and suttee, or widow immolation, was practiced. Law and order were not so well maintained as in Gupta times. Hsüan Tsang was twice robbed by bandits in India, and in the heart of the empire on one occasion he was nearly sacrificed by river pirates to the goddess Durga, one of the appellations of Siva's wife.

Harsha left no heirs. After his passing, the partial unity of India was lost; in large measure it was not to be restored until the advent of the Moguls in the late twelfth century. The intervening five and a half centuries witnessed a long period of war and peace among the various Hindu kingdoms. But learning proceeded, and court life of the various states reflected cultural activity. Sanskrit became confirmed as the formal classical language. Other tongues as Hindi, Gujarati, and Bengali—achieved recognized status. In the lower Ganges valley, the Pala kings in the eighth century established themselves as the ruling power in Bengal and Magadha. They again turned to Buddhism but with Tantric accretions, as faith in magic and supernatural interventions. Tantrism, a combination of Buddhism and Hinduism, was a mixture of terror and sensuality, of mysticism and grossness. It worshiped ferocious new divinities, performed bloody animal sacrifices, and put faith into miraculous diagrams. From Bengal, Tantrism spread to Tibet, where it took permanent root. After 1125, the Palas were succeeded by the Sena dynasty, an orthodox Brahman line that remained in power until the Muslims arrived.

Other states arose in the northwest, west, and central Deccan. Occasionally, Deccan rulers pushed into the Gangetic plain, but no northern king crossed the Vindhyas to conquer the Deccan. The Tamils formed a world of their own. In Kashmir, a strong kingdom rose in the seventh and eighth centuries. In Rajputana, a number of principalities arose, and the Rajput princes revived the power of Hindu culture. In Maharashtra, the Chalukyas, composed of Gujar princes, became important for some two centuries, between 550 and 753. Their rulers exchanged embassies with Persia and maintained relations with the Arabs. Their kings were staunchly Hindu, though they tolerated Buddhism. Their primary enemy was the Hindu kingdom of Pallava, but they met their nemesis in the Rashtrakutas, who gained Deccan ascendancy in the mid-eighth century. The new line sprang from petty tribal chiefs, who also favored Hinduism. During its period of eminence, the Ellora cave temples were cut out, as well as that on Elephanta island in the Bay of Bombay, with the striking three-headed statue portraying the trinity of Brahma, Vishnu, and Siva. Buddhism disappeared, but the Jains persisted. The Rashtrakutas continued the perennial campaigns against Pallava, but it was a revived Chaluyka dynasty that came back to power in 973, to rule over Maharasthra until 1318, only to be destroyed by the Muslims.

The Hindu Pallavas straddled Tamil land and the Deccan. Between the mid-sixth and the mid-eighth centuries, they were the dominant power in the Madras area. From their capital of Kanchi and the great temple city of Mamallapuram, merchants and missionaries carried Indian goods and ideas into Southeast Asia, where south Indo-Chinese states adopted Pallavan structural forms. In time, the Pallavas, as well as the Tamil states of Pandya and Chera, became subject to the more powerful Cholas, which became the leading south Indian state in the tenth and the eleventh centuries. Possessing a strong navy, the Cholas controlled the Bay of Bengal, and they sent expeditions to Malaya and Indonesia. Their kings worshiped Siva as the main deity, and they erected great stone temples in his honor. During the thirteenth century, the Cholas disintegrated, and the dynasty was extinguished in the following century by the Muslims and another Hindu state in the central Deccan.

As deduced from inscriptions written between 800 and 1300, Chola administration was highly systematized. The kingdom was divided into six provinces; each province was broken down into a group of districts which, in turn, constituted a number of village unions. A union of villages, rather than an individual village, was the basic unit of administration. Each union managed local affairs through an assembly, elected for one-year terms, that held power subject to control of royal officials. Each union had its own treasury and exercised jurisdiction over village lands. Union committees discharged such routine functions of village life as the supervision of justice, maintenance of law and order, and planting of gardens and crops. The state received an average of one-sixth of land revenue, but higher imposts ranging up to one-third were placed on more fertile lands. Payment was usually in kind, sometimes in gold. Dams were built and roads maintained.

Tamil culture contributed much to the growth of popular Hinduism, which added its concepts to the core of a purer Brahmanism of an earlier time. The Aryan gods fell into desuetude and even Brahma the creator receded in importance. Vishnu and Siva emerged as the popular main Hindu gods, and their avatars, or incarnations, appeared in several forms. The newer Hinduism became decidedly anthropomorphic, and even royal personages were identified through stone sculptures with Vishnu or Siva. Derived from early Dravidian background, emotional theism was stressed by medieval Tamil theologians. Among its more persuasive exponents was the ascetic, Sankara, who traveled throughout India in the course of the ninth century. He preached the doctrine of the ultimate reality of Brahman, the world soul. All objects of the senses, he claimed, were *maya*, or illusions. To liberate oneself, one had to strip away the illusion and identify his soul with that of the world soul. Ramanuja, a later Tamil philosopher and poet, who flourished about 1100, agreed that Brahman constituted total reality, but he emphasized the concept of *bhakti*, or personal devotion to the world soul. The idea of bhakti had ancient roots in Indian thought; the *Bhagavad Gita* had advanced the concept of salvation through devotion to a deity. But Ramanuja, also traveling throughout India, helped to popularize the doctrine of salvation by faith. He himself deified Vishnu. Such basic tenets became a recognizable part of popular Hinduism. Out of the political turmoil that constituted the early centuries of medieval India after the fall of the Guptas, these religious doctrines helped shape the intellectual currents usually associated with traditional India.

Traditional India

The main outlines of traditional Indian life had emerged by the time Islam arrived in force in India around A.D. 1000. In politics, though no coherent formal philosophy had developed, Indian political leaders pursued the science of statecraft. From sources such as the *Arthasastra*, *Mahabharata*, the sacred laws, and Gupta writings, some ideas, contradictory in part, can be discovered on Indian politics. Both the contractual and the divine theories of kingship were developed in India. The concept of a universal emperor was always present, but seldom, and then imperfectly, realized. Royal pretentions grew through time, but various checks—such as the Brahmans, the sacred laws, the councillors, and the mobs—tended to compel kingly restraint.

Kings usually rose from the Kshatriya class, but they might also have originated from the Brahman and the Vaisya classes. Normally male, kings held succession generally through primogeniture. A kingdom might extend over vassals, but oligarchies or "republics" and confederacies also existed. The king was charged with many powers, including that of performing royal sacrifices. A major duty of the ruler was to control and to regulate the caste system, to punish violations of caste rules, and to use royal power to maintain the caste system unimpaired. On advice from Brahman ministers, the king could even elevate or lower a caste in the hierarchy in his kingdom. Government by discussion was also present.

Where "national" bureaucracy temporarily prevailed, subunits included provinces and divisions or districts. In periods of strong kingdoms, the provincial governors were appointed by the king, who usually designated a member of the royal family. District governors were appointed by those on the provincial level, and these in turn were assisted by a council, whose generally hereditary members were heads of castes and guilds. Cities had councils and governors, whose chief duties included the collection of taxes and the preservation of order. The village was always the basic unit of government. Villages had their headman, usually hereditary in office and held by wealthier peasants. In literature, the headman was sometimes portrayed as an oppressive tyrant. Village councils, more prominent in the south than in the north, varied in size, number, and function. They collected revenue, arbitrated disputes, and regulated communal activities, as irrigation and other local public works.

Justice was meted out by a single judge or by a bench of magistrates, inflicting a wide array of punishments. Espionage systems existed and were widespread. While nonviolence was pronounced in certain aspects, as with regard to the taking of animal life, in Indian life war and capital punishment were not forbidden. The use of force and coercion by the ruler was explicit in all classical texts. The military was included as a major arm of government. Among traditional Indian leaders, a militaristic spirit was apparent, for armies were large and warfare was endemic. Elephants were utilized, as well as infantry, with bowmen in the center of the ranks and cavalry on the flanks. The main point of warfare was to demoralize the enemy by capturing kings and elephants. Standing troops were sometimes augmented by mercenaries. Battering rams, siege machines, and fortified cities complicated war patterns. Despite recurrent warfare by monarchs to increase their domains, India was never united, at least to the extent of modern-day India. The size of the land militated against union, and no bureaucracy on a continuing permanent basis was created to ensure survival of a political unit over an extended area. With scattered kingdoms, changing alliances, amorphously massed armies, and rigid theories of warfare, India was easily overrun by foreign invaders.

In religious affairs, regulation, rather than creation, became the watchword. To Vedic sacrifices and Hindu worship were added a multitude of demigods and spirits, as the *nagas* or snake spirits, the *yaksas* or gnomes and fairies, the *gandharvas* or male heavenly musicians, and their consorts, the beautifully seductive heavenly female *apsarases*. Vishnu and Siva emerged as the most important gods; caste became increasingly more rigid; pilgrimages, probably with impetus gained from Buddhism and Jainism, were widespread. On the one hand, indices of spiritual degeneration, as temple prostitution, became pronounced; on the other, the concept of bhakti as the doctrine of compassionate grace and love also grew. But no matter the expression or form, religion and a purported religious base for life pervaded traditional India.

In society, class and caste strictly governed behavior and

customs. Caste was based chiefly on three aspects: endogamy, or marriage within the group; commensality, or food habits that stressed food was to be received from and eaten with members of the same or higher groups; and occupation. Within this closed system, the joint family existed. It was patriarchal in structure, and it possessed rites commemorating up to seven generations of living and dead. Property was held communally, though it could be divided, if available, among male heirs. Marriage was generally monogamous, and widows could not remarry. The cow was held sacred, and while Asoka did not forbid slaughter of cattle, the *Arthasastra* suggested that those who did kill cattle should be put to death, a reference apparently to poachers killing cattle stolen from royal herds. The early spread of Mahayana Buddhism and Jainism also promoted vegetarianism.

In social and economic life, as in the political, the villages were the most important unit. Then, as now, the greatest proportion of India's population, estimated between 100 and 140 millions in medieval times, lived in the villages. These consisted of a cluster of huts, small and large, sometimes grouped around a source of water, as a well or a pond. In earlier times, they were usually stockaded. The villages often contained clubrooms or temples as a focal point for social and religious affairs. Villagers engaged in communal and corporate activities through their councils. Most villagers owned their land to all intents and purposes, though the distant monarch at the capital might claim its ultimate possession. Most holdings were quite small, and they were worked over by the peasant owner and members of his family. Landless peasants also existed, and they eked out a hard, subsistence living. Land taxation practices varied, but the basic tax, usually in kind, varied between one-sixth to one-third of the crop. Other taxes might include special assessments, house taxes, shop taxes, and road tolls. Taxes were to be in return for protection by the king as the ultimate landowner.

The shading between villages and small towns was slight. Of the latter, by the time of the Buddha, many were scattered throughout north India. But large cities were few in number; usually the metropolis was the concurrent center of government, commerce, and religion. In the city were the palaces and the temples. Temples, if they were famous shrines in sacred cities, were wealthy, and they provided employment to numerous persons servicing the buildings and the pilgrims. The wealthy lived in several-storeyed edifices, usually built around a square courtyard containing gardens, with whitewashed walls and thatched or tile roofs. The humble dwelt in huts of reed, brick, or wood, and thatched with straw. City folk and townsmen enjoyed numerous festivals, of which the most popular one was *Holi*, or the spring festival, a time of merrymaking in which rich and poor alike played practical jokes on each other, as scattering powder and squirting water.

In towns and cities, commercial life flourished. In theory, the government controlled and regulated economic life. Though trade in kind or barter was the usual practice, a money economy, utilizing silver or bronze with punchmarks, existed in India from the time of the Buddha. In the second century B.C., such coins were minted and gold and nickel specimens were added later. The basis of Indian industry was the individual craftsman, helped by members of his family. A great portion of his work was sold at the door directly to the buyer. Usually, each trade or craft was concentrated in a separate market or street, as in medieval Europe. Guilds existed and they, as well as the state, controlled the price and the quality of the product. They fixed hours of work and wages, and they presided over their own members in judicial matters, a practice that was accepted by the state. Guild courts could penalize erring members, and sometimes they even interfered in family relations of their members. Guilds were headed by hereditary, wealthy chiefs, who were assisted by small councils of elder members. The corporate bodies had their own heralds and banners and sometimes they maintained their own militia.

In external affairs, by A.D. 1000 contacts were falling off between India and foreign lands. Prior to that time, trade routes existed from west India to the Persian Gulf, Africa, and Europe. From east India they extended to Southeast Asia and China. From north India they stretched into central Asia and again into China. As early as 712, Arabs arrived in the Sind area. There they developed settlements, as well as around present-day Bombay; though under Muslim rule, they did not expand at that time. In Southeast Asia, Buddhist- and Hindu-inspired kingdoms continued to rise in Indo-China, Thailand, Burma, Malaya, and Indonesia. As early as A.D. 192, a Hindu kingdom was established in central Vietnam. At least three other major kingdoms arose in present-day Cambodia, whose modern name is derived from the Kambuja, or Khmer, kingdom. Its kings in the twelfth century erected the royal city of Angkor Thom and the magnificent royal temple of Angkor Vat, probably the largest religious edifice in the world. The Cambodian kings, as the Indian, identified themselves with Hindu or Buddhist deities and were semi-divine in nature. Minor kingdoms arose in Thailand and in Burma. The Mons, who inhabited lower Thailand and Burma, were in great measure responsible for the spread in the twelfth century on mainland Southeast Asia of Hinayana Buddhism that emanated from Ceylon. Hinayana came to replace the earlier Mahayana, and this form of Buddhism became the state religion of modern Burma, Thailand, Laos, and Cambodia. On Sumatra and Java, the Srivijaya kingdom, which lasted from the eighth to the fourteenth centuries, borrowed religious and secular Indian ideas. In the eighth century, its ally, the Sailendra kingdom on central Java, erected the Mahayana Buddhist monument of Borobudur.

Relations with China, sporadic but significant, continued through pilgrims and merchants. Developing in northwest India, Mahayana Buddhism spread into China in the first centuries of the Christian era. Legend relates that Buddhist missionaries from India made their first appearance in 217 B.C. in the Chinese capital. In 121 B.C., a golden statue of the Buddha was taken by a Chinese general from the Huns. In A.D. 65, the Chinese emperor dreamed of a golden man; his courtiers informed him that it was the Buddha. Ambassadors accordingly were sent to invite Buddhist missionaries from India; two returned. Fa Hsien and Hsüan Tsang were only the most famous of the early Chinese Buddhist pilgrims. In the seventh century, I Ching traveled via sea from Canton in south China to and from India in search of the latest Buddhist doctrines. In the second half of the same century, fifty more pilgrimages were recorded of other Chinese. Until about A.D. 1000, Indian missionaries also went to China. After 1036, Chinese chronicles have nothing more to report on the arrival of Indians to the Chinese court. By that time, the faith was dying out in India and simultaneously was losing its hold in China, but only after it had been exported in turn to Korea and to Japan.

So India received from and gave to neighboring states. It possessed a complex civilization that had evolved from one dominant religion with many facets. It had been fashioned through the fusion of many races, with their babel of tongues, in a geographically varied area. And traditional India was yet to enter even more kaleidoscopeic eras under further foreign rule, first that of the Muslims and then that of the British.

Chronology

B.C.

185–73	Sunga dynasty replaces Mauryan in north
184	Menander raids Gangetic plains from central Asia; two Greek dynasties established in northwest India
135	Scythians or Sakas commence invasions of India, replace Greeks
73–28	Kanva dynasty succeeds Sunga
28–A.D. 225	Andhra empire in the Deccan
20	Embassy from Tamil kingdom of Pandya to Rome
end of 1st century	Parthians or Pahlavas replace Sakas; gain suzerainty over northwest India; rule of Gondophernes

A.D.

45	Monsoon winds discovered as sailing aid in Indian Ocean
1st century	Kushans take over northwest India from Parthian domination
78–96	Rule of Kushan king, Kanishka
99	Kushan embassy to Rome
192	Hindu kingdom established in central Vietnam; Southeast Asia subjected to historic Hindu and Buddhist influences over next millennium
225	Pallava dynasty replaces Andhra in Deccan
3rd century	Rise of Tamil kingdoms in south: Chola, Kerala, Pandya

320–480	Gupta empire in Gangetic plain, founded by Chandragupta I, ruling 320–330
400–455	Poet and playwright Kalidasa flourishes
404–410	Chinese Buddhist pilgrim Fa Hsien in India
mid-5th century	Hun raids into north India, Rajputs and Gujars descendants
mid-6th to 8th century	Pallavas dominant in Madras area
550–753	First Chalukya kingdom in Maharashtra or Bombay area
606–647	Harsha's kingdom in north
630–647	Travels of Chinese Buddhist pilgrim Hsuan Tsang
712	Arabs arrive in Sind
8th century	Pala kings in Bengali; Tantrism rises
973–1318	Revived Chaluyka dynasty
10th–11th century	Height of Chola dynasty; Tamils in Ceylon
1125	Sena dynasty succeeds Pala in Bengal

Muslim India

Chapter 4

Muslim India

Islam Introduced

In A.D. 1018, Mahmud of Ghazni invaded India from his base in Afghanistan. He marched into the Punjab and conquered the north central kingdom of Kanauj. From this date, Muslim rule commenced on the Indian subcontinent. Muslim domination was real or nominal and wide or constricted, depending on the power of the reigning houses. For some seven centuries, until A.D. 1707, upon the death of the last and great Mogul emperor, Aurangzeb, Muslim kingdoms were a feature of Indian history. Though generally they were confined to north India, some of them ephemerally spread into south India as well. The Muslims generally settled down to live permanently in India. They conquered, intermarried with, or alternately left alone, the Hindu inhabitants of their domains. Their historical record was mixed. Muslim India, after an initial five centuries of Turkish sultans and a subsequent two centuries of Mogul emperors, showed a pattern that revealed some traits of compromise and some of amalgamation with native life. But the pattern revealed a more basic and fundamental cultural disparity between Hinduism and Islam.

Islam came late to India. The founder of the new religion was Muhammad, who lived from A.D. 570 to 632 in Arabia. He was a camel dealer in Mecca who, in middle age, received revelations through visions which he recorded in the Koran, the holy book of Islam. He called his faith Islam, or resignation to the will of God or of Allah. His followers were termed Muslims, or the resigned ones. He clearly defined his dogma in the *kalima* or creed, "There is no God but God and Muhammad is the prophet of God." He emphasized the unity and greatness of God and the absolute authority of the Koran. Muhammad's creed was monotheistic. Puritanical, it disclaimed idolatry, it frowned on music in mosques, it posited a strong belief in destiny, and it propounded a fatalism to the "will of Allah." Its five pillars were ritual purification, prayer, alms, fasting, and pilgrimage. Its followers constituted a brotherhood, and every man (but not woman) was equal before God.

Partly reflecting Arab times and environment, Islam permitted polygamy in social affairs. The Koran allowed four wives and subordinate wives or concubines. Woman's estate was an inferior one. She could not worship in mosques or take part in public life. She received little education, lived a secluded life, and dressed in a *burda,* or sacklike shroud. In early Islamic political theory, all Muslims formed one congregation that elected a caliph as the prophet's successor. He was a temporal rather than a spiritual leader. This principle of political universality did not last long in incipient Islam, for with the rapid spread of the faith the caliph of the day became the one who commanded the widest allegiance. But all true believers belonged to the world of Islam, and *jihad* or holy war was one means to extend it or to defend it. Some unbelievers, as Jews or Christians, who believed in the Old Testament, could purchase protection without conversion through the payment of *jizya,* or a poll tax. This process was later widely extended in India to Hindus, and it greatly facilitated Muslim rule.

Like other major world religions, Islam in its historical development was modified and was affected by the races and the nations accepting it. Arabs developed the *Shariat*, or Islamic law. Borrowing heavily from the classical Greek heritage, they returned Greek thought, particularly that of Aristotle, to the west through their academic channel at the University of Paris. The Turks, more experimentative, adapted the religion to their own needs. The Persians, more introspective, contributed a mystic and sensuous strain to Islam. With varying adaptations came differing interpretations of the Koran, an inevitable result of its evolution through time. While many sects arose in Islam, two main ones emerged, the orthodox

Sunnis, to which the ruling Turks in India generally adhered, and the more heterodox Shias, dominant in Persia, who through the Sufi movement propounded mysticism and free thought. Historical counter-claims to the caliphate among rulers of the Islamic states acerbated theological differences among them. After the prophet's death, leadership initially passed to the caliph, the first of whom was Abu Bakr, the prophet's earliest friend and the real founder of the Islamic empire. In 658, a split occurred, chiefly between the Arabs and the Persians for the line of succession. The former believed in free elections for the position, while the latter upheld apostolic continuity through Ali, Muhammad's son-in-law.

Despite internal political and doctrinal controversies, Islam exploded on the Middle Eastern, central Asian, and European scenes in its first century and a half of existence. Consolidation of the religion in the Middle East came first. In 635, the Arabs captured Damascus. This event took place only three years after Muhammad's death, while Harsha was ruling Kanauj and while the Chinese Buddhist pilgrim Hsüan Tsang was studying in India. The next year they entered Jerusalem and displaced the Byzantine Greeks. In 643, they wrested Egypt from the Greeks and overthrew the Persian Sassanids. In 650, they established the caliphate at Damascus. The Arabs could have pushed on into India, but they did not do so at the time because they were occupied elsewhere. In 711, they conquered Spain, but they were stopped in 732 at the fateful battle of Tours in France. They overran Asia Minor, but they were repulsed in 717 from Constantinople. In 751, they met the Chinese in central Asia at Talas—a significant event because it crystallized the boundaries of the Sinic and the Islamic spheres of culture in central Asia into contemporary times. In 762, the caliphate was transferred to Baghdad, and while the first Arabs arrived in the lower Sind about 712, India received a respite of three centuries from Muslim rule. Instead it was the Turks, indebted to Persian cultural influences, who introduced Islam from Afghanistan into northwest India in the eleventh century.

The Muslims, who began as traders in the lower Sind and as military troops in the Punjab, in time became one-fourth in numbers of the total population on the Indian subcontinent. The expansion of Islam in India is as intriguing a story as that of early Muslim expansion outside of India. In India, as elsewhere, conversion took place through several means. Undoubtedly, conversions proceeded by the sword, but this was the exception rather than the rule in India. Political motivation accounted for some conversions, for the path to highest fame and position was through adoption of the new faith. Migrations added to the numbers of Muslims in India because soldiers as individuals or as clans in the invading Turkish armies settled down to live in India. Theological persuasion, principally through dedicated Sufis as agents, won converts.

Indians reacted to conversions on an individual or on a corporate basis. Large-scale conversions took place mainly in the Punjab area, with its proximity and long historical subjugation to Afghan and central Asian Islamic kingdoms, and in east Bengal (now East Pakistan), where an oppressive Brahman rule under the Sena dynasty, whose founders had migrated into the area from south India, drove many into the Muslim fold. Muslim converts also probably came from among former non-Hindu and Buddhist groups who were low in status as far as the Hindus were concerned and who had been only inadequately assimilated into Hinduism. While other areas or tribes in north India turned to Islam, including some of the three dozen Rajput clans, Islam was mainly polarized east and west in north India. Indian Muslims were essentially Indian, but they were definitely Muslims.

The Muslims ruled over kingdoms of Hindu populations. Conversions and intermarriage proceeded through time. Some mutual influences, which were important, existed, as a strain of mysticism in both faiths, racial affinity, some social assimilation, a common speech, and a common body of secular intellectual knowledge. But Hinduism and Islam were fundamentally different ways of life, though some individuals and movements tried to bridge the gaps. Islam was theologically defined, while Hinduism was vague. Hinduism was polytheistic and idolatrous; Islam was monotheistic. Hindus had caste; Muslims posited equality of man. Muslims did not revere the sacred Hindu cow, and they saw nothing wrong in eating beef. On the other hand, Hindus ate pork and they loved music, playing it outside mosques. Because of deep feelings resulting from different ways of life, riots between adherents of the two dominant religions occurred and continued to occur into contemporary times. Though some in both camps accepted cultural coexistence, in the last analysis most Muslims and Hindus did not. The chief legacies of this state of affairs were cultural apartheid and political partition on the subcontinent.

Turks

The impact of Islam in India was delivered by the Turks. In a nomadic state, these peoples were restless and warlike. By the end of the first millennium A.D., they had established themselves in Turkestan, in what is now Soviet Asia. As far as this, Islam reached out from Persia and converted them. Complex in nature, the Turks were both destroyers and builders, ruthless conquerors and patrons of the arts. In 1071, they overthrew the Greek emperor and overran Asia Minor. Five years later, they took Jerusalem, and this action set the Crusades in motion. Simultaneously, they expanded east into Afghanistan, where some of them, having previously enlisted as bodyguards to Arab rulers, asserted their independence to form independent Turkish states. In 998, one such state was established in Afghanistan by a former Turkish slave and called Ghazni, located some 80 miles south of Kabul.

It was the founder's son, Mahmud of Ghazni, who first entered India in force. Between 1000 and 1030, Muslim sources record seventeen incursions of his into India. Of these, two were the most important and far-reaching. In 1018, he sallied forth from Ghazni, with a 100,000-horse army, seized Mathura, plundered temples, and then turned east to Kanauj, which submitted. Leaving behind administrators, he returned to Ghazni with an enormous booty. In this campaign we have reference of *jawhar*, the practice, usually associated with the Rajput clans, of warriors who, when faced with a hopeless campaign, killed their wives and children and sallied forth to certain death against overwhelming odds. From 1024 to 1026, a second major campaign led Mahmud, "the image breaker," looting and plundering, south to the Kathiawar coast. His destination was the great temple to Siva at Somnath. After fierce fighting, his men conquered the city and put to death over 50,000 in the battles. Mahmud himself destroyed the Siva idol and dispatched fragments back to Ghazni, where the faithful trod on them. In 1030, the conqueror died, but for more than a century his dynasty retained Ghazni and a large part of the Punjab. Because of his campaigns that involved widespread destruction and idol-breaking, one of Mahmud's legacies to Hindu India was the stereotype that pointed up Muslim intolerance and needless waste.

Despite his ravaging campaigns in India, Mahmud in his capital kept a well-ordered court. He erected mosques and collected libraries. He enjoyed the company of learned men, and Persian became the language of the court and of the literati. Some of Mahmud's personality and his rule is contained in the works of the scholar Alberuni, who resided in north India. Alberuni was a great literary and scientific figure of Islamic culture. A remarkably well-rounded man, he was interested in Hindu philosophy, and he versed himself with the Hindu classics. He studied Sanskrit. He composed a complex history of India which, in a rather unusual way for a Muslim, dealt at great lengths with the customs of the infidels. He recorded the relatively high position of women, but also noted suttee. He mentioned the increasing incidence of child marriages. He portrayed the strong role of the Brahmans, though he was silent on Buddhist activities.

In the twelfth century, Mahmud's successors were replaced by another Turkish dynasty centered at Ghur, also in Afghanistan. In 1175, Muhammad of Ghur, having overcome his overlords, went into Multan, captured Lahore in 1186, and sent plundering raids as far as Bengal. He made Delhi his capital, and extended his kingdom throughout the traditional Hindustan area. Local rajahs went down into defeat through their conservative military tactics, inter-clan jealousies, and social and religious tensions between the rulers and their subjects. To many peasants of north India, Turkish horrors, while aggravated, were no worse than those perpetrated by Hindus. It was chiefly the Brahmans and the few remaining Buddhist monks who suffered at Muhammad's hands. For three decades, the Ghuris ruled from Ghazni to the Bay of Bengal, until Muhammad was assassinated in 1206. Effective rule then passed to Aibak, his most trusted general and viceroy, a former slave, who set up a new Turkish dynasty at Delhi.

Over the next three centuries, some three dozen sultans or rulers in five dynasties ruled from Delhi. Known collectively as the Delhi sultanate, the monarchs revealed varying personalities and programs. The Delhi sultanate was an autocratic state with unlimited powers in the monarch. He maintained a royal army and utilized the armed forces of the military nobility, who served him as governors or overlords of provinces. Some of the sultans continued the vindictive policies of the earliest Turkish rulers, while others practiced more conciliatory measures. But they, and their Muslim followers, constituted only a minority in Hindu India. They had to evolve a modus vivendi with the Hindus in the land they had conquered and which they ruled from Delhi, a relatively new focus of political power in north India. Though the territory in the vicinity of Delhi is recorded by other names in the *Mahabharata*, it was never a source of major Indian governmental power until the Turks established themselves there. Located strategically between the Punjabi and the Gangetic plains, Delhi faced east and west.

As the first of the five lines, the Slave Dynasty (1206 to 1290) consolidated the north Indian kingdom. It finally obliterated organized Buddhism, which was already in precipitous decline; it overthrew Brahman rule in Bengal as well as Rajput dominance in north and central India; and it kept the Mongols, restive under Genghis Khan and his successors, at bay on India's borders. Aibak, the founder of the dynasty, had been on the throne only five years when he was killed in a polo accident in 1211. The Turkish nobles elected as his successor another general who had commenced life as a slave but had risen in status through ability. He nominated his daughter Raziya as his successor, and she was the first of Muslim princesses who were to take a prominent part in affairs of state. After ascending the throne, she proved to be a forceful leader. She commanded the troops in person, seated in full armor on an elephant. But she could not overcome prejudices and court intrigues, and she and her husband were murdered. After a period of temporary confusion, Balban, who ruled from 1266 to 1287, ascended the throne. Already advanced in years, he was a severe but just, temperate, and fairly tolerant man. He put minor posts into Hindu hands, and in his rule no general Hindu uprising occurred. After his death at the age of eighty, another period of anarchy resulted.

The Slave kings were supplanted by another tribe from Afghanistan, that of the Khalji sultans (1290 to 1320), who carried Islam south. The founder of the short-lived dynasty was another old man of over seventy. His wars were conducted mainly by his nephew Alauddin, who campaigned against the Mongols to the west and invaded Deccan to the south. An able but unscrupulous man, he murdered his uncle to ascend the throne. Calling himself a second Alexander, Alauddin, ruling from 1296 to 1315, repelled five Mongol invasions and campaigned against the Rajput princes. Generals carried his campaigns deep into Tamil land, where the Hindu temples of Madura were sacked. The sultan effected stern measures against both Muslims and Hindus. He strictly enforced Koranic law, and he forbade Hindus to carry arms or ride horses. He abolished grants and stipends to Muslim nobles, and levied compulsory taxes on Hindus at half their total incomes. He instituted a widespread espionage system. Under his rule, peace and prosperity prevailed, but only at heavy cost. Eventually, Alauddin was assassinated. His son followed on the throne, but after a three-year reign he too was killed, and more chaos resulted.

Under the Tughluqs (1320 to 1413), whose name derived from the founder of the new line, the Muslim breakup began, with the loss of the south and with the sack of north India and of Delhi in 1398 and 1399 by Timur. Muhammad Tughluq (ruling from 1325 to 1351), the son of the founder of the line, was one of the more noteworthy sultans. He was a mixture of opposites: arrogant and humble, generous and cruel, courageous and severe. A pious Muslim, he abstained from wine. A good scholar, he was skilled in letters and the sciences. He was brilliant but eccentric. One of his more drastic actions was the evacuation of Delhi in 1326–1327, partly for economic reasons as a result of famine conditions and partly to punish the inhabitants for disloyal behavior. Some of his personality and his acts were described in the works of Ibn Batuta, an Arab traveler from Africa who resided at the court of Delhi for five years, from 1342 to 1347. The monarch died of fever and his cousin ascended the throne.

The new sultan, Firoz Shah Tughluq, ruling from 1351 to 1388, was a just monarch in many ways. He abolished cruel punishments; he taxed lightly; he constructed and repaired canals and irrigation ditches. He utilized able ministers, one of whom was a Brahman who had accepted Islam. But, like his cousin, he was a strict Muslim. He forced the poll tax, and he forbade the erection of Hindu temples. He demolished others and used the materials to construct mosques. His administration evidenced the prototype of the Muslim political structure that existed during Turkish rule. The king was supreme, and he was commander-in-chief of the armed forces. The provinces were governed by generals, who were usually princes of the royal family. Officials were paid through the assignments of revenues of certain tracts of land. Provincial governors kept an elaborate system of accounts that were audited at regular intervals. Gold and silver coinage circulated. The chief sources of income were the land revenues and the poll taxes on non-Muslims.

Firoz Shah's rule was firm, but his territory shrank. He lost Sind, Bengal, and the Deccan. Upon his death, anarchy resulted, and the invasions by Timur within a decade effectively terminated Tughluq power. Timur, who had overrun central Asia, marched through north India on Delhi. In a five-day siege and pillage in the city he killed 50,000 and enslaved double that number. He returned to Samarkand, to leave famine and pestilence behind. In the ensuing politically turbulent decades, the Sayyid rulers (1414 to 1451) came into power. Three members of the dynasty, who claimed to be Sayyids, or descendants of the prophets, ascended the Delhi throne. The last of these abdicated in favor of the Lodis (1451 to 1526), an Afghan tribe. The founder of the last of the Delhi sultanate lines was a good ruler and a man of simple habits. But, in the course of Lodi rule, its territory shrank to Delhi and the countryside around the capital. North India became balkanized. Delhi rule was contested by other Muslim and Hindu rulers. It was left to the advent of the Moguls, who, again emanating from Afghanistan, effectively replaced the decadent Turkish lines in 1526.

The Muslim Turks with their Koran, their prophet, and their definite tenets could not be absorbed into Hinduism and Hindu castes as some earlier invaders had been. But certain Islamic ideas, which found counterparts in Hindu thought and life, provided a bridge between conquerors and conquered. The practice of purdah, or seclusion of women, already present in incipient form in Hindu life, was enhanced. A common linguistic basis was found in Urdu, the "camp" language, derived from the Turkish word for camp. Urdu was a Persianized form of western Hindi, especially spoken around Delhi. Urdu utilized Hindi grammar and structure, but it contributed Persian vocabulary, which, after the Muslim conquest of Persia, included Arabic words as well. Islamic monotheism and its devotional theistic approach could be equated with bhakti. Ramanand, who lived in the fourteenth century in south India and continued the work of the eleventh-century prophet Ramanuja, preached devotion to the deity in the form of Vishnu in incarnations as Rama and Krishna. He admitted the casteless and peoples of all castes to his orders. He had twelve apostles, including a Muslim weaver, Kabir (d. 1518). Kabir's own followers included both Muslims and Hindus. He condemned the worship of idols and the institution of caste. The essence of his teaching was that God, as a spirit, existed everywhere.

The legacy of Turkish rule was mixed. While the Turks could be severe, generally their severity was limited to Hindu leaders. On the other hand, there was not a great disturbance of the commoner's life. Peasants continued to sow or to reap, but they paid revenue either directly to Muslim rulers or through Hindu chiefs to the new overlords. The Turks, if not ruling directly over territories, utilized the traditional Hindu pattern of a number of vassal states acknowledging the supremacy of an overlord. Hindu rulers submitted, paid tribute, and retained position and authority. The Turks, as well as their successors the Moguls, generally sought paramountcy rather than empire, suzerainty rather than sovereignty, and superintendence rather than control.

The loose control of the Turks from Delhi in the latter course of their dynasties was reflected in the growth of independent states in the peripheral areas. Of the autonomous Muslim states that arose during the Delhi sultanate, some of the more prominent included those in Bengal (1338 to 1576), Malwa (1401 to 1564), Gujarat (1411 to 1572), and Kashmir (1346 to 1586). All were eventually conquered by the great Mogul ruler Akbar and reincorporated into centralized Muslim rule. The most important independent Muslim state was that of the Bahmani kingdom in the Deccan. In 1347, Muslim chiefs there had rebelled against Turkish domination and established the principality. The founder assumed the name of Bahman because he claimed descent from an early Persian king of the same name.

At its height, Bahmani stretched from sea to sea and included Hyderabad, as well as parts of Madras and Bombay. A sultan, assisted by a council of eight, administered the kingdom; an elaborate army conducted almost continual warfare and used artillery in its early campaigns for the first time in Indian history. The monarchs maintained huge armies that included unruly mobs and foreign adventurers. The kingdom had a bloody history, and its kings were fanatical and warlike. Some of them, however, gave encouragement to the pursuit of purely Muslim learning, and they undertook irrigation works in the eastern provinces. A Russian merchant, Athanasius Nikitin, who resided in Bahmani dominions between 1470 and 1474, recorded some aspects of political life for posterity. By 1518, the kingdom had broken up into five fragments, when the five provincial governors declared their independence. These successor states to Bahmani included Bidar to the south, Golconda and Berar to the east, and Ahmadnagar and Bijapur to the west. As the most important, Bijapur was a well-governed kingdom. Its rulers, one of whom married a Hindu princess, went on building sprees. The capital city of the same name boasted fine secular and sacred monuments, including a mosque with the second largest dome in the world. Eventually, the five kingdoms were absorbed by the powerful Moguls.

A concurrent Hindu political movement, directed against both Muslim and Turkish domination, resulted in the establishment of the empire of Vijayanagar ("City of Victory"). Lasting from 1336 to 1565, it controlled all of India south of the Kistna river, and it formed an effective barrier to the Islamic armies from the north. It engaged in continual warfare with its rival, Bahmani. Vijayanagar was founded by two brothers in what is now the state of Andhra in south central India. Originally Hindus, they were converted to Islam, but then they reverted to their original faith. They built up a powerful state, headed by a *raja* or king, and supported by a central bureaucracy and a mercenary army. The king presided over a brilliant court and lived in a palace enclosure with thirty-four streets. As supreme head, the king appointed a council of ministers and viceroys for each of the six principal provinces, which were again further subdivided. Some of the offices were hereditary, but their occupants were often related to the royal family. The officials contributed a fixed number of troops and a certain amount of revenue to the king's coffers. Land revenue assessments, in cash or in kind, varied according to the type of land under cultivation.

Inscriptions, coins, and accounts of indigenous, Muslim, and early European travelers, including the Italian, Nicolo Conti (1420), the Russian, Nikitin (1470), and the Portuguese, Domingo Paes (1552), described the riches of Vijayanagar. It amassed wealth from textiles, mining, metallurgy, perfumery, and crafts. The kingdom exported cloth, rice, iron, saltpeter, sugar, and spices; it imported horses, elephants, pearls, copper, coral, mercury, China silks, and velvet. It utilized gold, silver, and copper coins. With over half a million inhabitants, its capital spread 7 miles north to south. A type of decadent Hinduism was practiced in the kingdom, with suttee and numerous sacrificial and animistic rites practiced. Animal food, except beef, was eaten.

Though Vijayanagar was a Hindu state, it was rent by regionalism, for its rulers constituted a Telugu-speaking oligarchy that presided over Kanaras, Tamils, and Malayalis. While the kingdom lasted, it was prosperous and great. But the capital was destroyed in 1565 by its Muslim neighbors to the north, and it was never repopulated. The kingdom fell apart, in part because of the artificially imposed regional and centralized oligarchy. While little remains today of its former glory, Vijayanagar, as Hindu enclave in south India, managed to contain for some two centuries the further spread of Muslim rule into Tamil land, until the Moguls burst onto the scene.

Moguls

Like preceding Turkish dynasties, the Moguls rose to power in Afghanistan, outside of India. From there, the Moguls (a term loosely applied in India to all foreign Muslims from central Asia, and a term that is also spelled variously as Mongol, Mughal, or Mughul), spilled over into north India. They came to conquer and to hold, for varying interims, almost the whole of the country. The Mogul period in Indian history was one in which royal personalities dominated, particularly those of its founder Babur, his grandson Akbar, and the latter's great grandson Aurangzeb. Under the Moguls there was a general advance in refinement and elegance of life in India. The Mogul court, whether in Delhi, Agra, or on the move in the Deccan, was the nerve center of the empire. Scholarship and literature flourished; poetry abounded; painting proliferated; architecture luxuriated. Monuments are plentiful from this period. They include graceful buildings with bulbous domes, lofty vaulted gateways, cupolas, and slender pillars. Detailed records on Mogul rule include contemporary accounts by local historians and by rulers themselves, as Babur, who wrote his memoirs, and Aurangzeb, who conducted extensive correspondence and reports. European sources, as traders and priests, some transient, some resident, some keen, some less perspicacious, also recorded impressions. Under the Moguls, particularly the earlier rulers, India enjoyed its most impressive political and cultural life in a millennium.

In the early sixteenth century, India and central Asia were turbulent, divided, and restless. The backwash of Timur's invasions resulted in differing, bickering kingdoms. As first of the Mogul line, Babur ("The Tiger") himself was part Turk and part Mongol. He was fifth in descent from Timur, and, on his maternal side, traced an even earlier line back to Genghiz Khan. Born in 1483 in Ferghana in central Asia, Babur ascended the throne at the age of eleven, and he built up his kingdom in Afghanistan. After unsuccessful wars in expanding his domain in central Asia, he directed his energies to north India, which was then in loose confederation, or fighting with, the Lodis. Invited into Punjab by the governor of that province (as Alexander had been in an earlier day), the conqueror, after several compaigns in 1526, captured Delhi. With the aid of artillery and musketry, his troops of 8,000 defeated the Lodi's army of 50,000 men and 1,000 elephants. After this initial success, he spent the following four years, until his death in 1530, with few resources but formidable enemies, in consolidating north India.

Babur was a cultural link between the central Asian nomad and the refinement of north Indian court life. He was a great soldier and a courageous leader, as well as a poet, musician, and appreciative lover of beauty. Coming from a cooler climate, he disliked India as much as his men did. He tried to placate his discontented followers, who, in the hot, dry, dusty Indian countryside, longed for the high, cool Afghan retreats. He dealt vigorously in the Gangetic plain with the Afghan nobles, each of whom under the Lodis was practically supreme in his own territory. He defeated the Rajput clans, including the chief one at Mewar (Udaipur). Though military campaigns consumed much of his energy, he found time to write poetry, exercise a sense of chivalry and of humor in his undertakings, indulge in the good manners and taste of a Persian-influenced life, and write an autobiography. His *Memoirs*, written in Turkish and later translated into Persian, reveal the author as a likeable, vigorous personality, who shared both the hardships and the good life with his followers.

Humayun, Babur's eldest son and governor of one of the provinces, succeeded him. He was also a brave and refined man, but he lapsed into indolence and did not press his military campaigns to successful conclusions. Addicted to opium, he idled away his time at Agra. This proved conducive to promoting revolts among the Afghan nobles, one of whom, Sher Khan, an able and powerful general, drove Humayun into exile in Afghanistan. From there, the unlucky monarch was further pursued by a rival brother until Humayan ended up in Persia. There he managed to elicit help from the Shah, and with reinforcements he returned to expel his brother from Kabul, where he set himself up as ruler.

In India, after ascending the throne at Delhi, the rebel Sher Khan assumed the title of Sher Shah. A strong, effective ruler, he put down the disaffected Afghan nobles. His powerful central army consisted of some 150,000 horsemen, 25,000 infantry, and 5,000 elephants. To obviate the possibility of graft, he branded horses in government service. Sher Shah personally supervised a tightly knit political and administrative structure of government. His domains were divided into forty-seven provinces, each of which was again subdivided into districts consisting of groups of villages. Each district had a military governor, treasurer, judicial officer, and two accountants, one writing in Hindi and the other in Persian. The village communities bore responsibility for crimes committed within their borders.

The monarch promoted other strong economic and social measures. He enforced a strict collection of land revenue, which was settled directly with the cultivators at one-fourth or one-third of the average produce, payable either in kind or in cash, with the latter method of payment preferred. He built a network of roads throughout north India with shade trees, conveniently placed resthouses, and a system of horse-posts. Law and order were well maintained. Hindus were employed in office. There was no religious persecution and Hindus could practice their rites. An excellent silver coinage was issued, with the rupee standardized at 180 grains, a ratio that was adopted by the later Moguls and the British. In power only five short years, Sher Shah, with his administrative reforms and efficiency, paved the way for Akbar, into whose service passed many of the officials. Killed in battle in 1545, Sher Shah was succeeded by a son, who ruled for nine years. Upon his death, succession disputes broke out, and, taking advantage of the disorders, Humayun returned from Kabul to reoccupy Delhi. The fruits of victory were short-lived, for his second reign lasted only seven months before his death.

Humayun's son, Akbar, ascended the throne at the age of thirteen, to rule, initially through a regency, for half a century, from 1556 to 1605. As a contemporary of Philip II of Spain and of Queen Elizabeth of England, he ruled over a populous empire of some 100 million inhabitants. Akbar was the most famous of the Mogul line. A complex man, he was a soldier, administrator, statesman, leader, and artist. He was an intellectual with an inquiring mind, but, apparently through choice, he could neither read nor write. Physically, he was well equipped for the arduous task of empire building. He liked sports. He was decisive in action and ambitious in character. His personal magnetism attracted many men and loyal followers. He lived long and he reigned long, and, in a country were age was respected, he became a legend in his own lifetime. Akbar united north and central India, and gave to it a Persian form. The monarch extended his conquests south to Rajput and Gujarat, east to Bihar and Bengal, northwest to Punjab, Afghanistan and Kashmir, and southwest to the lower Sind and Baluchistan. In the latter years of his reign he pushed into the Deccan, but this proved to be an Achilles heel to the aging monarch, as it had been to previous conquerors.

Akbar's military conquests were aided by political policies of toleration and of accommodation. While initially proving unruly, the Rajputs were given personal privileges and concessions, class, and prestige. The proud Hindu clan leaders became partners with the Moguls in the joint enterprise of empire building. Some 50,000 of these best horsemen in India were won over by Akbar, who additionally cemented the alliance with a marriage to a Rajput lady. To achieve Hindu acquiescence, he deferred to veneration of the cow and decreed its slaughter a capital offense. He exempted Hindus from the jizya. He freely took Hindus into the imperial ranks, where he bestowed top civilian and military positions on them. He treated their temples with due respect. Akbar initially located his capital at Agra, but in 1569, considering that location unlucky, he moved 20 miles west to Fatehpur Sikri. There he built a new capital city at the site of the residence of a Muslim saint to whose intercession he attributed the birth of two sons. But in reality the effective capital of India moved with the emperor. In 1585, he left Sikri to spend the next twelve years in the northwest. When he returned, he relocated again at Agra, for reasons not precisely clear.

Akbar's state was established on bureaucratically organized lines. He built on the administrative skills of others, including those of Sher Shah, and he was fortunate in utilizing the excellent services of an able Hindu minister, Raja Todar Mal. The sources on Akbar's governmental structure are many. They include descriptions by visiting Jesuits and by Abul Fazl, a close friend of the emperor's, who spent seven years compiling the *Institutes of Akbar*, which provides detailed information on the operations of the far-flung Mogul empire. At the political apex, of course, was the emperor, with unlimited personal power, who was bound only by Koranic injunctions. His chief advisers in the central government included the prime minister and the ministers of revenue, war, and religion. The emperor maintained a brilliant court in which no hereditary nobility, in theory, existed, since court positions and ranks depended on grants or assignments of revenues by Akbar to them. The emperor was heir to the personal and real property left behind by deceased nobles, though generally portions of the estate were restored to the family. Recognizing the evils inherent in the established practice of granting fiefs to followers, Akbar sought wherever possible to diminish the power of holders of revenue assignments by converting these lands into crown property.

Akbar's administrative structure consisted of the major divisions of court, army, and the general imperial and revenue administrations. Court functions included the operations of the imperial household, the mint, the imperial bodyguard, and public works. The army structure found Akbar as commander-in-chief of the forces, with the position of paymaster general as another top rank. The cavalry and the artillery were the most favored and the most remunerative of the branches of service. The regular standing military forces were small in number, but militia and irregular contingents, utilizing the decimal system from commanders of 10,000 horsemen to those of 10, were called up in time of war.

The prime minister was responsible for the general administration of the empire. The country was divided, by Akbar's death, into fifteen provinces. Each was headed by a governor, who was responsible for law and order but not for financial affairs. The provinces were divided into districts and into groups of villages. Large cities had their own city governors. The provincial governors were great nobles and usually members of the imperial family. Under the governors were *mansabdars*, a carefully graded body of officials, who were classified, in terms of cavalry commands, according to the number of horsemen they were supposed to supply to the imperial army upon request. This imperial service was graded into thirty-three ranks, in which officials received fixed salaries, paid in cash. The three highest grades, reserved for royal princes, included commanders of 10,000 to 7,000 horsemen; below these were thirty grades in which commanders headed 5,000 to 10 horsemen. The mansabdars, responsible for peace and security of their areas, were both civil and military officials.

In keeping with Sher Shah's innovation, as further developed and refined by Todar Mal, the revenue administration was kept separate from the general political administration of the empire. The revenue administration was headed by the *diwan*, or revenue minister, who had direct access, as had the prime minister, to the emperor. In the provinces, the revenue officials or commissioners were independent of the governors.

Each commissioner had a staff of collectors. The revenue administration was charged with the assessment and collection of land revenue, as well as custom duties, the salt tax, and some other minor financial items. Except for Bengal and for some areas that were reserved for the imperial treasury, all land in India was taxed on the principle that the cultivator was responsible for the payment of taxes. The assessment took into consideration the area under cultivation, the nature of the crop, and the fertility of the soil. The tax amounted to one-third of the average produce, and it was paid in cash to the local treasury office. Local collectors were given discretionary powers to vary the system and to reduce rates. Newly cultivated lands were given preferential tax considerations. Later in Akbar's reign, provisions were made for lump-sum payments assessed on whole villages, in which arrangement the village headman was made responsible for the revenue collected.

Akbar's genius was manifested in religious affairs as well as in political and economic matters. A mystic by nature, the emperor had become increasingly disenchanted with orthodox Islam, whose role and status he reduced during his lifetime. In 1579, he issued an infallibility decree that appropriated to him the power to issue religious orders and to judge doctrinal disputes. The next year, he overthrew Islam as the state religion and proclaimed the Divine Faith, to which the court, rather than the populace, was to adhere. Centered on the monarch himself, the new religion involved a simple monotheism. It stressed the four virtues of justice, chastity, courage, and wisdom. Of eclectic nature, it borrowed baptism from Christianity, fire worship from Persia, and prostration from Islam. A syncretic cult, it ranged above Hinduism and Islam. It was to provide a focus for a higher loyalty than the two faiths, but the new religion so enraged orthodox Muslims that they rallied around the monarch's younger brother to conduct an abortive rebellion against Akbar.

Akbar's religion died with him, but his political and cultural legacies were more enduring. The bureaucratic structure that he founded continued to function after his death, and the Persian character of his reign continued on as reflected in Urdu, which attained the status of a separate language. Expanding, experimenting, and excelling, Akbar in some ways prepared the way for the British, who borrowed and adapted Mogul territorial, administrative, and governmental systems from him.

Succession disputes marred the reigns of the later Moguls. Suspected of poisoning his father Akbar, Jahangir ascended the throne and reigned for twenty-two years, from 1605 to 1627. His administration was generally conducted along the lines inherited from Akbar, but there was some deterioration in its effectiveness. Central control became more slack, and the practice grew of assigning revenue collection privileges through grants to favorites or through purchase and bribes by officials. The emperor's memoirs, which cover nineteen years of his reign, give an insight into the monarch's character as a mixture of good and evil. He was a patron of the arts, and he appreciated music and song. He could be kind and generous at times, but often he gave in to fits of excessive intemperance and of savagery. He was married to an ambitious Persian woman, who, with her father as well as her brother as the prime minister, in effect ruled the empire. Court ceremonials were ostentatious and costly, and Jahangir immersed himself in them. Occupied with these matters, he lost the territory of Kandahar in the west to the Persians, but he managed to retain the loyalty of the Rajput chiefs. He displayed a partiality for Christian ritual as it was practiced by the Jesuits at his court, and though he was on close terms with the fathers, he was not converted to the foreign faith. The Jesuits were harbingers of only one foreign interest, and, more important for the future course of Indian history, Dutch and English merchants settled on coastal areas during Jahangir's reign.

In the latter years of Jahangir's rule, his son, Shah Jahan, turned against him. To ensure his imperial position, the new monarch massacred male collaterals to the throne. Shah Jahan, who was on the throne from 1628 until his deposition thirty years later in 1658, is best known for the construction of the Taj Mahal in Agra. This beautiful structure was a mausoleum erected for his wife by unknown architects. The project employed 20,000 workmen, who labored daily over a fifteen-year period (1632 to 1647). Shah Jahan embarked on other large-scale and expensive projects, including that of constructing the Peacock Throne, the coastliest of eleven in use. The reign of Shah Jahan is usually considered as the golden period of Mogul rule in India because of its cultural brilliance and because of the lack of any major external or internal threats, at least prior to the wars of succession toward the end of his reign. The court was famed for its splendor and its magnificence, but the imperial splendor by this time was becoming more static rather than creative. Thought was conforming to habit, and art was bowing to stereotypes. Behind the pomp and circumstance lay the poverty of the peasant. In the revenue areas assigned to officials and in those reserved for imperial use, much money was taken from the harassed peasants. Law and order became relaxed, and officials proved tyrannical. In 1656, the monarch became ill. Four sons struggled for power, and the third one, Aurangzeb, won out after he had imprisoned his father, killed one brother, and executed the other two brothers, a son, and a nephew.

Having gained power in a throne-or-coffin campaign, Aurangzeb, like his great-grandfather, was on the throne for half a century, from 1658 to 1707. In the course of the first half of his rule, he consolidated north India, pursued a policy of toleration to potential enemies, and employed Rajputs. As a newly installed ruler, he sought to garner the goodwill of his subjects by abolishing excessive taxes. He remitted nearly eighty taxes, though, according to local chronicles, the officials continued to collect excessive revenues for their own benefit. From about 1680, when Aurangzeb was past sixty, he moved his costly campaigns, his huge entourages, and his capital into the Deccan, where he spent the last twenty-six years of his reign. He also became a Muslim fanatic, and endeavored to transfer India into a Muslim state. He followed Koranic law and Islamic traditions in every detail of his personal life. He learned the whole Koran by heart, and became well acquainted with the prominent Muslim theologians. He prohibited music in public; he reimposed the jizya; he sporadically destroyed temples. Alienating Hindus generally through intolerant policies, he caused breaches with the Rajputs as well as with other new and emerging states.

In the latter years of Aurangzeb's reign, the Mogul empire reached its greatest territorial extent. The fifteen provinces of Akbar's time were increased to twenty-one. But while substantially similar in nature to that which existed in Akbar's reign, the administrative system was more enfeebled. Aurangzeb could not maintain a high degree of effective and respected rule among his subordinates spread throughout the extensive realm. Decentralization set in, and it was in his rule that the practice became quite widespread of farming out revenue assignments for tax collection purposes. Despite the wide range of his empire, however, as a sovereign Aurangzeb might be considered a failure in both public and private life. His imperial structure rested on shaky ground, and he could not maintain, much as he desired, the high degree of personal rule that was necessary to cement the kingdom. He trusted no one; he relied on his own sheer cunning to win and to keep power. He did next to nothing to enrich Indian, or Muslim, cultural life. After his death in 1707, the Mogul line, though it persisted on the Delhi throne until 1858, became progressively weaker with the growth of other Indian states and with the steady territorial and commercial expansion of the English East India Company.

Aurangzeb's direct actions helped to rearrange Indian political patterns, and, in the ensuing flux, new principalities were formed, including that of Hyderabad, originally a center of Mogul rule in the Deccan, which, from about 1724, gradually became independent of Delhi. Mogul rule practically ended with the death of Aurangzeb. The succeeding twelve years were marked by five reigns and three wars of succession. In 1739, the Persians invaded north India; Westerners began to arrive in numbers, and other indigenous powers shared the political forefront. That the height of Mogul political power lasted as long as it did was due in great measure to the administrative structure that Akbar utilized. It outlived him to persist in main form into the unusually long reigns of three successors. But the Moguls, essentially foreigners wielding despotic rule, had no roots in Indian soil. Their vast military operations were expensive and unsound, and economic causes, as excessive taxation and revenue decentralization, hastened the end.

One important Hindu state that arose in the political flux that existed during the latter years of Aurangzeb's rule was the Maratha kingdom or Maharashtra (the Sanskrit form). It sprawled along the Western Ghats and the Deccan in the territory between Goa and Bombay. It provided a thorn in the side of the Muslims and later gave the British staunch military opposition. The term Maratha is defined but vaguely. Strictly speaking, it connotes one agricultural caste living in the area, but sometimes it is used as a generic term to cover a group of such castes or the entire population of the region. Its inhabitants occupy a marginal land, out of which they eke a hard and frugal life. In history they proved to be excellent military men whose services were in great demand by other Indian kingdoms.

The rise of Maharashtra was connected with one such dominating military personality, that of Sivaji, who lived from 1627 to 1670. His father was a military adventurer who enlisted first in the forces of the Muslim kingdom of Ahmadnagar, and then of Bijapur. Sivaji was brought up, mainly at Poona, by his mother on an assignment held by his father, who was usually off fighting wars. From early life, Sivaji was imbued with a love of country and of Hinduism. At the age of twenty, he was managing the assignment and gathering adherents. Expanding in power, he came into collision with Bijapur state and with Aurangzeb, who temporarily brought him under vassalage. In 1675, Sivaji declared the independence of his people. By his death five years later, he was master of a vigorous, compact kingdom with an organized bureaucracy, though his successors did not maintain it.

Sivaji provided for a structured administration to govern the areas under his rule. He governed through a council of ministers, composed of military leaders and civilians, including Brahmans. The chief minister was a Brahman prime minister with the title of Peshwa. Other ministers were placed in charge of finance, foreign affairs, army, records, religious matters, and justice. Revenue farming was stopped, and regular assessments were placed on land. Sivaji prevented the possibility of encouraging independently minded officials by paying them directly from the treasury rather than assigning them revenues from land. All offices were appointive in nature, and none was hereditary. After Sivaji, the importance of the king declined. As time went on, the Brahman prime minister consolidated more and more power into his own position, which became hereditary and fixed at Poona, the capital, while the military leaders carved out such dominions as they could for themselves. There developed a loose Maratha confederacy, which, with internal divisions and with external pressures from Moguls and Afghans, was not able to succeed to the Mogul Delhi throne.

Another rising indigenous political and religious power was that of the Sikhs ("Disciples"). Dating to the fifteenth century, the Sikh religion was founded in the Punjab by Nanak, who lived from 1469 to 1538. He was born a Hindu of the Kshatriya class. The son of a corn merchant, he was a follower of Kabir, who tried to find a common bond between Hinduism and Islam. Nanak married a Hindu girl, sired two sons and possibly a daughter. Becoming increasingly absorbed in the problem of fundamental truths underlying differing religions, he abandoned his wife and family in search of answers to theologically perplexing questions. He wandered over India and Ceylon, and went to Medina and to Mecca. Affected by the bhakti and the sufi movements, he subordinated doctrine to a mystical communion with God. He propounded a monotheistic creed. He sought to abolish the idolatry and the caste distinctions of Hinduism, as well as the rigid orthodoxies of Muslim theology and institutions.

Nanak appointed one of his disciples as his successor or *guru*, of whom subsequently there were ten. The fourth guru founded Amritsar as a sacred city for the Sikhs. The fifth, put to death by Jahangir in 1606, compiled a sacred book. The tenth, murdered in 1708, made a final recension of the Sikh scriptures, called the *Granth* (the Sanskrit word for treatise). He started to organize his followers in the form of a military fraternity, who wore turbans, carried daggers, never cut their hair or beards, and adopted surnames of *singh* or lion. By the late eighteenth century, the militant Sikhs had conquered most of the Punjab, where they remained of importance into contemporary times.

As evidenced by the rise of independent states and peoples, the political face of India had changed. By the eighteenth century, strong Mogul personalities had departed from the scene. The political vacuum thus created resulted in the jockeying of various domestic and foreign groups for power. The balance of power that usually had been maintained in the west between India and Persia was upset. The Rajputs, while powerful and alienated by the later Moguls, continued as a powerful military confederacy, but they existed in a disunited state. The Sikhs and the Marathas, who arrived to stay in the Indian political arena, grew in power. But none could succeed to the imperial Mogul role. Yet, despite kaleidoscopic political changes, village India continued in its traditional life. It persisted in its self-sufficient subsistence economy, independent of kingdoms and of states coming and going. Village panchayats, headmen, priests, artisans, and police—all continued to function. As agriculturists, villagers produced wheat, corn, and rice. As craftsmen, they spun cotton, they engaged in pottery, and they promoted metal and woodwork. The drudgery of daily life was their inevitable and unenviable lot.

Cities, sprinkled throughout India, were becoming more important in commercial life during Mogul rule. Some of them were strictly commercial ones, like Surat, located on the west coast, north of Bombay. Other cities were ancient religious centers, as Benares. Still others were such royal cities as Delhi, Agra, Hyderabad, and Poona. Surat exported bulk products, as sugar, indigo, oil seeds, and tobacco, to destinations in India and abroad. From Kashmir came silk; from the north and west coastal plains and the Deccan came cotton; from the Malabar coast pepper; from Gujarat indigo; from Bengal rice, more sugar, and silk. In return for produce exported in international trade, Indians imported mainly luxury goods and raw materials, as copper, tin, zinc, mercury, ivory, horses, slaves, wines, and art objects. Though this import trade remained marginal to Indian economic life, the commercial activity proved to be a magnet to Europeans, who were beginning to burst the confines of their newly emerging nation-states. In the early sixteenth century, the Portuguese, as the first of the Europeans, began to arrive. India was to experience increasing contact with western powers and strong western national interests. Another era dawned, to add new foreign dimensions to Indian history.

Chronology

1018	Turks under Mahmud of Ghazni invade India
1175–1206	Muhammud of Ghur invades and rules India
1206–1290	Slave dynasty established at Delhi; first of five in Delhi sultanate

MUSLIM INDIA

1290–1320	Khalji rule
1320–1413	Tughluq rule
1336–1565	Vijayanagar Hindu empire in south
1347–1518	Independent Bahmani Muslim empire in Deccan
1398–1399	Timur sacks Delhi and north India
1414–1451	Sayyid rulers
1451–1526	Lodi rule
1469–1538	Nanak and establishment of Sikh religion
1526–1530	Babur consolidates Mogul rule in Delhi and north India
1530–1554	Humayun's rule in Delhi and in exile; Sher Shah on throne, 1540–1545
1556–1605	Akbar's rule
1605–1627	Jahangir on throne
1627–1680	Sivaji and rise of Maharashtra
1628–1658	Shah Jahan's rule; Taj Mahal constructed
1658–1707	Aurangzeb on throne
1724	State of Hyderabad founded

India and the West

INDIA AND THE WEST

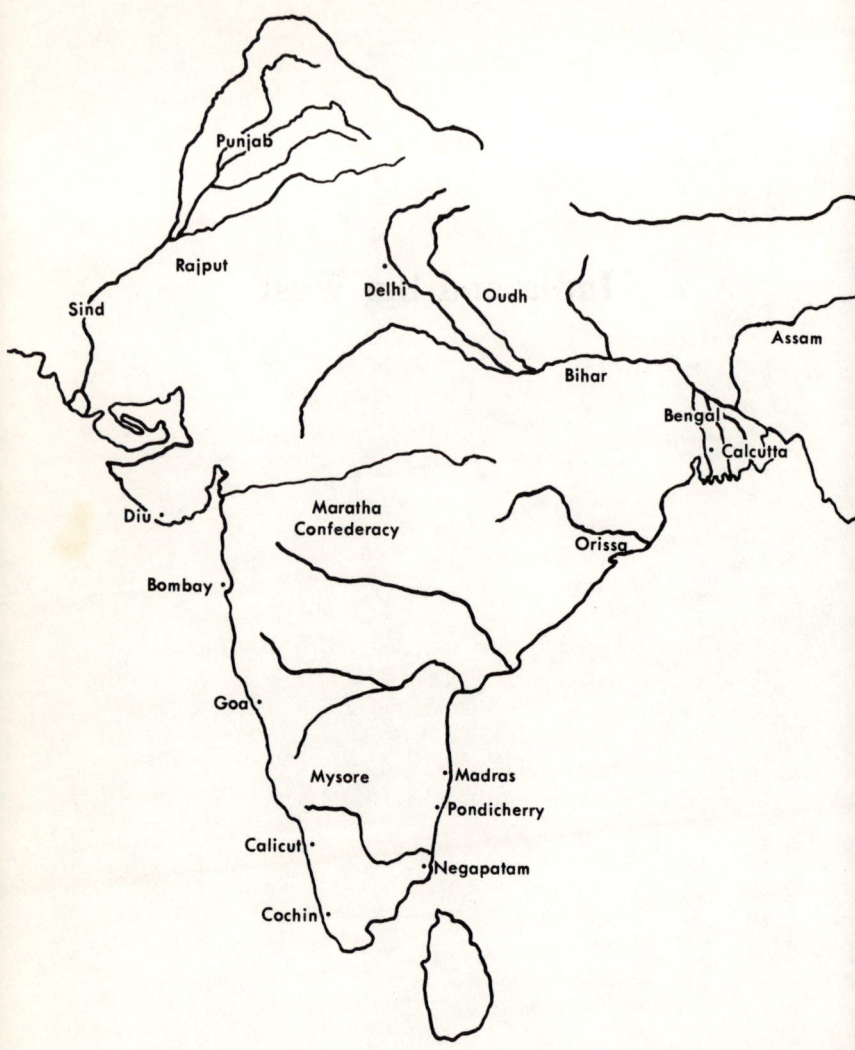

Chapter 5

India and the West

Early Europeans

Europeans arrived in India by sea, rather than by the traditional land invasion routes from the west and the northwest. Riches drew them on; prospects for religious converts proved to be attractive; fear of powerful Muslim kingdoms in central Asia and the Middle East led the monarchs of Christendom on a search for Asian allies. The reason that India, rather than China or Japan, was the first major Asian country into which the West intruded is explained by certain factors. Of the Asian "Big Three," India was the closest to Europe. The subcontinent consisted of a long peninsula, easily accessible by sea. It was divided politically, and it was culturally heterogeneous, as China and Japan were not. India eventually was conquered by the West, but the process of conquest extended over three centuries. Europeans did not have the available forces to master the subcontinent until technological improvements in Europe had been realized to sustain large-scale conquests. Europeans themselves were divided, and they fought against each other in India; the British had to eliminate rival powers to achieve dominant position. Moreover, it was long-standing Company policy to disapprove officially of territorial aggrandizement, a policy that was not always countenanced by Company representatives in India. India was conquered, but the task was involved and difficult.

The European connection with India dated to the Greeks, and a degree of interchange occurred until after the fall of Rome.

Subsequently with unstable political conditions in the intervening areas, only occasional European travelers came to India. The long central Asian trade lanes through deserts and mountains, controlled by Mongols and Turks, were difficult to traverse. The alternate route through Egypt, while open, was cumbersome. Long circuitous routes passed through middlemen, who included Arabs and Italians, and who exacted large tolls. To obviate these problems, an incentive existed for European Atlantic powers to strike directly at the heart of the producing areas of the desired items of trade. High on the list were spices, introduced into Europe by the Crusades and so necessary for the preservation and flavoring of food and drink. In the resulting search for alternate but direct routes to the East, the Portuguese took the lead.

The Portuguese had already commenced probes down the west coast of Africa in search of slaves and trade. By 1486, Bartholomeu Diaz rounded the Cape of Good Hope at the tip of the continent. The next step was to sail directly on to eastern kingdoms. Twelve years later, in 1498, Vasco da Gama with three small ships arrived at the Malabar coast. He cast anchor off a small village a few miles north of Calicut. He loaded spices there, which was a thriving center of pepper production as well as a traditional area for the re-export of spices from the East Indies. After an absence of twenty-six months, he returned to Lisbon with a cargo valued at sixty times the cost of the voyage. In 1500, a second and larger Portuguese expedition of thirteen ships set sail under Pedro Cabral, the discoverer of Brazil. In 1502, da Gama returned in force to India with a fleet of twenty ships. He established a trading post south of Calicut at Cochin, where a better harbor and more friendly Indians existed.

To conserve growing Portuguese commercial interests and to drive the Arabs out of the Indian Ocean, in 1505 the Portuguese government appointed Francisco de Almeida as viceroy. Four years later, his successor Affonso de Albuquerque assumed office. His aim was to establish a Portuguese empire in the east. In the ensuing six years as viceroy, he implemented Portuguese policy of acquiring key islands and ports in order to control the sea lanes and trade between Southeast Asia, India, Africa, and the Arab Middle East. Through this policy of establishing fortresses and of maintaining supremacy on the sea, he conquered Socotra off the entrance to the Red Sea, though Aden was never secured. In 1510, he annexed and established headquarters at Goa, the main port of the sultan of Bijapur. This was the first piece of Indian territory directly taken by Europeans since the invasion of Alexander the Great. In 1511, in a nine-day campaign, he captured Muslim-held Malacca, on the Malayan peninsula, which was a major center of trade through which the goods of China and Japan as well as the spices of the East Indies were funneled to the West. In 1515, Ormuz off the Arabian coast was taken. The Portuguese fixed posts at Diu and Daman on the western Indian coast, north of Goa. They located also in Colombo in Ceylon.

The Portuguese territories on the west coast, obtained by conquest or cession, were confirmed as integral parts of the kingdom of Portugal. On the east coast, less regular Portuguese establishments, often unruly and sometimes independent of the viceroy's rule, were founded. To the new colonies on both coasts came soldiers, merchants, and priests. In 1520, a bishop of Goa was appointed. Saint Francis Xavier labored at Goa before he proceeded to Malacca, China, and Japan in search of converts. In 1560, the Inquisition was introduced, and Jesuits appeared at Akbar's court in 1579. Through a combination of effective early leadership, zealousness, naval force, and use of arms, the Portuguese consolidated their holdings in India. Since women did not emigrate in numbers from Europe, intermarriage was encouraged, and a race known as Goanese (Portuguese-Indian-Catholic) arose in Portuguese territories.

For over a century the Portuguese ruled the Indian sea lanes, to be replaced by the Dutch and other powers. Portuguese decline was as rapid as its rise, for its inner strength had been sapped long before the rivals appeared. In 1622, Ormuz fell to the Persians and the English. To the Dutch, the Portuguese lost Malacca in 1641, Colombo in 1656, Negapatam, a port south of Madras, in 1658, and Cochin in 1663. The reasons for Portuguese decline were several. The hostility of indigenous peoples to the Portuguese never died out. This hostility was engendered in part by the Portuguese themselves, who believed that no faith had to be kept with unbelievers. The Portuguese received little support from home in financial and military undertakings, and the colonies had to be self-sufficient in their operations. The Marathas helped to contain the advantages of the Portuguese, and the political activities of the Jesuits and of the Inquisition gave rise to reactions against spiritual pressures. Moreover, with the political amalgamation in 1580 of Portugal and Spain, the former power became subordinated to that of the latter in an arrangement that lasted until 1640.

The Portuguese legacy in India was mixed. Because of their forced conversions and frequent opportunistic and perfidious actions in the colonies, the image that was left smacked of notoriety. Other heritages were more tangible. A corrupt Portuguese language remained the lingua franca of the ports into the eighteenth century. The Goan race persisted into the twentieth. The Portuguese brought in new crops, as tobacco, corn, and potatoes, and they imported Renaissance art and architecture in their cathedrals. They left their stamp on Catholic missions, on the three remaining colonial territories of Goa, Diu, and Daman (which the Indians took by force in 1961), and in two records narrating their exploits in the east: the work *Asia* of the historian João de Barros and the epic *Lusiad* of the poet Luiz Vaz de Camoëns.

The Dutch assumed control over some Portuguese ports in India, but their main interest was in the consolidation of their holdings in the East Indies, which was the center of spice production. Their opportunity to realize commercial and territorial gains was not granted until the early seventeenth century. Prior to that time, the spices destined for northern Europe had come from Lisbon to Antwerp for distribution. After the Protestant Dutch in 1580 revolted against Catholic Spain, and particularly after the defeat in 1588 of the Spanish Armada by the English, the Dutch began to strike out on their own. In 1595, four ships under Cornelius van Houtman sailed from Amsterdam for the Indies. Within seven years, many rival Dutch companies had been formed, and, with diverse and competing ships plying to the Indies, ruinous intra-Dutch competition resulted in the spice trade. In 1602, the Estates-General, or the Dutch parliament, granted a charter and a twenty-one-year monopoly, which was renewed periodically, to a single joint stock enterprise. This was the United Company, or, as it was familiarly known, the Dutch East India

Company. Though private, it was a national organization, and it was practically sovereign in its rights to develop Dutch commercial interests.

The formation of the Company regularized Dutch trade in Asia, and it was a timely action. In 1601, the year before its establishment, Dutch buyers from Acheh in north Sumatra had begun to appear in Gujarat. Though that initial venture in India was a commercial failure, the Dutch renewed their efforts. Two years later, they settled on the Coromandel coast, where they established headquarters at Negapatam and where they competed with the Portuguese. They planted a factory (a widespread term of the day used to denote a warehouse-residence-office complex) in Bengal, some stations in the Malabar coast, and another factory at Surat. The Dutch particularly sought cotton piece goods in India that were in great demand throughout the Malayan world, but the Moguls and the rulers of Golconda were too powerful to permit the newcomers to operate freely. Yet the Dutch, with their spice-producing areas in the East Indies, the amassed wealth of the monopolistic Company, and the ability of their representatives, managed to retain a great share of European trade in India.

Despite these footholds and some advantages in India, the Dutch concentrated their efforts in the East Indies. In 1618, they established their main Company base at Batavia, now Djakarta, the Indonesian capital city. From the spice islands they drove out the Portuguese as well as the English, who were compelled to concentrate in other Asian lands. From their center at Batavia, the Dutch expanded their interests throughout the islands that now constitute Indonesia. They contracted their holdings in India, in part because of growing English pressures and hostility against them there. By 1759, they had pulled out of the subcontinent. Remaining Dutch influence in India was negligible. Concentrating on trade, the Dutch conducted no religious propaganda in India, but Company officials kept extensive records, some of which contain valuable economic information.

In the course of the seventeenth century, other European countries established toeholds in India. In 1616, the Danish East India Company was organized, but Danish operations remained on a small scale. The Company founded two settlements. One was at Tranquebar, on the southeast coast, where the first Protestant missionary activity was effected. The other was at Serampore, near present-day Calcutta, on the Hooghly river. The Danish factories were never of importance at any time, and in 1845 they were finally sold to the British. The French arrived late on the Indian scene. In 1664, Colbert, Louis XIV's minister, founded the French East India Company. Four years later, at Surat, the first French factory was established in India. Another six years later, they purchased Pondicherry, a town seventy miles south of Madras. They turned this into a main base of operations in India. Though colonially ambitious, the French never garnered a major share of the Indian trade, and their overseas settlements seldom received adequate support from home. The French colonies persisted on into an independent India, and it was not until 1954 that the French Republic handed over its last remaining territories to the Indian Republic.

The English, who eventually won out over other European national interests in India, entered inauspiciously. In 1600, two years before the Dutch United Company was formed, Queen Elizabeth granted a fifteen-year charter, later renewed periodically, to develop East Asian trade to the "Governor and Company of Merchants of London Trading into the East Indies," or the London East India Company, as it was commonly called. The initial Company dispatched twelve separate voyages, chiefly to the spice islands, in as many years until 1613, when it was transformed into a joint stock organization like its Dutch counterpart. In the course of the seventeenth century, the new Company had its ups and downs. In 1698, a rival company, "The English Company Trading to the East Indies," was formed. In 1707, the two were amalgamated into "The United Company of Merchants of England Trading to the East Indies," popularly known as the English East India Company. Through the three commercial organizations, English-chartered trade in the Far East lasted for over two and a half centuries.

The English pattern in India followed the usual succession of the initial separate voyages, the resident factories, and the established forts on leased or ceded land. Following the early voyages sponsored by the London Trading Company, a permanent factory was established in 1612 at Surat, where the first

English had landed in India four years previously. The English managed to stave off the Portuguese and to obtain the right to trade from Gujarati officials. Surat remained as headquarters of the Company for some seventy years until it was superseded in importance by Bombay to the south. In the early 1600's, other ports were founded at various points along the west coast. In the course of colonial expansion in India, intra-European struggles and alliances ensued among the English, the Dutch, and the Portuguese.

The English factories also sprang up in various places along the east coast. The Company established two settlements on the Bay of Bengal, but trade there was so hampered by the local rulers that one of the factors, or Company representatives, explored the possibility of another site. In 1639, with the breakup of the Vijayanagar empire, the local ruler at Madras ceded a strip to the British on which to erect a fort. This was their first territorial grant in India. The land at the time looked uninviting, bare and inhospitable, for it consisted of only wastes of sand, without an adequate harbor. But the Company built up the settlement and called it Fort St. George, the patron saint of England. The growing town attracted Indian merchants and artisans from the politically disturbed surrounding areas, and Madras came to flourish as one of the important British centers.

For two decades after the founding of Madras, England was rent by civil wars and the Company's activities declined in India. In 1660, with the Stuart restoration, fresh energy resulted. In 1668, Charles II gave Bombay to the Company on perpetual lease at the nominal rent of ten pounds a year. He had received Bombay as dowry on his marriage seven years earlier to Catherine of Braganza, of the ruling house of Portugal. The area at first was quite unhealthy, but the first governor went to work to drain swamps and to reclaim land. The town was fortified, and a policy of religious tolerance attracted Hindu and Parsi merchants. Company activities on the west coast subsequently were centered at Bombay, but the port remained undeveloped for some decades. It was too far north for transshipment lanes, a profitable hinterland was precluded by the nearby forbidding mountainous Western Ghats, and the Marathas circumscribed British activity.

A third area of British commercial endeavor was in Bengal,

strategically located at the mouth of the Ganges with a vast hinterland to tap. The rich province offered products as silk, cotton piece goods, rice, indigo, and saltpeter for trade. Various factories had been established in Bengal, but because of qurrels with the Moguls the British had to withdraw. When they were permitted to return in 1691, they leased an area on the delta marshlands but with deep-water anchorage. It was an unpromising site, muddy and fever-stricken, but the delta land with swamps offered the British protection. The settlement was founded as Ft. William, so named after King William III, but it came to be called Calcutta, derived from Kalikata, the most important of three nearby leased villages.

By 1700, the British were entrenched in the three centers of Bombay, Madras, and Calcutta. These grew in importance in the course of Company activities in the eighteenth century. In these settlements senior merchants, sitting as select committees, appointed one of their number as president or governor. All matters of general importance in the three presidencies were supervised by Company directors in London. But the first step in local self-government was taken at Madras as early as 1688, when a municipal corporation was established with Indian and European aldermen. It dealt only with functions of local municipal administration, and it did not affect the power or the authority of the directors in London over the affairs of the Company. Early Company life was communal to a great extent. Members ate corporate meals in a common hall, worshiped in chapels, and intermarried with Indians. They adopted some Indian customs, for they lounged in Indian clothes and pajamas, ate Indian dishes, and smoked cigars and cheroots. They sent home detailed reports, which later became a major source of intelligence and historical insight on Indian-European relations in these early decades.

As a major European power in India, expanding England met ambitious France in head-on clashes in southern and eastern India during the eighteenth century. Though the conflict was long-drawn-out and registered initial French successes, it was the English who finally emerged triumphant. In India, the contest between the two nations, through their respective companies, was in part a result of their struggles in Europe, notably in the War of the Austrian Succession (1740 to 1748) and the Seven Years' War (1756 to 1763).

In the course of the first European war, the French sent out a remarkable man, Joseph Dupleix, as governor of Pondicherry. Of many talents, Dupleix was an astute manager, trader, and politician. In 1748, the French fleet under his command captured Madras, but the Treaty of Aix-la-Chapelle restored Madras to the British in return for Cape Breton island off the mouth of the St. Lawrence river in Canada. The French governor not only fought the British but he interfered as well in the succession disputes of Hyderabad. Through force or intrigue, he achieved success in turning the Muslim Indian state into what amounted to a French-sponsored entity. For five years, his own French representative was the de facto ruler of Hyderabad. The governor built up contingents, under foreign commanders, of native troops known as sepoys (which had been used by the French on the Malabar coast dating back to about 1720), and he utilized two of these companies in the War of the Austrian Succession. Dupleix and his representatives secured for the French company unique and important trading privileges as against the British, whom they sought to exclude from trade in south India. He also desired the native potentates to pay the overhead costs of the French establishment in India. These aims were important, for they had a fall-out effect on the English who emulated them.

The English counterpart to Dupleix was Robert Clive (1725 to 1774). A year after Dupleix came to Pondicherry as governor, Clive, at the age of eighteen, arrived at Madras as a writer or clerk in the civil service of the English East India Company. Quite energetic in nature, Clive rose to prominence in the southern campaigns and in Bengal operations of the Company. In 1756, the youthful new *nawab*, or governor of Bengal, theoretically under Muslim rule but practically independent, had attacked the English. He imprisoned the foreigners in their own fort in what came to be known as the "Black Hole" of Calcutta incident (an event that was greatly exaggerated in scope and in importance by later historians of the British empire). The English brought up reinforcements from Madras of ships and men, including Clive. With renewed forces, the English seized the French center in Bengal as a potential ally of the nawab, and, in June, 1757, they defeated the nawab himself in the historic Battle of Plassey.

As a result of their victory, the English placed in the post of nawab a claimant friendly to themselves. In turn, they received concessions from the newly sponsored state. In Clive's first tenure as governor, from 1758 to 1760, the Company's trading privileges were renewed. Permission was granted to fortify Calcutta, to coin money, and to receive landlord rights over some 900 square miles of territory south of Calcutta. Two years later, the Mogul emperor confirmed the revenue assignment in this district. At the same time that Company interests were expanding in Bengal, they were growing similarly in the other two presidencies. The Madras presidency and the nawab of the Carnatic arranged joint rule over additional territories along the southeast Indian coast. In Bombay, the English in 1755 received more territory from the Marathas, with whom they had joined in campaigns against the French. Two and a half decades later, after another war (and this time against the Marathas), a treaty of 1782 gave the Company still more land on the western Indian mainland.

In Bengal, the new nawab proved to be slippery. He fell out with the English, who, in 1764, defeated him and his allies that included the ruler of adjoining Oudh, farther up the Gangetic plain, and the Mogul emperor. Clive returned for a second term of office as governor from 1765 to 1767. He faced the inter-related problems of the Company, its operations in Bengal and the Ganges area, and its relations with the Mogul emperor. Already possessing general administrative rights in Bengal through earlier arrangements, in 1765 the Company, subject to annual payments to the ruler of Bengal and to the emperor, received the *diwani* grant, or the right to receive and to administer revenue in perpetuity in the provinces of Bengal, Bihar, and Orissa. For the next seven years, the Company appointed officers who posed as deputies of the nawab of Bengal in revenue collections. In 1771, the directors in London decided to forego this fiction and have the Company itself constituted as the diwan. The next year, with the establishment of the Board of Revenue, consisting of the governor and the council at Calcutta, the Company became effective sovereign power with both general administrative and revenue rights over three of the richest provinces in India.

Clive had escalated the French policy of a sponsored state to one of a directly ruled state. The English East India Company, with territorial and trading rights, was firmly ensconced in east, south, and west India. Company officials received great compensation and huge estates from Indian rulers and, since they received only nominal salaries as Company employees, they engaged on the side in lucrative private trade. Much of this was exempted from the numerous local tolls through agreement with local Indian officials. From these extra-cirricular activities, some Company officials amassed big fortunes. Clive himself received extensive gifts of land and of money from Bengali rulers and from Hindu traders and merchants in return for privileges granted. A dynamic personality with insights into the local Indian scene, Clive was a complex man. He was naturally ambitious, but his career was marked by a certain lack of integrity. Making many enemies, he was attacked on several counts that clouded both his private and his public record. Upon his return to England, he advocated a policy that suggested the crown take over Company possessions in India. At the time, this possibility was not seriously considered, though it was implemented later. Embittered and frustrated by prolonged criticisms, Clive committed suicide under the age of fifty. He took his life prematurely, but his lasting contribution was that he helped to lay the foundations for the British empire in India.

East India Company

Interpretations of British intentions in India differ. One general theme leaves impressions that the English came humbly and diffidently, that empire was thrust on them, and that it was acquired in fits of absence of mind. A contrary thesis holds that they were out for deliberate planned conquest and that their eventual supremacy in India resulted from cold, calculated policy. Accuracy lies somewhere in between, for the empire builders made maximum use of opportunities presented. Their conquest of India was amazing. A large, populous country with ancient traditions, India came under the royal scepter of Britain, located thousands of miles away, a country small in size and with a differing culture. The conquest was effected through the East India Company, which inaugurated and expedited British rule in a politically divided country accustomed to foreign rulers.

In political affairs, the Company followed two approaches. Through direct rule, the Company itself became the sovereign power over certain territories. In these it administered all major functions of government, as the collection of revenue, the administration of justice, and the exercise of police powers. Through a second policy of indirect rule, while not appropriating territory, the Company exerted various pressures on and placed advisers in the princely states. This twofold political division of directly ruled British India and paramountcy in the princely states persisted after 1858, when the crown took over Company activities in India. Parliament did not specifically detail in any public document theories of Company rule. But the spirit of parliamentary laws maintained that the Company, as guardian of the Indian realm, was to wield unlimited power in disinterested use to advance public welfare.

Commendable theory was imperfectly translated into action through Company bureaucracy, known as the Indian Civil Service. Many of these British public servants were dedicated, conscientious men, while others played the role of *sahib* master, keeping to their separate British ways. Since the Company was a complex structure embracing a variety of personalities and policies, disparate criteria exist in judging its record. Politically, the Company inherited a fragmented India on the decline, and it restored a considerable degree of political and administrative unity to the country. Perhaps as important, the British gave to India an unaccustomed freedom from internecine wars, rebellions, and brigandage, as well as improved transport and communications media of major importance to unification. Economically, it enhanced and revived economic activity, though in the process it impoverished certain segments of the economy and populace. Socially, the traditional fabric of Indian life was disrupted by the "acids of modernization" through its introduction to the modern world. But the British had come to stay, and the Company was their agent.

With Clive's second governorship in Bengal, Company interests were put on a secure footing. But Company abuses led to increased parliamentary control and supervision that culminated in the takeover of Company territory and interests by the crown. This final act was but the last in a succession of previous laws designed cumulatively to supervise and to regulate Company activities. As first of these restricting bills, the Regulating Act of 1773 limited the Company charter to twenty-year periods, subject to review upon renewal. It gave the government supervisory rights over the presidencies of Bombay, Madras, and Bengal. Bengal was made the most important of the three, the governor there was elevated to the position of governor general, and the seat of Company government was established at Calcutta, where it remained, after crown takeover, to 1911, when it moved to Delhi.

In a second major India act, passed in 1784 during the prime ministership of William Pitt the Younger, the government, while continuing to leave commercial matters to the Company's directors, assumed its political powers. A Board of Control with six commissioners was appointed by the crown to review, modify, or veto instructions that the Company directors sent to their representatives in India. In the first twenty-year review, the Charter Act of 1793 confirmed existing arrangements. But, in the Charter Act of 1813, advocates in England of laissez-faire and of free trade won their point of view when the Company's commercial monopoly in India was abolished and trade was thrown open to all British subjects. Evangelical spokesmen also won permission for missionaries to enter India and to secure a church establishment there. The act further appropriated a sum of ten thousand pounds a year for education. This was significant since it was the first recognition by the government through the Company to ameliorate the condition of the Indian people. In 1833, the Company was permitted to retain for another twenty years administrative and political control, but only in trust for the crown and its successors. In 1853, the arrangement was reconfirmed without the twenty-year stipulation of review.

Though the Company came under more government control at home, after Clive it broadened its territorial scope in India. Expanding commerce, securing border areas, and containing the French in India and the Russians in central Asia were primary considerations in policies of expansion. In addition to minor campaigns, the Company engaged in four wars with Mysore state (1767–69, 1780–84, 1790–92, 1799), which had risen to power in south India in the latter decades of Mogul rule, three with the Maratha confederacy (1775–82, 1803–05, 1817–19), two with the Sikhs (1845–46, 1848–

49) and the Burmese (1824–26, 1852), and one each with Nepal (1814–16) and the Afghans (1839–42). Other areas were absorbed by political expedients. Since at least four-fifths of the Company's army were sepoys, and since military expenses were met by taxes collected in India, the extension of British rule was accomplished at little or no cost to the English people.

Succeeding Clive as governors general of the Company were a number of outstanding administrators who, despite parliamentary restrictions placed on them, expanded British commercial, political, and territorial interests. As Clive had earlier done, so Warren Hastings went to India as a clerk to better his own and his family's fortunes. An able man, he advanced rapidly to the position of governor, then to that of the governor generalship in Bengal from 1772 to 1785. Under him the Company consolidated its holdings in Bengal. It stopped payment of tribute to the Mogul emperor and it took over the entire civil administration of the great province. Hastings pushed into Mysore and Maratha, and he persuaded the Rajput states to barter away their independence for British protection. Upon his return to England, he was involved in attacks on his policies and person, as Clive also had been. Partly a victim of changing times in an England disenchanted with the loss of the American colonies, disillusioned with further territorial expansion, and continued fear of Company power, Hastings faced seven years of hearings in the House of Lords. Eventually acquitted, he lost his fortune defending himself.

In 1786, Lord Cornwallis, the defeated British general at Yorktown, was dispatched, without any subsequent loss of prestige, as governor general to Bengal. For seven years in that post, he took directions from the crown on political and administrative matters as provided for in the newly passed India Act. Renowned for good administration, he hired men of integrity and of public responsibility, and he laid the merit basis for the Indian Civil Service. He discouraged out-of-office fiscal activities, increased salaries, and tried to modify patronage. He stressed character qualifications rather than family connections for jobs. Because Cornwallis came from outside Company ranks, rather than moving up through them, he could the easier effect reforms. Moreover, in Britain a rising public conscience and the growth of a utilitarian philosophy in political affairs demanded not only Company reforms but also more equitable treatment of Indians.

At the turn of the nineteenth century, Lord Wellesley, elder brother of the Duke of Wellington, who defeated Napoleon at Waterloo, became governor general. He held office from 1798 to 1805. In keeping with another change in European attitudes, that now favored expansionism and annexation as expressed during the revolutionary wars, territorial aggrandizement became the keynote of his administration. Wellesley wanted the British to be the dominant power in India, and he sought that end through the promotion of either direct or indirect rule. He reduced Maratha strength. He ended the wars with Mysore, whose boundaries he whittled down. He annexed the southern coasts of Kanara, Malabar, and the Carnatic, and he established control over Delhi, the traditional seat of the Mogul dynasty. Through subsidiary alliances, including those with Hyderabad and Oudh, he extended British influence through local rulers. A principal means of effecting this was the arrangement by which Indian princes accepted and financed British garrisons in their territory. As a result of these forceful measures, after his tenure, only Rajputana, Sind, and the Punjab remained outside effective Company domination. Wellesley also tried vigorously to patronize native learning and scholarship. Importantly, he established a college at Ft. William to train Company officers in their duties and in knowledge of India. Wellesley found scattered British possessions; he bequeathed the basis of the future British empire. The British were succeeding to the Mogul heritage.

After Wellesley came the Napoleonic wars, in which the British completed the suppression of the last pretensions in India of the French, who retained only minor colonies. In the succeeding decades, further conquests expanded Company borders. To the southwest, in the third and last Maratha campaign, that confederacy of five states (Poona, Baroda, Nagpur, Gwalior, and Indore) was finally defeated and assimilated. Maratha downfall, in addition to persistent British military campaigns, resulted from internal disunity, intrigues and quarrels among the states, an outmoded military organization, unsound economic policies, and a poor agricultural base with natural resources too meager to sustain expanding territorial commitments. To the north, as a result of a campaign against the ruling Gurkha dynasty in Nepal, the British in an 1816 treaty received certain Gangetic areas, where hill stations and summer resorts were later established. They stationed a British resident at Katmandu, and they replaced the Nepalis as overseers in neighboring Sikkim.

To the east, Company interests clashed with those of neighboring Burma's. In 1824, the Burmese moved into Assam, which had been subject in the past to Burmese kings but which the Company now proclaimed as enjoying British protection. That year, the first Anglo-Burmese war broke out over the Burmese invasion of Assam. In retaliation, the Company landed in Burma some 40,000 troops, of whom 15,000 died of dysentery and fever. After a desultory two-year war in Burma, in a treaty of 1826, the defeated Burmese paid an indemnity, ceded Assam and two southern Burmese provinces, accepted a British resident at their capital of Ava in central Burma, and sent an ambassador to Company headquarters at Calcutta.

When Lord Bentinck, the next great administrator, had acceded to office, Company commercial operations had been curtailed and the waves of reform from Europe lapped in India. As governor general from 1828 to 1835, Bentinck revealed a humane philosophy through his motto of "British greatness upon Indian happiness." He opened subordinate government positions to qualified Indians. He cut Company administrative costs and exercised strict supervision over the Indian states. The governor general abolished the practice of suttee, especially prevalent in Bengal. He suppressed thuggee, or ritual strangling. He tried to prevent female infanticide by giving presents to tribes that kept their daughters and by financing dowries for marriageable girls. His record was summed up in the inscription on his statue in Calcutta, "He abolished cruel rites; he effaced humiliating distinctions; he gave liberty to the expression of public opinion; his constant study was to elevate the intellectual and moral character of the nation committed to his charge." Though Bentinck concentrated more on internal than on external policies, the Company absorbed Mysore in 1831, but the crown returned it fifty years later to the royal family of that state. In 1842, after Bentinck's tenure of duty, Sind, under loose rule of a confederation of *amirs*, was annexed. This annexation was a direct result of an earlier disastrous war, inspired by fear of Russia in central Asia, with Afghanistan. The British had proceeded to that kingdom through Sind, but, upon retreating in defeat, they conquered the amirs and stayed on in Sind.

Earl Dalhousie, the last of the great personalities and the last but one of the governors general under the Company, held the top position from 1848 to 1856. Trained in England under Sir Robert Peel and William Gladstone, Dalhousie, an energetic man and reformer, did not know much about India but he had had considerable administrative experience in England. His goal was a modernized India with public schools, trained Indians, civil and criminal law codes, and decent jails. His heart was in constructing public works, as roads, harbors, railways, telegraph lines, and irrigation systems. His energies spilled over into additional territorial conquests. In the east, through the second Anglo-Burmese War, the British in 1852 received territory in central Burma. In the west, the warlike but divided Sikhs succumbed. Once strong under the national leadership of Ranjit Singh (1780–1839), they had kept peace with the British at the territorial boundary of the Sutlej river. Now they were disorganized into a confederacy of some dozen anarchic entities that could not contain British expansion. In 1849, after defeating them, Dalhousie on his own responsibility annexed the Punjab by simple proclamation.

The governor general augmented direct military expansion with indirect political measures. In 1848, he enunciated the doctrine of lapse in which rights of sovereignty, as separate from those of personal property rights, of adopted sons of deceased princes lapsed to the Company. Through this measure, which was reversed a decade later under the first royal governor general, as well as the earlier doctrine of paramountcy, in which the Company as paramount power unilaterally defined misgovernment and interfered in a princely state to correct conditions, additional territory passed to the British. Accomplishing much, Dalhousie believed that his successor would have nothing more to do but to carry on with his reforms. Instead, his successor reaped the whirlwind in the mutiny of 1857.

Men executed policies that expanded Company interests in India. As foreign agents using a foreign language, observing religious neutrality, and giving strict attention to administrative problems, English Company rule replaced Mogul imperial rule. Company administration was tight. In the civil service and army, all posts paying more than five hundred pounds annually were reserved to European members of the service. Not until 1864 did an Indian actually enter the civil service in higher ranks. The governor general exercised control over Company troops, which were augmented by regiments of royal troops from the home country in times of crises. Sepoys were universally used, but no Indian in military office passed beyond the rank of non-commissioned officer. By 1857, the Company's army totaled 238,000, of which 38,000 were Europeans.

In judicial matters on local levels, the Company utilized Hindu and Muslim customary law. Hindu or Muslim law applied according to the faith of the defendant. British law filled the gaps with miscellaneous codes on rules of evidence, contracts, and court procedures. At first unclear as to what constituted native law, British scholars, including Sir William Jones, the first European to know Sanskrit effectively, studied and translated native texts. Until 1864, *pandits* or Hindu lawyers were attached to courts to advise the British. In the judiciary, Indians held lower positions, to the rank of subordinate judge. The net result in the legal field was the development of an Indian juridical profession, highly educated and often vocal, versed in a hybrid Anglo-Indian law.

At first, the Company was against the introduction of education, which might give rise to ideas of independence among Indian subjects and Indian troops. Also predicated on this possibility, the Company endeavored to keep missionaries out of the country, but when the Charter Act of 1813 permitted their entry, many of them went out to India to preach the Gospel and to establish presses, hospitals, orphanages, and schools. Debates arose in England over the nature of education that was to be extended to Indians. Orientalists advocated a combination of Indian languages and history with western sciences. Others, including the historian Thomas Macauley, who headed the Committee on Public Instruction that was created to study the problem, advanced European superiority and western learning. The latter view prevailed. In 1835, English replaced Persian as the official language in India, and the Indian intelligentsia became familiar with western ideas through the medium of the English language. Education in the lower grades continued to emphasize the vernaculars, but the study of English, which had commercial value and social prestige, led to the most remunerative rewards.

Along with the promotion of education went the growth of the press. Prior to the eighteenth century, presses were lacking in India. Books were hand-copied, and Brahmans exercised a monopoly of the written word. Printing broke down this monopoly. Hindu reformers now could also use against the priestly class the same religious texts, where they found no religious sanctions for such rites as purdah, suttee, and child marriage. In 1801, because of Company proscription on mission activity at the time, the British Baptist William Carey set up the first press for both English and the vernacular in the Danish settlement of Serampore. In 1816, the first Indian newspaper was founded; seven years later there were four in Calcutta. But the influence of the press at the time was small, and the Company had a tendency to arrest editors and return them to England. At first, the native press stuck closely to noncontroversial subjects, but later it turned to nationalistic issues with an aim eventually to oust the British. The press kept up its role of opposition, which it maintained into an independent India.

The best early example of an Indian steeped in western education but without compromising the good in indigenous life was Ram Mohan Roy, who lived from 1772 to 1833. Roy was one of the most outstanding Indians of the nineteenth century. Of catholic tastes, he was a blend of the positive elements in Hindu culture and western ideas. Born of devout Brahman parents, he broke with them over his sister's suttee. He showed an early interest in religion and in languages. As a youth, he wandered through India in search of knowledge. Eventually, he entered British employ, acquired a skill in the English language, and rose as high as was possible for an Indian in the Bengal civil service. Being independently wealthy, he retired at forty-two and settled to live in Calcutta, the intellectual as well as the political capital of India. Over the next decade and a half, Roy worked on a number of projects. He founded, edited, and published newspapers in Persian, Bengali, and English. He organized secondary schools, and he translated some of the Upanishads into English and New Testament commentaries into the vernacular. He advocated the use of western techniques, as the press and education, to change internal customs. He organized a religious society, the *Brahmo Samaj*, or Divine Society, to adopt commendable ways of the West and to abolish less desirable aspects of Hinduism, as purdah, child marriage, and image worship. With his variety of causes that promoted change or synthesis, Roy demonstrated that it was possible to be Indian and yet agitate for more egalitarianism and democracy in Indian society.

In economic affairs, because the agrarian community was important as the chief source of income, Company administration concentrated on the collection of land revenue in cash. To achieve maximum effectivity in taxation, after preliminary country-wide surveys of soil and crop conditions, three systems were introduced. In 1793, Cornwallis in Bengal had made a permanent settlement of three million pounds annually in the province. This tax demand was fixed in perpetuity on landlords, and in this system, in order to facilitate collections, the *zamindars*, or hereditary tax gathers under the Moguls, were transformed, if they did not already hold land, into landlords with proprietary rights to retain, sell, or purchase land. Though this eased Company tax collections, many agriculturalists became helpless tenants and their hereditary rights were ignored. In Madras and a good part of Bombay, where less Muslim tradition prevailed, another system was introduced, that of the *ryotwari* (*ryot* for peasant), in which the tax settlement was fixed directly with the cultivators. In central India, Delhi, and the Punjab, the *mahalwari* (*mahal* for subdistrict or estate) tax demands were made on villages or estates, whose authorities then apportioned the demands among the joint owners of the land.

Having commenced Indian operations in trade and commerce, the Company developed those economic sectors. Where previously Indian trade had been mainly internal and in luxury goods, the British emphasized exports of cheap goods for mass markets. While British policy kept tariffs on Indian goods and refused to permit India to import machinery, the British flooded the Indian market with their machine-made goods. India became a dumping ground for cheap manufactured items, principally cotton textiles. These goods penetrated the country and helped to undermine village handicraft industries, thus eliminating a source of cash for the already hard-pressed peasant, who had to meet tax and other demands in money. Exports from India increased, but their commodity composition changed. As the nineteenth century wore on, Indian exports increasingly consisted of raw materials, especially agricultural raw materials. The traditional international trading pattern of India had now been reversed, for Indians were buying more from abroad than they were selling in foreign markets. Many hardships ensued from the changing patterns of trade, and while more wealth accrued in the British period of Indian history, few shared in this increase. To regularize an ever-growing money economy, in 1835 a single rupee, carrying a portrait of the sovereign of Britain, replaced the mixed coinage of the three presidencies.

The Company achieved mixed progress in communications and public works. In 1825, the first steam voyage, which lasted 113 days via the Cape of Good Hope, took place from England to India. Steamships were introduced on the Ganges river and later on the Indus and the Brahmaputra. Navigable for long distances, these river routes opened up out-of-the-way areas in India to world markets, world goods, and world prices. Some road building was under way by the 1830's, but results were meager. More progress was registered in postal services. By 1836, some 276 post offices had been established. Each province had its own postal administration, with letters carried by runners, who were sometimes held up by bandits. In 1854, a unified postal service was created, and mails left at stated intervals. That same year, the first telegraph line was constructed between Calcutta and Agra, and India became linked to the outside world. Railroads came late to India. By 1857, only 200 miles of track had been laid in the country.

Into this background of a changing India came the sepoy mutiny of 1857, a watershed in modern Indian history. Though British secretiveness has rendered difficult access to official documentation, much has been written on the topic. The event has been variously interpreted as a simple military revolt, as a planned conspiracy against the British, as the first Indian war for independence, and as the culmination of social, economic, political, and religious unrest in India. The mutiny contained elements of civil rebellion, yet there was little cooperation among the leaders of the various uprisings, and no unified Indian plan existed as to immediate or long-range goals. But the mutiny did indicate indigenous restlessness over the rapid expansion and changes caused by British rule. Princes were unhappy at the loss of privileges, prestige, and sovereignty, as well as over the Dalhousie doctrine of lapse. Landlords were uneasy over Company regulations. Brahmans resented this subordination to foreign authority. They feared the implicit challenge to their ancient ascendency from English ways as well as the leveling influence in English law. They tended to fear the implications of the new education, which seemed to subvert Hindu orthodoxy. Company reform measures were appearing to break up the traditional Indian social fabric, and the gulf between the English and the Indians in race, color, customs, and religion proved to be deep.

There had been previous mutinies in Indian military annals. In 1806, the British had ordered sepoys in Vellore, Madras, to give up caste marks, trim their beards, and wear special turbans. The regiment refused, and the ringleaders were given nine hundred lashes apiece. After this punishment, the sepoys massacred two companies of European troops. In 1824, a regiment refused to go to Burma by sea because it felt that caste would be endangered by such a voyage. A court martial condemned six to death and sentenced hundreds to hard labor. In 1856, another regiment balked at service in Burma, but the punishment, which was light, was merely transfer of the unit to Dacca, in East Bengal.

The immediate cause of the 1857 mutiny was the offense taken by troops at a new type of cartridge issued for the Enfield rifle. The cartridge, reportedly greased with the fat of beef or of swine, had to be bitten before use. This involved ceremonial defilement to either Hindu or Muslim. On May 9, 1857, sepoys at Meerut, near Delhi, mutinied, and refused to touch the new cartridges. They were given prison sentences. The next day, in retaliation, three Indian regiments on the station shot their officers, broke open the jail, and marched off to Delhi. This signaled the beginning of a more widespread resistance. The mutiny was confined chiefly to the Ganges valley, where princes and landlords, Hindus and Muslims joined the mutinous armies. Some native troops remained loyal. With their help, as well as with the aid received from imperial British reinforcements, the eighteen-month rebellion, which registered brutality on both sides, was finally suppressed.

By the end of the campaigns, northern India lay prostrate. The more immediate results of the mutiny recorded that most of the rebel leaders were killed in battle, were executed, or disappeared. A number of implicated princes lost their territories and their lives. The Mogul empire, which had been only a legal fiction for a century and a half, came to an end. The imperial family was shorn of its royal status, and the last emperor was exiled to Burma, where he died at the age of eighty-seven. Of more long-range importance was the transfer of Company possessions and authority in India to the crown. In 1858, British interests in India were placed directly under the crown. On November 1st of that year, a royal proclamation announced to the princes and the people of India the transfer of sovereign authority from the East India Company to the British crown. Nearly twenty years later, in 1877, Queen Victoria was proclaimed Empress of India. Though she was not present, formal ceremonies were staged at Delhi, the traditional center of Mogul might and grandeur. British hands had changed, but the personal element in British rule continued to accord with Indian tradition. The British crown had simply become the successor to the last of the Hindu and Muslim dynasties. The Queen-Empress reigned over a larger area of India, either directly or indirectly, than had the greatest of the Indian or Mogul monarchs, as Asoka and Akbar. Thanks to the British, Indian political boundaries were defined to their greatest extent.

Chronology

1498	Vasco da Gama arrives at Malabar coast
1510–1962	Portuguese colonies in India: Goa, Diu, and Daman
1600	First English East India trading company established
1601–1759	Dutch interests in India
1608	First British trading venture in India at Surat
1616–1845	Danish interests in India
1639	First territorial grant to British Company in India, at Madras (Fort St. George)
1668	Company established at Bombay

1668–1954	French colonies in India
1691	Company founds Calcutta (Ft. William)
1756	"Black Hole" incident at Calcutta
1757	Battle of Plassey; British defeat French and Bengalis
1758–1760, 1765–1767	Robert Clive as governor of Company
1772–1755	Warren Hastings as governor (then governor general) of Company
1772	Company appropriates administrative and revenue rights in Bengal and two other provinces in north India
1772–1833	Ram Mohan Roy
1773	Regulating Act: Company charter limited to twenty-year periods; post of governor general established at Calcutta
1780–1839	Ranjit Singh, leader of Sikhs
1784	India Act: British government assumes Company political powers
1786–1793	Lord Cornwallis as governor general
1798–1805	Lord Wellesley as governor general
1813	Charter Act opens India trade and missions to all
1816	Treaty with Nepal
1824–1826	First Burmese War
1828–1835	Lord Bentinck as governor general
1835	English becomes official language; unified coinage introduced
1848–1856	Earl Dalhousie as governor general
1857–1858	Sepoy mutiny
1858	Fictional Mogul empire comes to end; crown replaces Company rule in India

Chapter 6

Indian Nationalism and the British Crown

Setting

In the course of the post-mutiny years, the British developed a new respect for Indian traditions, which seemed to them to be ingrained in their subjects. Advancing a trusteeship concept and tempering zeal with prudence, the British tolerated their traditionalist partner. For their part, realizing that they could not oust the British by force, Indians put up with the overlords as well. Yet, conditions of mutual toleration could not remain static. On the subcontinent, new westernized classes were emerging, and, while the British continued to persist in looking to the usual traditional leaders for Indian guidance, new spokesmen were emerging from new classes. These groups, sometimes ignored by the British, were to be a potent force in the growth of Indian national consciousness.

Under the crown, in political affairs, India was administered from England through the Secretary of State for India, the Council of India, and the India Office. In India, three political categories emerged. First, there were the remnants of Portuguese and French possessions, the most important of which were Goa and Pondicherry, respectively. Then, there were the native princely states, consisting of one-third of the land area with one-fifth of the population. Many of the states were quite small, but a few, as Kashmir and Hyderabad, were as large as some European nations. Spread throughout India like a crazy patchquilt, the states were subject to British control through various treaties and precedents. Usually a British resident was maintained at the courts, and foreign affairs were in the hands of the British. The principle of paramountcy continued, but the queen's proclamation of November, 1858, revealed a British disinclination to expand territory at the expense of the existing princely territories. To enhance relations with the princes, the British canceled the doctrine of lapse, recognized adoption, guaranteed existing boundaries, and encouraged Indian princes to think in terms of all-Indian problems and issues. In turn, the princes, usually loyal, constituted a main prop of support for the British.

Finally, as the largest political division, there was British India under direct crown rule. At the top of the administrative hierarchy in India was the governor general or viceroy. He was assisted by an advisory Executive Council, all of whose members were appointed by the crown, and a Legislative Council, which was composed of the full Executive Council along with additional members as appointed by the viceroy. Under the viceroy, depending on the importance of the area concerned, provinces were ruled by governors, lieutenant governors, or commissioners. By 1935, when Burma was detached as a province but two others were added to the roll, eleven so-called governor's provinces were listed in the last twelve years of British rule: Assam, Bengal, Bihar, Bombay, Central Provinces, Madras, Northwest Frontier Province, Orissa, Punjab, Sind, and United Provinces. As a third administrative layer, provinces were divided into districts, each headed by a deputy commissioner and district magistrates. Commissioners ruled over three or more districts.

Filling in the administrative structure was the Indian Civil Service, about one thousand in number. Recruited from Great Britain through competitive examinations instituted in 1853 in London, young men went to India for a life-time government career. With its high tradition, prestige, power, ample salaries, and retirement allowances, the Service attracted a high type of hard-working, honest candidate. In 1858, the examinations, based on an English education, were opened to Indians. In 1878, the minimum age limit was reduced from twenty-two to nineteen, and candidates were now drawn from the schools rather than from the universities, a procedure that gave the English added opportunity in the civil service competition but reduced the opportunity of Indians to compete. In 1893, the House of Commons passed a resolution favoring simultaneous examinations in India, but the Liberal Government in office at that time did not implement the recommendation. Not until after the First World War was the idea put into effect, though for many years previously Indians had been admitted to lower, less competitive posts and a few of them to higher ranks in the Service.

After the crown takeover, an outstanding fact in Indian history was the gradual extension and consolidation of British authority in the border areas. Three major considerations motivated continued British expansion outward: to open new areas to commerce, to end border raids by frontier tribes, and to contain Russian expansion in central Asia. Until 1870, the first two considerations were paramount. After that date, the Russian advance toward Indian mountain passes in the northwest frontier caused apprehension to the British government and its representatives in India—an apprehension only somewhat mitigated by the defeat of the Russians in 1905 by the Japanese.

In the northeast, border warfare erupted in 1865 with Bhutan, which was forced to cede to the British some 4,000 square miles of territory along the frontier. In the northwest, the protected state of Baluchistan was induced to cede to the crown the district of Quetta, which extended the full length of the northern frontier. In 1878, the second Afghan War broke out when the British invaded Afghanistan after the ruler there had received a Russian envoy but declined to see a British representative. The ruler fled, and his successor ceded Kalat, the Khyber Pass, and the valley of Kurram to the British, whose losses had been severe in this second campaign. The new amir, or ruler, continued to parlay between the Russians and the British, whose policy it was to give him a generous annual subsidy rather than to station troops in Kabul. When the Russians in 1891 and 1892 seized the Pamirs, the British counteracted and occupied certain areas in the Gilgit valley and Hindu Kush passes in the northwest.

To the east, in the third Anglo-Burmese war of 1885–1886, the British occupied upper Burma, and, in 1897, despite its separate history, peoples and problems, Burma was united into a single administrative unit of the Indian empire. To the north, in Tibet, in a pattern reminiscent of that which previously had been effected in Afghanistan, when the Dalai Lama appeared to play Russians off against the British, the viceroy, the energetic Lord Curzon, in 1904 dispatched the Younghusband expedition to Lhasa. The Tibetans were forced to pay a small indemnity, and the British government received rights to trade and to maintain a representative in the capital. Though this treaty recognized China's suzerainty in Tibet, the British government intervened to prevent any close incorporation of that region into China. The inaccessible mountain region became a pivot for British, Russian, and Chinese diplomatic intrigues.

As they expanded frontiers, the British modernized India. Under the accepted educational theory of westernizing the country rather than compromising with indigenous thought, the government emphasized higher education, at least until the First World War, as over primary and secondary. But most of the schools were aided by grants from the government. In 1857, the first three major universities of Calcutta, Bombay, and Madras were opened. The government operated some of the institutions and supervised others, as local private and mission schools, which provided for some coeducational programs as well. Schools trained Indians for employment in the government and in the professions, though by the turn of the twentieth century an oversupply of graduates had resulted. The school system was a potent force for westernization, and from the high social classes and professions, Indians including the top political triumvirate of India and Pakistan, Nehru and Gandhi as Hindus and Muhammad Ali Jinnah as a Muslim studied in England. Widely spoken by educated classes, English was the lingua franca. Nationalists advanced their claims against the British in the English linguistic medium and in the major vernacular languages.

In agriculture, the British placed emphasis in expanding irrigation systems, particularly those in the Punjab and Sind. By the early 1900's, 12 million acres of irrigated land, which permitted double cropping and so further increased yields, had been added. By 1940, irrigated lands in British India totaled 50 to 60 million acres, or one-fifth of the total cultivated area. Agrarian legislation was enacted to benefit cultivators, and agricultural cooperative credit societies were established, which provided for low interest rates to their members. Research programs delved into improving crop strains and more efficient methods of agriculture. Land tenure was modified in permanent settlement areas. The Bengal Rent Act of 1859 gave occupancy rights to all tenants of twelve years' standing, and other provinces followed suit. The British engaged in a persistent battle to prevent starvation. With undernourishment chronic in India, acute famine killed thousands and sometimes millions. The failure of a monsoon to arrive on schedule reduced the already narrow margin of subsistence in dry land farming areas.

Modernization proceeded in other fields. In public health, the fight continued against prevalent diseases, which included bubonic plague, cholera, tuberculosis, malaria, influenza, and dysentery. Extreme poverty, undernourishment, and the absence of elementary sanitary precautions exacted heavy tolls. Hospitals and dispensaries opened; pure drinking water supplies were developed in the main cities; inoculation and vaccination, which engendered some Hindu opposition, were practiced. But better health meant more people, and a discouraging increase of population was recorded in India. Where Akbar's dominion in 1600 had some 100 million, in 1881 the population totaled 253 million, in 1921, 319 million, in 1931, 352 million, and in 1941, 389 million.

In transportation, after a slow start under the Company, the railway system, with its strategic and commercial implications, rapidly expanded. At first the state guaranteed construction by private companies, but by 1870 the policy of state development was adopted, with an over-all state railway blueprint for the country. The government bought up privately owned mileage. By the Second World War, 43,000 miles of railroads were operative, to give India the most extensive and most efficient system for any Asian country its size. Railways provided speedy travel, encouraged pilgrimages, and helped indirectly to break down caste barriers. The state also operated the post office system, which provided as well for savings banks and life insurance departments. The state managed telegraph and telephone systems.

In finance, after initial failure with gold coins, the government put currency on a silver standard, with the circulation of silver coins. The rupee was made the standard unit of currency, and it became closely tied to sterling as early as the 1880's. By 1864, India enjoyed a balanced budget, and the country paid its own way in ordinary years, though loans were floated to finance wars, famine relief, and railway and canal construction, which latter projects amortized themselves in time. Half the central and provincial budgets came from land taxes; the remainder was raised through a miscellany of taxes, including a compulsory salt tax on all inhabitants. In legal affairs, a high standard of judicial impartiality and even-handed justice was the ideal. Codes of law, based variously on English tradition, common law, French codes, or Asian precedents, were framed. A modified form of trial by jury was introduced. Much of native law was retained, especially in family matters, but these were modified from time to time, as in the raising of the ages of majority and of consent to marriage.

Progress was achieved in economic autonomy. In 1919, India fixed its own tariffs, and home industries were encouraged as against British manufacturers. India benefited from the system of imperial preferences, adopted in 1927 to encourage intra-empire trade and to assist British industry. The depression of the early 1930's affected India, which experienced a sharp decline in its chief exports of raw materials, but economic and industrial growth had recovered by the end of that decade. Chief of the new industries was the textile industry, centered on cotton and jute. Tea and coffee plantations, indigo and spice cultures, were developed. The steel industry sprouted. With large coal and iron deposits in the east, and capitalizing on an ancient Indian knowledge of iron smelting, India produced the first steel in 1913. By the Second World War, India ranked sixth in world steel production. The factories of the Tata family of Parsi background were producing one million tons of steel a year. Their Jamshedpur operations in Bihar constituted the largest single steel mill in the British empire.

The defense system was modernized, but it was opened only slowly in higher ranks to Indians. After the mutiny, the designated Army in India consisted of Indian cavalry and infantry serving under British officers, who were stationed permanently in the country. Additional units of artillery, cavalry, and infantry troops of the British army were transferred to India for designated periods of time. In 1903, a unified Indian army was created, to replace the various British and

Indian contingents, as well as the three separate military commands, dating back to Company days, that were centered in Calcutta, Bombay, and Madras. With Lord Kitchener as moving spirit in the reorganization, the commander-in-chief replaced the civilian member dealing with military matters on the viceroy's council. This move, which split top British policy in India, resulted in the resignation of Lord Curzon as viceroy, who opted for civilian supremacy but was overruled by London in this matter.

To serve in the royal army, border people of martial races were recruited. Princes were permitted separate military units, which became, in 1889, fixed contingents. Trained under British officers, they participated mainly in local ceremonial affairs, though they could be mustered under the commander-in-chief when need arose. At the end of the First World War, the Indian Army numbered some 150,000 troops, of which one-third were British. Indians continued to serve in the infantry and the cavalry under British officers, but few Indians or Pakistanis had risen above the rank of major by 1947. No Indians served in the artillery or in the air force until the 1930's, when selected young Indians were sent to England for training. By the end of the Second World War, in terms of numbers Indian defense forces had grown tremendously. They totaled almost 2 million, a figure that included 30,000 in the Royal Indian Navy and 23,000 in the Royal Indian Air Force. Upon independence and partition, India and Pakistan inherited well-trained and well-organized indigenous troops under some native leadership.

Through the decades, because of the multiplying effects of westernization that proceeded along diverse civilian and military lines, India modernized in part. The process was long and diffuse. First affecting those Indians who had initially ministered to Company needs in the three main cities, in the course of time more Indians were exposed to western externals and western ideas, with the growth of Company and crown interests. More and more Indians were brought into the English orbit. A middle class emerged, as merchants, subordinate government officials, lawyers, journalists, professors, doctors, and military leaders. They lent an air of homogeneity to the country through various links of education, language, occupation, press, and communications. Yet, only a small percentage of Indians were westernized—probably less than 5 per cent. Modern and traditional groups, sectors, and peoples were juxtaposed and coexisted in a discontinuous and bewildering fashion in society.

The westernized minority might have contributed to the formation of a new India image, but what type of India was it to be, Hindu or Muslim, westernized or indigenous, religious or secular? While westernization had provided some common bonds among a new and rising class, plural loyalties still provided brakes on unity. Loyalties to family, to region, to country, and to religion tore people asunder. Particularly noteworthy were Hindu-Muslim relations. Some common bonds existed between the adherents of the two major religions. Physically alike, Hindus and Muslims derived from the same racial stocks. In matters of dress, wedding ceremonies, and purdah, some social similarities were obvious. Adherents of both faiths shared common speech in local areas, a body of common intellectual material as in mathematics and astronomy, some common religious ideas as in mysticism, and much common history.

Yet, differences between the two faiths proved great. In religion, Muslims adhered to one basic religious form that stressed one God, one interpretation, one set of prophets, one book, one revelation. Hindus, on the other hand, could accommodate many religious viewpoints. In Islam, the religious community and congregational worship prevailed. In Hinduism, one offered individual prayers. In political theory, Muslims advanced a theocracy, or a religious state where Islam could govern only Muslims under one divine will. Hindus, more accommodating, believed that different faiths could exist under one government, and not even necessarily under Hindu rule. Cultural differences exacerbated religious and political differences. Basic historic enmity, with past Muslim rule over Hindus, widened schisms.

Economic strains prevailed in the countryside, with Hindu peasants residing under Muslim landlords, or in reverse arrangements. Hindus, more willing to receive an English education, filled governmental ranks. Avoiding education or filling lesser posts, Muslims held secondary positions. The Hindu bourgeoisie filled professional ranks, wrote a different script, and pursued different art and architectural forms from

Muslims. Whereas Hinduism claimed that it could absorb Muslims, Islam posited that its faith could not be reconciled with Hindus. Rivalry grew between the leadership of the two communities over jobs, preferment, political rights, and over control of the modern sectors of life. The stark issue came to be whether the Muslim minority could risk its future in a nation dominated by a Hindu majority, who could monopolize political power and its benefits via the ballot box. The Muslim leaders posited a strong negative reaction to this arrangement. Basic and apparently unreconcilable differences existed.

Hindu nationalism was probably more nationalistic and more secular than that of Islam. To many Indians, Hinduism, embodying concepts associated with old India, appealed as a national way of life. With many of their persuasion in the civil service and government bureaus, Hindus looked upon themselves as the heirs of the British. More progressive and more receptive to foreign ideas, Hindu leadership derived from its professional and business classes. The reconstruction of the Hindu past helped their cause, for objective historical and archeological reasoning enhanced the antiquity of Hindu India. Two chief geographical centers of Hindu nationalism prevailed. In the east, Bengal was one, with Calcutta its nucleus, and with the University of Calcutta the focus of intellectual and nationalistic activity. In the West, the Maratha country with its religious dogmatism and warlike people, who had fought both British and Muslims, provided another center for nationalism.

Some early Hindu nationalist leaders came from Maratha. Epitomizing a militant approach, Bal Gangadhar Tilak (1856–1920) was dominant in Hindu nationalist circles in the early 1900's. A passionate agitator from Poona, he founded newspapers, advocated noncooperation with the British, and advanced a program of orthodox Hinduism. His counterpart, Gopal Krishna Gokhale (1866–1915), also from Poona, was of a liberal, tolerant, and persuasive bent. Desiring to preserve only the better values of Hinduism, he founded the Servants of India Society with forward-looking, secular objectives and programs. Three subsidiary geographic centers of nationalist activities included the Punjab, where the Sikhs resided; Gujarat, economically depressed, and the home of Gandhi; and south India, with its splinter groups arranged on regional, linguistic lines. Not until 1885, with the formation of the Indian National Congress as the first major Indian political party, was a start made toward a coherent, unified, and secular stand.

Augmenting varying Hindu nationalist outlooks were diverse Hindu philosophic responses to the challenge of modernization. One reaction was that of conservatism, which was espoused by Brahmanical exclusiveness endeavoring to hold the English at bay. A contrary approach accepted western forms, but tried to reconcile Indian substance and western usage. The *Brahmo Samaj* had been Ram Mohan Roy's attempt along accommodating lines. A third variant was the militant *Arya Samaj*. Founded in 1875, it accepted the necessity of western education, but it desired to revert to ancient times of the Vedas and the Aryans. It attacked such Hindu customs as caste and idolatry as well as Christian and Islamic tenets. A fourth reaction essayed yet another attempt at blending East and West. Through a life of contemplation and renunciation, the ascetic Ramakrishna (1836–1886), borrowing eclectically from various religious, sought to identify himself with the ideals of each great religion until he had attained divinity within himself. His disciple, Vivekananda (1863–1902), supplemented contemplation with a gospel of social action. He founded a monastic order called the Ramakrishan mission in which he proclaimed the essential oneness of all relgions. In 1893, he attended the World Congress of Religions at Chicago, and there he put Hinduism on the map of the western world. Vedanta missions in the United States date from his mission. Still another philosophical influence was that of the Theosophical Society, which allied itself with the Hindu revival movement. Founded in 1875 in the United States by a Russian lady, Madam H. P. Blavatsky, the movement spread to India. There its leadership was centered near Madras in the Englishwoman, Mrs. Annie Besant, who interested herself as well in political causes. The Society held that the problems of India could be solved by the reintroduction of its ancient institutions.

Muslim thought and nationalism also enjoyed a pluralistic approach, but to a lesser degree. From the right came Wahhabiism, which originated in late eighteenth-century Arabia and spread to India. Actually retarding the progress of the Muslim community, it attacked western learning and restored the concept of holy war. Pleading for the moderate cause was Sir Syed Ahmad Khan (1817–1898), probably the most influential Indian Muslim of the nineteenth century. Faithful to British rule, and remaining loyal during the mutiny when some Muslims turned against the British, he advocated a doctrine of toleration for all and propounded the peaceful teaching of Islam. He sought Islamic ideological links with the West by combining western science with Aristotelian elements in Islamic thought. In 1875, he founded the Anglo-Muhammedan College at Aligarh, near Delhi, but, despite claims of toleration, he remained aloof from the Indian National Congress, which he stated was too Hindu in outlook. Another Muslim, Muhammed Ali (1878–1930), as leader of pan-Muslim policy and intellectual Islam, helped to shape Muslim sentiment in the early twentieth century.

Nationalism in India took root, but it was divided. Hindus, claiming to speak for all Indians, themselves propounded several approaches toward British rule and the question of independence. Gandhi himself could not speak for all Hindus; he was assassinated by a fanatical one. Muslims, as a numerous but perennial minority, also were disunited in outlook in political matters into the twentieth century. The princes, over five hundred of them, generally kept themselves and their states aloof from nationalistic struggles. The British, with an obligation of fair play to all parties concerned, keenly felt their responsibility for maintaining orderly procedures, yet they too did not unanimously agree on policies with which to meet Indian nationalism. The struggles built up over the years between the British and the Indians and among the Indians themselves.

The course of the complex political power plays might be conveniently periodized into several epochs between 1858 and 1947. For the first few decades under crown rule, into the 1880's, Indians played a role of loyal opposition. Constitutional in procedures and moderate in demands, Indian nationalists remained loyal to the British. From the 1880's to the First World War, this moderate phase waned in the face of ardent pleas from advocates for direct action against the British. Relations became more strained, and in this interim the major political organs of both Hindus and Muslims were formed. During the First World War, with Wilsonian pronouncements of self-determination and British announcements for a self-governing dominion status in India, fresh impetus was given to nationalism and to the movement for political autonomy. The interwar period of the 1920's and the 1930's belonged to Gandhi. In cycles of conflict and of truce with the British, he came forward to assume leadership of the Indian nationalist movement. He transformed the Congress Party from a select group into a mass national party; simultaneously, he drew world attention to the Indian struggles for independence. But neither Gandhi nor his protégé, Nehru, could speak for the Muslims, who plead their own cause through Jinnah. By the Second World War, Hindus, Muslims, and British had come to agree on the reality of independence, but the varying proposals for its implementation and realization proved to be troublesome.

Incipient Nationalism (1858–1921)

With the assumption of sovereignty by the crown over India came a series of gradual and guarded extensions of limited rights to Indians to participate in central and provincial executive and legislative organs. The first major parliamentary act affecting Indian affairs at the center and provincial levels after the transfer of power was the Indian Councils Act of 1861. Though the Councils had less power than those created by the Act of 1853, the viceroy's Executive Council (an already existent body of five members) was enlarged to six. His Legislative Council, created by a previous law, which also consisted of members of the Executive Council, was expanded to include an additional six to twelve members. These were appointed for two-year terms, and the following year the viceroy appointed three Indians to the Legislative Council.

At the provincial level, the Act of 1861 restored the executive councils to the governors of Bombay and Madras, provided an additional legislative council to consist of the executive council with five to eight more members, and authorized similar councils for other provinces as they were created. Taking the hint from the central government, the governors of the two great provinces of Bombay and Madras adopted the policy of appointing Indian members to provincial legislative councils. All councils, executive and legislative, were advisory in nature, subject to gubernatorial or viceregal veto and parliamentary direction from London, as fountainhead of authority.

Indians demanded more voice in their political affairs. Spearheading the drive, the vernacular nationalist press was particularly vocal in Bengal, Bombay, and Madras, though the Vernacular Press Act of 1878, in effect four years, provided press censorship on native language papers. The most significant development was the establishment of the Indian National Congress in 1885 as the first sign of concrete awareness, on a country scale, of nationalism. As a party of the middle classes, the Congress desired to replace British control with their own control. Claiming to speak for the will of all India, the party initially advanced moderate claims, but splits developed in time between the moderates, who wanted self-government, and the extremists, who desired independence. The Indian masses were not consulted by and did not participate in this coroprate form of nationalist endeavor, and the Indian aristocracy, as the princes and great landlords, by choice remained aloof from it.

The buildup to such a party organ had been gradual. As early as 1851, the British Indian Association was formed. As the first recognizable political body in the country, two years later it submitted to parliament the first proposals for Indian participation in government affairs. In 1876, a young Bengali, Surendranath Banerjea, who had been ejected from the civil service on grounds that some considered to be insufficient, founded the Indian Association. In 1883, this organ changed its name to the Indian National Conference. That same year witnessed a significant event in spurring Indian nationalist aims. The Ilbert Bill, named after the law member who had introduced it, was submitted to empower Indian judges, who were by then reaching senior status in the civil service, to try Europeans in the districts, a power they already enjoyed in the presidency cities. Europeans vociferously protested the bill. In part to meet their objections, the viceroy amended the bill so that, were Europeans to be tried, they could claim at least a jury composed of half Europeans in number. In the end, few were satisfied with the compromise arrangement. As a result of this episode and of effective organized agitation, the Indian National Congress, into which the Indian National Conference merged, sprang into existence.

The main figure involved in the formation of the Congress was an Englishman, Alan Hume, who in 1849 had gone to India in the civil service. Serving as a district officer over the years, he retired in 1882. Staying on in India after his retirement, he devoted time, not only to ornithological studies (he wrote the first book on Indian birds), but also to political reforms. In 1884, he wrote to graduates of Calcutta University asking for volunteers to join in a movement to regenerate India. He averred that this was a task to be done by Indians themselves, which was a new concept. The first session of the Congress convened at Poona, where it displayed an almost diffident temper. Over the years, as a self-constituted body drawing mainly on European and Hindu membership, the party assembled to discuss the political conditions of the country and to suggest reforms.

As part of their early platform, they advanced the desirability of elected legislative councils in the provinces, civil service examinations to be held in India as well as in England, limitations on military expenditures, the abolition of the Council of India, and the commissioning of Indian officers in the Indian army. During the first two decades of its existence, the Congress steadily increased its prestige, though Muslims, who constituted one quarter of its membership, remained on its fringes. From a small group of some seventy dues-paying members, the party grew into a larger body of several hundred, elected by various groups all over the country. During the early years, moderate leaders were able to retain control. By the turn of the century there appeared a strong militant minority, led by Tilak, many of whom were orthodox and traditionalist Hindus, who wanted speedy achievement of self-rule and who emphasized self-reliance and an independent spirit.

The British, in the meantime, had extended some political rights. The Indian Councils Act of 1892 enlarged the viceroy's Legislative Council to eighteen members, to draw a dozen Britishers from the civil service and to include some Indians nominated by certain groups. The provincial legislative councils were similarly structured, with parties nominated by such hybrid groups as municipalities, district boards, chambers of commerce, universities, and other special interests.

On the heels of this act came one of India's most outstanding viceroys, Lord Curzon, into office from 1899 to 1905. Able, arrogant, eloquent, and industrious, the viceroy epitomized the imperialist of the day. He worked for the good of the Indians as he defined it; he interpreted this as a policy of trusteeship to develop the colony, but not to grant self-government. With pomp and panoply, visiting provinces and princes, he traveled throughout the country, and into the Persian Gulf as well, displaying British might. Of strong will and great courage, he accomplished much and alienated many. Two of his policies were particularly controversial. The Universities Act of 1904 modified the constitution of the executive bodies of schools in such a way as to provide for nominated members, usually government officials or educationalists, with powers of official inspection in the affiliated colleges. Indian faculty members, as part of the new middle classes, jealous of hardwon prerogatives and mindful of the issue of academic freedom, strongly protested the move.

Curzon's second policy was the partition of Bengal, along with Bihar and Orissa, into halves. Containing almost 80 million people, the large unwieldy unit was divided into West Bengal and the new province of East Bengal (essentially East Pakistan later), which was amalgamated with Assam. The results of this partition were several and basic. The Bengali-speaking area was cut in half. The division heightened communalism, for Hindus were in the majority in the western half and Muslims in the eastern half. Because of this, the division pleased Muslims but inflamed Hindus. Some of the latter embarked on a program of terroristic methods, which for practically the first time in British Indian history, were practiced on a fairly wide scale. Rioting broke out not only in Bengal, but also in western India and the Punjab. Other nationalists, in another first, launched a *swadeshi* or "buy Indian" campaign. Tilak also coined the word *swaraj*, or self-rule, which in 1906 was declared to be the objective of Congress. To help preserve their rights, in the same year in Dacca the Muslim League was organized by the Aga Khan and the brothers Mohammed and Shaukat Ali, who declared for nonviolence and moderation.

Moderate Congress elements under Gokhale also opted for a similar program, though in its annual meeting in 1907 at Surat the party split into moderate and militant wings on the question of cooperating with the British.

When the Liberals in 1905 came to power to England, Lord Morley, biographer of the Liberal William Gladstone, was appointed Secretary of State for India. The path was cleared for more Indian rights. In 1907, two Indians were appointed to the Council of India. With Lord Minto in office as viceroy, further reforms were enacted into law. The Morley-Minto reforms of 1909 provided for the appointment of an Indian to the inner sanctum of the viceroy's Executive Council. His Legislative Council was enlarged from eighteen to sixty, with twenty-eight appointed official representatives, five appointed nonofficial Indians, and twenty-seven elected Indians (seven landlords, five Muslims, two from chambers of commerce, and the rest from provincial legislative councils). Indians also were appointed to provincial executive councils, and fifty members each were elected (not nominated) to legislative councils in Bombay, Bengal, Madras, and the United Provinces by a franchise which was extended to some one million voters on property qualifications. The legislative councils could not pass laws, for they could only discuss measures proposed by the government. The reforms conceded the demands of the Muslim community by providing for separate representation of members chosen by the voters of a Muslim electorate. This principle of communal representation was to have profound effects over time. To reassert the personal nature of British rule, in 1911 King George V and Queen Mary came to Delhi, where they reversed the Bengal partition and announced the transfer of the Indian capital from Calcutta to Delhi.

By the First World War, the nationalist movement was more than ever the preserve of the Congress party, dominated by the English-speaking urban middle classes. They sought political objectives for India; social and economic benefits for the people, they argued, would come only if power passed into the hands of Indians. Hoping for rewards by cooperating with the British during the war, the party temporarily relegated politics to a back seat. The hard-pressed British welcomed the respite because they faced the problems of keeping

Indian antagonisms in bounds during the emergency and raising funds and men for the war effort. The British succeeded to a degree in their objective of expanding Indian participation in the war, for 800,000 Indian soldiers and 400,000 auxiliaries were recruited. Indian troops participated in European and in Middle Eastern campaigns, in which some 26,000 Indians were killed and 70,000 were wounded. In 1917, a munitions board was established in India to develop local industries and to furnish supplies for allied operations in south and west Asia. In August that year, Lord Montagu, Secretary of State for India, after consultations with Viceroy Chelmsford in India, announced, in a definite but open dated policy, that Britain would provide for "the increasing association of Indians in every branch of the administration and the gradual development of self-governing institutions with a view to the progressive realisation of responsible government in India as an integral part of the Empire." This possibility of Indian self-rule was fanned by the fires of self-determination as expressed in the outbreak of the Russian revolution, which saw the fall of despotism in that country, and in the enunciation of the Wilsonian fourteen points, which were predicated on a world-wide basis.

Assisting the Indian movement for self-government at home was the Home Rule League founded by Mrs. Besant. Relating the political movement to religious overtones, she launched the League with the aim of self-rule for a Commonwealth of India within the British Empire. Cooperating with the Congress, in 1917 she was elected president of that organ. So active was she in politics that the British restricted her to the Madras area. Additionally, there was some cooperation during the war between Hindus and Muslims. Congress supported the League in the Khilafat movement, which was directed against British actions in Turkey. Muslims looked to the caliphate in Istanbul as their political and religious center, but the Turks were on the losing side in the war. Though Muslims in India supported the British, they disliked what appeared to be a British dismemberment of Turkey. Both Hindus and Muslims in India were temporarily thrown together in this anti-British cause, centered outside India. In the Lucknow Pact of December, 1916, they agreed to cooperate in the cause of Indian unity and self-government. The agreement did not outlive the war, for natural antagonisms revived and the Turkish cause collapsed. In 1922, the sultan was deposed by revolution and two years later the caliphate was abolished.

The Congress and the League continued to press for more rights from the British. In 1916, they suggested a national parliament and legislative assemblies, responsible to an electorate, for all provinces. Partly as a result of this, the British government appointed a royal commission to study the question. The Act of 1919, based on the Montagu-Chelmsford report, provided for further participation of Indians in the central and provincial governments. The viceroy's Executive Council was enlarged to seven members, to include three Indians. The central Legislative Council was transformed into a bicameral national parliament. Its upper house, the Council of State, had sixty members with five-year terms. Twenty-six members were appointed and thirty-four were elected by a restricted electorate of 17,000 voters at the time. As the lower house, the Legislative Assembly of 146 members sat for three-year terms. Roughly one-third of them were appointed and two-thirds, or 106, were elected by an electorate of some 5 million voters. A Chamber of Princes, to act as a common consultative body for the princely states, was established. Eight governor's provinces were created, each with executive and unicameral councils (with 30 per cent appointive and the rest elected membership).

At the provincial level, dyarchy or dual government was established. Councillors, responsible to the governor, handled "reserved" matters, such as finance, land revenue, canal construction, and law and order. Ministers, responsible to the governor and assemblies, were charged with less important "transferred" functions, as agriculture, health, and education. At all times, the governors and the viceroy maintained the residual power of certification, the approval or veto of all measures. Among the electorate, the principle of communalism continued. Muslims, Sikhs, Europeans, Anglo-Indians, and Indian Christians constituted separate electorates. In February, 1921, the new government structure became effective and immediately came under fire from several quarters. The reforms were attacked by right-wing British opinion, which claimed that they undermined the powers of the viceroy.

Others contrarily maintained that such features as certification, reserved powers, communalism, and the lack of real ministerial responsibility inhibited parliamentary operations. The Congress abstained from participation in the reorganized structure. Some reforms were effected by a few other local parties that participated, as the Justice Party in Madras, which reformed the administration of wealthy south Indian temples, and the Unionist Party in Punjab, which extended education benefits and passed protective laws for cultivators of land.

Where the British gave on the one hand, they took away with the other. In 1918, as part of wartime security measures to curb German activities in the northwest frontier, in Punjab, and in Bengal, the Rowlatt bills, named after the English justice who framed them, were formulated. One never passed and the other was enacted when few could prophesy its unpopularity. The act, valid for three years, provided that in political cases judges could conduct trials without juries, and that provincial authorities could intern persons suspected of disloyalty or subversion without benefit of trial. Never invoked, the measure nonetheless stirred up strong sentiment and fomented more anti-British feeling. Reacting to the bill and advocating a policy of nonviolent noncooperation, Gandhi on February 23, 1919, at a meeting of the Ahmadabad branch of the Home Rule League, appealed to Indians to observe a day of national humiliation and prayer.

To add fuel to the fire, on April 13th in the Punjab, the tragic Amritsar affair occurred. Concerned with security measures and acting with military directness, General Reginald Dyer, the commander of the area, ordered a throng of Indians, mainly Sikhs, listening to political speeches, to disperse. When the assembly did not appear to do so, the general commanded his troops to fire upon it. The action resulted in 379 killed and 1200 wounded. Indian reaction was immediate, angry, and nation-wide. Because of Amritsar, titled Indians renounced their honors, students left school, and boycotts of British goods were effected. The massacre engendered adverse global publicity as well to British policies in India. The British government censured Dyer, but a large sum of money, raised among Europeans in England and in India, was presented to him along with a sword of honor as the "Saviour of the Punjab."

After Amritsar there was no going back for nationalism.

Protests and boycotts were the order of the day. By the end of the First World War, noncooperation became pronounced, despite British gestures toward indigenous representative rights. Indian demands outplaced British concessions. On the issue of British concessions Indians united in principle though they varied in tactics to achieve them. Nationalism now existed on a broader base, and a new set of Hindu and Muslim leaders emerged as its spokesmen.

Militant Nationalism (1921-1941)

Mohandas Karamchand Gandhi (1869-1948) was born into the Vaisya class in Porbandar, a port on the Kathiawar peninsula in western India and the capital of a small Hindu state. His father was the hereditary prime minister of the state, and the youth had an early association with politics and state service. He was sent to London to study law and qualified there as a barrister. Returning home, he practiced his profession for a time, but in 1893 he proceeded to South Africa. There he remained over twenty years to defend Indian immigrants against racial prejudice and to evolve his political philosophy, which included the doctrine of ahimsa or nonviolent noncooperation. Returning to India in 1915, he joined the Congress, outlived his teacher Gokhale, and climbed to leadership in the party over Tilak. He retained this position, in or out of party office, during the interwar period. Called *mahatma* ("great soul"), he promoted the first civil disobedience movement, which lasted from 1920 to 1922. It got out of hand and Gandhi deplored the bloodshed. After a trial in which he took responsibility for the violence, he was sentenced to two years' imprisonment. Because of ill health, he was released after a year. He then remained aloof in his Gujarat *ashram*, or retreat from political quarrels, over the next several years.

For Gandhi, cooperation in any form with the "satanic government" was "sinful." He lived the simple life, and to dramatize swadeshi and swaraj he burned foreign clothes. Endearing him to the people were his religious habits and language, his simple vegetarian diet and poverty. His emblem was the *charkha*, or hand spinning machine that turned out *khaddar*, or handspun cotton cloth. Not against caste distinctions so much as caste restrictions, he championed the cause of the untouchables, whom he termed *harijans*, or sons of God. Through *satyagraha*, or soul force, he related religious ideas to political tactics. Strikes were moral protests, passive resistance was a campaign for truth, and opposition to the government was noncooperation with evil. It was fortunate that Gandhi was around to advocate pacifism at a time when India appeared to be heading for bloodshed. He diverted nationalism into constructive channels, though it got out of control at times. He identified nationalism with the common people and related it to India's past and modern needs. He desired pacific relations between the English and the Indians and among Indians themselves. He elevated the Indian cause to worldwide attention and he gave to it a moral and spiritual standing. His idealized aims were high, but the reality of practical politics sometimes charted a contrary course.

The Congress accepted Gandhi's leadership, but nationalists were not of one mind on how to react to British policies. The party boycotted the elections as provided for in the Act of 1919, and, because of the campaigns of nonviolent noncooperation, most of its leaders were put in jail. As the movement grew, many of Gandhi's followers sought a more activist role, and they desired to use physical force. The mahatma did not countenance such an extreme, and some of his followers became disillusioned. But out of noncooperation, as masterminded by Gandhi, came some positive results. It showed that Indians could unite to a great degree—a unity which elicited respect from the British. The colonial power sought allies from among the princes and granted more rights to Indians. Representatives from the untouchables were appointed to legislative councils, more Muslims entered administrative ranks, and business groups received economic concessions.

In the mid-1920's, Chitta Ranjan Das and Motilal Nehru, father of Jawaharlal, came to the fore as spokesmen of the moderate nationalist cause. With neither approval nor hindrance from Gandhi, they founded the *Swaraj* party, as a Congress parliamentary party. They entered candidates for elective offices in provincial assemblies, where, if majorities were gained, legislation was introduced favoring extension of Indian rights. Such laws, unpopular with the British government, were then usually nullified through the certification process. In several provinces where the Swaraj operated, its tactics of council-wrecking proved to be successful. In another definition of noncooperation, the Swarajists demonstrated the effectiveness of parliamentary procedures. But, at the same time, the schism deepened between Hindus and Muslims. The Muslim League intensified its demands for separate electorates, provincial autonomy, and weighted representatives. To counter these Muslim demands, Hindu extremists within the Congress organized a Hindu *Mahasabha,* or association to promote their own communal and special interests.

The political spectrum was broadened further with the introduction of Socialist and Communist movements, though these remained, in organized form, on the fringes of Indian political life. In 1923, the first Socialist weekly was founded in Bengal. Within the Congress itself, a Socialist youth movement called the All-India Independence League, which embraced the younger Nehru, advocated a program of complete independence, liquidation of landlords, and the establishment of a Socialist state. In 1925, Communists called the first all-India Communist Conference in Cawnpore. Five hundred delegates attended the meeting, elected an executive committee, and transferred their headquarters to Delhi. The Communists immediately came under handicaps. The chief Communist, S. A. Dange, and other leaders, were put in jail on charges of conspiracy against the British government. In 1926–1927, several British Communists and an Indian elected to the British Parliament came to India, in line with Moscow policy, to establish cells of farm workers and peasant parties in Bombay, Bengal, the Punjab, and the United Provinces. In 1928, the Communists held another conference in Calcutta, where they allied themselves with the program of the Comintern (Communist International). Organizing a militant left-wing labor movement, they participated in many strikes. In March, 1929, the Indian government arrested thirty-one leaders, of whom all but two were Communists, in the Meerut Conspiracy Case. Most of them were released in 1933, though four of the most prominent were held longer. In 1934, another wave of strikes occurred, and the government banned the Communist Party, which went underground until 1942.

Best known of the Indian Communists was M. N. Roy (1898–1954). Born as Narendranath Bhattacharya, he slipped out of India in 1915 to Java to contact German agents bringing arms for an Indian insurrection. The plot failed, and the youth went on to the United States and to Mexico under his assumed name. When news of the Bolshevik revolution reached him, he helped to found the Mexican Communist Party and then proceeded to Moscow. He registered a favorable impression on Lenin, who put him on the Executive Committee of the Comintern. An international and widely traveled Communist in the 1920's, he was busy for a time in Tashkent in central Asia training Indians. He published papers in Berlin and in Paris, and he appeared in China in 1927. Two years later, he severed his connection with the Comintern and returned incognito to India, where he was arrested by the British and served a six-year prison term. During the Second World War he opposed Gandhi and Nehru. After independence, he abandoned Marxism and founded a Radical Humanist group. But he kept his belief in materialism and continued to preach against religion, possibly the most important aspect of traditional Indian life.

As the political scene broadened in India, the British government re-examined Indian policy. The Act of 1919 had provided for a review of its results at the end of a decade, and, in 1927, the Simon Commission of seven, including the later British prime minister Clement Attlee, was appointed. No Indians were appointed on the Commission, which was instructed to study the Indian governmental structure and to recommend appropriate legislation to broaden Indian participation. After a five-year study, the resulting report became part of the basis for the monumental Government of India Act of 1935. The Simon mission worked in an Indian atmosphere of resentment, because of the lack of Indian representation on it as well as greater Indian demands. Nationalists insisted on full and complete independence. The British were unwilling to go this far. In October, 1929, after consultations with London, the viceroy reiterated the British stand of dominion status that was implicit in the declaration of 1917. This fell short of nationalist aims, and in December, 1929, the Congress at Lahore resolved that "we must sever all connections with the British and attain complete independence. We will prepare ourselves by withdrawing so far as we can all voluntary association from the British government and we will prepare for civil disobedience, including nonpayment of taxes."

The next month the Congress party members reiterated this pledge of independence on January 26th, a date celebrated after independence as Republic Day. As leaders of the radical wing, Subhas Chandra Bose (1897–1945) and Jawaharlal Nehru (1889–1964) came to the forefront.

Nehru described himself as a "queer mixture of the East and the West, out of place everywhere, at home nowhere—perhaps my thoughts and approach to life are more akin to what is called Western than Eastern, but India clings to me." Of Kashmiri Brahman background, the younger Nehru was born at Allahabad, where the Ganges and the Jumna rivers converge. As Motilal's only son, he later wrote that "an only son of prosperous parents is apt to be spoilt, especially so in India." At home he studied under tutors; at fifteen he was sent to Harrow; two years later he entered Cambridge. At twenty he went to London to take a law degree where Gandhi had studied two decades earlier. Sojourning seven years in England, he returned to India in 1912 to practice law with his father. Jawaharlal joined the Congress and toured his country. But he was disappointed by Gandhi's sudden suspension of the non-cooperation movement in 1922, after the outbreak of violence. In 1926–1927, with his wife he toured Europe, where he conversed with Socialists and Communists. In Russia for a week's stay, he was impressed by Soviet achievements, and professed to see a common opposition to imperialism.

Back in India, Nehru plunged into national struggles again. He demanded as the goal of Congress not dominion status, as his more moderate father wished, but rather complete independence. To keep the political movement splitting, as had been the case in 1907, Gandhi yielded to such a demand. In 1930, the mahatma persuaded the Congress to accept Jawaharlal, forty years old, as party president. From that time, Nehru was regarded as Gandhi's heir apparent. But the two men were poles apart in several ways. Nehru, a man with secular emphasis, held little brief for religious ways. He took nonviolence as a means, not an end. As a Socialist living in the modern day, he wanted a centralized state with a planned industrial economy rather than the Gandhian ideal of self-sufficient villages with hand spinning looms in cottages.

As other leaders from Hindu India came to the limelight, so the Muslim cause was furthered by new champions. In

1929, the Aga Khan, the head of a small unorthodox Muslim sect, promulgated the concepts of continued separate Muslim electorates, a loose federation of provinces in order to ensure Muslim predominance in provinces where Muslims enjoyed a majority, and Muslim membership in all cabinets. The next year, as president of the Muslim League, the poet-politician Muhammad Iqbal (1873–1938) reiterated the uniqueness of the Muslim religious ideal and way of life, which in time he came to feel could be realized only in a separate Muslim political state. Later canonized by Muslims for developing this political concept of Pakistan, Iqbal provided the poetic and philosophic bases for the future state.

Born in the Punjab of devout parents, Iqbal was educated at Lahore College. Later he went to Europe to study philosophy and law in Germany and in England, though he was interested chiefly in writing. As the greatest Urdu poet of the time, he composed, with a vein of mysticism, in the Islamic tradition. Advocating the cause of Islam, which he claimed would cure most of the world's ills, he devoted himself to a program that stressed the cultivation of the innate greatness of the human self, and of developing the individual through a true understanding of the relationship between God and man. This would be most effective, he claimed, through a community of similar outlooks as in the community of Islam. In 1922, he accepted knighthood for his poetry, but he continued to dabble in politics, for which he was not temperamentally suited. Toward the end of his life, Iqbal became convinced that Muslims were threatened with extinction, and he single out as his successor in the political field Muhammad Ali Jinnah (1876–1948).

Jinnah, the real architect of Pakistan, was born in Karachi, into a small and unorthodox Muslim sect. During the first forty-five years or so of his life, he had no reputation of Muslim piety or for any special interests. Educated in London, he returned to live in Bombay, where he developed a brilliant and financially remunerative law practice. He entered politics and began his rise to power. He joined the Congress in the interests of promoting Muslim-Hindu unity. He was elected by the Muslim constituency of Bombay to the viceroy's Legislative Council, where his ability gained him recognition. In 1913, Jinnah also took out membership in the Muslim League, because it appeared to have aims similar at that time to those of the moderates in the Congress. Throughout the First World War he worked for Indian unity. He remained faithful to the Congress, but, when Gandhi emerged as leader, Jinnah resigned. He had little use for the policies of noncooperation and of civil disobedience, which he characterized as unrealistic and as jeopardizing Muslim interests. He devoted his political energies toward the League, and, in 1934, was elected its permanent president. In time, he became its virtual dictator, and his followers bestowed upon him the title of Great Leader. Living up to this designation, he brooked no opposition in the League. Fastidious, stately, imperious, and a cold realist, he pushed the Muslim cause to partition.

Gandhi, back in politics in the late 1920's, threatened a second civil disobedience campaign were nationalist demands not met. These consisted of full home rule and a conference to frame a constitution in which Indian interests would be duly represented. In reply, the viceroy reiterated the 1917 pronouncement, but he invited Gandhi and some other Indian leaders to meet with him to discuss the composition of a conference that might adopt constitutional proposals for parliamentary consideration. The meeting was held in December, 1929, but it ended in stalemate since the Congress representatives demanded immediate home rule, which a constitution as adopted by a conference would simply confirm. The British would not go this far, and they gained the acquiescence of minority groups on the issue of discussing cooperative measures through a round table conference.

The promised civil disobedience campaign was initiated with an attack on the government's salt monopoly. In defiance of the salt tax imposed on all, in March of 1930 Gandhi set out on a three-week, 170-mile march to the sea. He waded into waves, dipped a cupful of water, and poured it onto red-hot rocks on the beach. In this symbolic defiance of the monopoly, he began a nationwide movement of nonviolent noncooperation which lasted for four years. Government officials resigned from office, foreign businesses were boycotted, *hartals* or cessation of business activities took place. As had been the case in the first civil disobedience campaign, rioting and violence erupted. Two months after the salt march, Gandhi was again imprisoned. By that midsummer, 60,000 Indians were in jail;

a prison sentence became a mark of distinction for Indian nationalists.

It was into this seething atmosphere that the recommendations of the Simon report were publicized. They advocated the enlargement of the provincial legislatures, the further development of dyarchy in the provinces, the election of members of both houses in the central· legislature by provincial councils, the extension of the franchise, and the ultimate creation of an all-India federation. With the publication of the report, the British Labour government, then in power, also announced that it was convening in London a conference to represent all sections of Indian opinion, including princes, to consider what steps to take next toward dominion status.

At the first round table conference from November, 1930, to January, 1931, Prime Minister Ramsay MacDonald chaired the meetings. Proposals were presented from all Indian political groups except the Congress, the most important one, which boycotted the sessions. The conference recommended a federal India to be organized loosely enough to embrace a British-dominated center, the princely states, the British provinces. The final recommendation was preliminary and tentative, for, without the cooperation of the Congress, no plan could be workable. After the conference, MacDonald ordered the release of political prisoners, including Gandhi, from jail. He authorized the viceroy to talk with the mahatma, who announced, after some hesitation, that he would attend the second round of talks.

In late 1931, Gandhi, as sole representative of the Congress at the second round table conference, went to London dressed in his loincloth via third-class steamship accommodations. Discussions centered on the issues of dyarchy and of separate electorates for communities, which the Congress opposed. It pressed for a general electorate, but Indians were divided, for the minorities advocated separate and communal representation. The gap between Indians and between the British and Indians remained. The conference broke up, and, back in India, Gandhi returned to prison. Just before the Labour government left office, the prime minister announced the Communal Award in which separate electorates were decreed for minorities, including the depressed classes or untouchables. Gandhi disliked this arrangement that persisted in communal approaches and additionally made a distinction within the Hindu community between untouchables and the traditional classes. His vow of a fast unto death on this issue was broken only when he and Dr. B. R. Ambedkar, chief leader of the depressed classes, worked out a scheme to give the untouchables a larger representation and which eliminated the principle of separate electorates at least within the Hindu fold. In 1932, the third and last session of the round table conferences brought forth a white paper which, after parliamentary discussions, helped to frame the Government of India Act of 1935.

As the last major organic law to govern British India, the Act of 1935 was voluminous. Consisting of four published volumes, it was the longest bill in British legislative history. It accepted a federal concept for India, extended autonomy in the provinces, provided for dyarchy at the center, separated Burma from India, maintained separate communal electorates, and promulgated a new constitution. Proceeding from negotiations between the British rulers and Indian subjects, the Act was a compromise, and, as such, completely satisfied no one. India remained a colony, responsible to parliament through the Secretary of State for India. An all-India federation was stipulated, to be comprised of the eleven governors' provinces; the six commissioners' provinces, administered by the viceroy through a chief commissioner appointed by him; and federating princely states. Those states that federated were to surrender their power over foreign affairs, defense, and communications in exchange for a substantial voice in the central government, but their line of responsibility to the crown lay through the viceroy rather than through the government of India.

The Act of 1935 further provided for a bicameral federal legislature. The lower chamber, termed the House of Assembly or the Federal Assembly, was indirectly elected by provincial legislative assemblies on a communal basis for five-year terms. It consisted of 250 representatives from British India and half that number from the princely states. The upper house, or Council of State, as a permanent body of members with nine-year terms and one-third retiring every third year, had representation also from British India and the federated princely states. That from British India consisted of 156 members, of which six were nominated by the viceroy on a communal base and the rest elected directly or in a few cases indirectly on high franchise qualifications but also through communal electorates. The federating princely states sent 104 representatives, who were appointed by the rulers.

In the provinces, the franchise in elections was extended to 35 million, or 12 per cent of the total adult population. Provincial legislatures were enlarged and second chambers were provided for in six of the eleven provinces. Representation also continued on communal lines, including that for the scheduled classes, the new term given to untouchables. More ministerial responsibility devolved upon provincial governments, but the very considerable reserve and veto powers that remained safely in the hands of governors and of the viceroy severely limited such power. Nor did the ministers have a decisive vote in finances. Dyarchy, abandoned in the provinces, was adopted instead in the central government. Defense and external affairs were reserved matters, to be administered by councilors responsible only to the viceroy. Salaries of the viceroy, judges, and the civil service were outside legislative authority. The viceroy had to give previous approval to bills relating to coinage, currency, and constitutional changes.

The provincial provisions of the Act of 1935 were shortly implemented. Early in 1937, provincial assemblies were elected. The Congress participated in strength. By this time, the party was an effectivee nation-wide organ, ranging from grass roots level to the national, of some 3 million members that included 100,000 Muslims. It won 711 of 1585 contested seats, and it achieved a clear majority in five provinces and a dominant position in two others. More responsible government in the provinces had been initiated. Provincial legislation directed primarily toward the welfare of the masses was enacted, as the reduction of rents, improvement of working conditions, efforts to eradicate mass illiteracy, and promotion of educational reforms. But it was impossible to effect federation at the center, and the viceroy continued with his Executive Council. Princes turned down federation, the Congress left wing displayed little patience with the moderates, and those members who cooperated with the British fell under suspicion. Impatient and militantly nationalist elements within the Congress under Bose lost patience with both the British and

Gandhi. They broke with Nehru and directed their admiration toward Hitler and the Japanese military, with whom Bose later collaborated abroad in the Second World War.

Relations worsened between Hindus and Muslims. In 1938, Jinnah and Nehru endeavored to hammer out schemes for communal cooperation, but their efforts came to nothing. Congress would not admit Muslims to posts in provincial cabinets unless they joined that party. For their part, Muslims disliked the singing of the Hindu national anthem, the favored use of Hindi over Urdu, and the choicest political appointments going to Hindus. After two years of implementing provincial provisions of the Act of 1935, the Congress ministries resigned in November, 1939, as part of their opposition to circumstances under which the British brought India into the Second World War. Taking note of the action, the Muslim League chose to celebrate Deliverance Day on December 22nd, and on that date in subsequent years until partition, they thanked God in the name of Muslims for freeing them from the oppression of the Congress. Yet, in the Punjab and Bengal, where Muslims had the upper hand and controlled provincial legislatures, they reversed the advantages of Hindus and appeared only slowly to evolve social or economic programs for the community.

As the possibility of war approached in England, the Congress warned the mother country that it would not fight other people's wars. Britishers thought otherwise, and on September 3, 1939, when England declared war on Germany, the viceroy proclaimed that India also was at war. With the Congress members absent from the session, the central legislature of India approved the defense of India bill. The princes affirmed their loyalty and offered aid. The Muslim League promised support on the condition that no constitutional changes in the Act of 1935 would be made without its approval. In October, 1939, the British government reaffirmed the pledge it had given ten years earlier to grant India the status of a self-governing dominion. To gain Indian participation in the war, it suggested the formation of a consultative group, presided over by the viceroy, of all political parties in British India and of the Indian princes. In March, 1940, the Congress reiterated its decision not to support the war, advanced the possibility of a third civil disobedience campaign, and demanded an immediate declaration of the independence of India. That same month, the Muslim League at Lahore under Jinnah formally adopted partition, the "vivisection of India" as Gandhi termed it, in which the northwestern and the eastern zones of India, each with four and two provinces respectively, were to be independent states.

After the fall of France in autumn of 1940, when the British were in dire straits, they promised dominion status in even stronger terms. They proposed a purely Indian constitutional assembly to frame the postwar form of government. Both the Congress and the League rejected the proposals, and the former authorized another campaign of civil disobedience in September of 1940, to be conducted on an individual, rather than on a mass, basis. To compromise on a middle way that would embrace more Indian participation in government, some Indians of moderate persuasion met in early 1941 and suggested that the viceroy's Executive Council be enlarged. The viceroy eventually enlarged the countil to twelve, with seven Indian representatives. He also established a National Defense Council of thirty, drawn from British India and the princely states. But the British continued to hesitate in granting independence to India, and they did not essentially change their position during the Second World War.

When the Atlantic Charter was drawn up in August of 1941 by President Franklin D. Roosevelt and Prime Minister Winston Churchill, its third paragraph indicated the right of people to choose the form of government under which they cared to live and to restore self-government and sovereign rights to those deprived of them. Indians naturally inquired whether the paragraph referred to them. In a House of Commons speech Churchill clearly answered the question in the negative. He affirmed that the paragraph referred only to nations conquered by the Axis powers and that it did not apply to India (or to Burma). As the Pacific war clouds lowered, the British remained frozen in their concept of dominion status for India, the princes continued noncommittal, the Indian National Congress demanded independence, and the Muslim League insisted on partition. The Indian "problem" proved to be complex.

Divided Nationalism (1941-1947)

The primary aim of the British was to remain solvent in Europe during the war, but there were more efforts to find solutions to the Indian problem. In March of 1942, a mission was dispatched under Sir Stafford Cripps, a lawyer and statesman noted for his liberal views and one presumed sympathetic to Indian nationalism. In keeping with British war cabinet proposals, the Cripps mission sought generally to create a new dominion, that of the Indian Union, which was to be associated with the United Kingdom and with other dominions through a common allegiance to the crown. The Union was to be equal to the other members in every respect and in no way subordinate in any aspect of its domestic or external affairs. Mission members talked extensively with leaders, including Gandhi, from all chief political Indian groups. After consultations, the mission published its specific proposals in a draft declaration. Included as the main points in the proposals were the British retention of the defense portfolio during the war, the Indianization of the viceroy's Executive Council, the convening of a postwar constituent assembly, the revision of treaties with the Indian states, the extension of Indian Union dominion status to those provinces and those princes desiring it, the provision of separate dominion status for those provinces not acceding, and the safeguarding of minority rights in all instances.

The Cripps proposals were unfortunately timed. British prestige was at a low ebb, and Gandhi was eager to keep India out of the war. Seven major political groups replied to the Cripps proposals. Five of the seven rejected them, while the princely states were noncommittal. Rejection, as advanced by the Congress as the chief political party, proceeded from several grounds. It objected to continued British control of the defense position, for it desired at least a civilian Indian minister or secretary of war, though military components under British command would continue in the field. It thought Indianization of the viceroy's Executive Council was inadequate, since Indians would remain in only an appointive advisory capacity, not subject to the electorate. The possibility of partition of the country into two or more political entities was feared. The Congress, demanding more democratic procedures in the autocratic princely states, criticized the constitutional arrangement by which representatives for the states were to be nominated rather than elected.

As a result of the proposals, Gandhi went into another fast, the Muslim League was encouraged by the British acceptance of the concept of a politically independent Pakistan, and the princely states were caught in the middle between the alternatives of absorption into an Indian Union or existence as separate and potentially not viable dominions. In August, 1942, the Congress passed a resolution that the British should quit India, and it demanded that a national government with real power be established immediately. As its reply, the British government declared the Congress an unlawful association and clamped its leaders into jail.

After Pearl Harbor and United States entrance into the war, Americans concerned themselves with Indian affairs. Because India was a major base for allied operations to aid Chiang Kai-shek's China in the war effort against the Japanese, it was believed that Indian resistance to the British would hamper high-priority military operations. With additional American concern for the independence of colonial countries (the Philippines, as the only major United States colony left, had already been promised independence for 1946), the idea of continued and acerbated Indian-British differences posed a possible threat to postwar peace. In late 1941, an American Mission was established in New Delhi, and an Indian Agency General was set up in Washington. Discussions for a treaty of commerce and navigation with the Government of India proceeded, but they did not lead to fruition. The United States ambassador in London tried to persuade Churchill to eliminate the passage interpreting the Atlantic Charter as not including India and Burma from his House of Commons speech. This was to no avail, for the prime minister, seconded by his cabinet, informed him that the Indian question was one solely of internal British policy.

The day before Churchill announced the Cripps mission, President Roosevelt sent him a cable offering as a political suggestion, on which to pattern Indian-British transitory relations on the way to Indian independence, the American experience under the Articles of Confederation, which had effected a federation approach prior to American national existence. The President suggested that representatives of different Indian religions, areas, and castes meet to consider the structure of such a government, which would temporarily operate for some five to six years in a move toward union. During the Cripps mission, the United States tried to smooth feelings between the British and the Indians. Colonel Louis Johnson, a former Assistant Secretary of War and later President Harry Truman's Secretary of Defense, was in New Delhi during the stay of the mission, and he tried to facilitate a satisfactory settlement. Succeeding Johnson, as another personal representative of Roosevelt, was William Phillips, a former Under Secretary of State and Ambassador to Italy. His report to the President of April, 1943, written at a low point in Indian-British affairs, concluded negatively that India was in a state of inertia; that it was prostrate, helpless, full of divided counsels; and that no pronounced war spirit existed, even on the part of the British, against Japan. When an American columnist later leaked part of the report, it elicited public excitement and British protest.

With the defeat of Germany, tension eased slightly, and the ban on activities of the Congress was lifted. In June, 1945, the viceroy convened a conference at Simla for all Indian leaders to discuss the prosecution of the war against Japan and the nature of a constituent assembly. The conference resulted in deadlock. The Muslim League insisted that only the League could speak for Indian Muslims and that the Congress could speak only for caste Hindus. The Congress could not accept this definition of its role or allow itself to be relegated to the status of a caste Hindu body. When the Labour government won the July, 1945, elections in Great Britain, its platform called for Indian self-government in friendly association with the United Kingdom. In India, elections were held for central and provincial legislatures. The League won practically all seats reserved for Muslims and demanded nothing less than the concept of Pakistan. Equally successful in non-Muslim constituencies, the Congress demanded immediate independence. The British formed an all-Indian executive council and a national assembly to draw up a new constitution.

In some ways, despite politically divergent views, the Second World War promoted a measure of Indian unity. A large Indian army of about 2 million, from all classes, areas, and castes, was recruited through voluntary enlistments. This great expansion of armed forces provided a stimulant of social change as well as promoting industry and transportation growth. Indian industrial production greatly increased, and it provided for nine-tenths of the military equipment for Indian and Middle Eastern armies. Indian troops served in campaigns in North Africa, Italy, the Middle East, and Southeast Asia, in which 180,000 Indian casualties were recorded. The debtor-creditor relations of India and the United Kingdom were reversed, for, with large British wartime purchases from and in India, India passed from the former stage to the latter. Huge credits, which were blocked for the duration of the war, piled up in London in favor of India. In sum, the war accelerated the achievement of political and economic autonomy of India.

In February, 1946, another British mission of three was sent, consisting of Cripps, the secretary of state for India, and the first lord of the admiralty, to draw up a plan for Indian self-government. The mission rejected Muslim demands for Pakistan, and it narrowed the proposed Indian Union's powers in certain affairs, as in foreign relations, defense, communications, and finance. Its report advocated a constituent assembly to draft a new constitution, with the princes to make their own arrangements with India. In effect the mission advocated that the British get out of India, but to whom would power be transferred? The Congress demanded a strong central government; the League wanted Pakistan in loose federation. Jinnah told the British first to divide and then to quit India; Nehru asked the British to quit and then let the Indians divide if need be. The viceroy tried to form an interim government, but when Jinnah designated August 16, 1946, as Direct Action Day in protest against nonaction on League demands, riots broke out in Calcutta. Communal hatred reached new heights in the months that followed.

In December, 1946, an all-Indian constitutional convention was called, but Muslims did not attend. Finally, to give the shock treatment, and in keeping with general retrenchments of British interests in the Middle East as well, the Labour government under Prime Minister Attlee in February, 1947, announced the complete withdrawal of British interests in India no later than June, 1948. A new viceroy, Lord Mountbatten, was dispatched. Believing the Congress would by now be receptive to partition, and holding that the League would settle for less territory for Pakistan, he cut short the sixteen-month transition period. On June 3, 1947, he announced the plan for partition, and those predominantly Muslim territories that might constitute a separate state. Areas with a Muslim majority, if they so desired, would form a separate dominion. Bengal and the Punjab, as combined Hindu-Muslim areas, were to be divided by boundary commissions. In the Northwest Frontier Province, a referendum would be held on whether to join the new Pakistan. Similarly, the Sylhet region in Assam would hold a referendum on the issue of joining a Muslim Bengal. The date for transfer of power was fixed for August 14, 1947.

Boundary commissions were immediately established, a supreme partition council was formed, and over the next two months ten expert committees consisting of senior Indian officials worked to divide assets between India and Pakistan-to-be, presenting their recommendations to the partition council. In July, 1947, an act of parliament ratified the partition and dominion status of India and of Pakistan. The princely states were left free to accede to either dominion. Amid cheers and bloodshed, by the morning of August 15, 1947, independence and partition had been achieved on the Indian subcontinent with the creation of the new states of Pakistan and the Union of India. For this end result, praise and blame have been assessed on various individuals, parties, or events. But the four major parties concerned—the British, the princely states, the Hindus, and the Muslims—through various degrees of action or inaction taken, helped to shape history that day.

Chronology

1817–1898	Sir Syed Ahmad Khan
1856–1920	Bal Gangadhar Tilak
1857	Universities at Calcutta, Bombay, and Madras opened
1861	India Councils Act: expansion of viceroy's executive and legislative councils; provincial councils established
1866–1915	Gopal Krishna Gokhale

INDIAN NATIONALISM AND THE BRITISH CROWN

1869–1948	Mohandas Karamchad Gandhi
1873–1938	Muhammad Iqbal
1876–1948	Muhammand Ali Jinnah
1885	Indian National Congress party established
1889–1964	Jawaharlal Nehru
1892	India Councils Act: further enlargement of central and provincial legislative councils
1897–1935	Burma incorporated into Indian empire
1899–1905	Lord Curzon as viceroy
1903	Unified Indian army created
1904	Younghusband expedition to Tibet
1905	Bengal partition
1906	Muslim League formed
1909	Morley-Minto reforms: election of Indians to central and provincial legislative councils
1911	Political capital transferred from Calcutta to Delhi; Bengal partition reversed
1916	Lucknow pact: Hindu-Muslim unity on self-government issue
1917	British pronouncement of Indian dominion status in future
1918	Rowlatt bills
1919	Indian tariff autonomy; India Act: more Indian participation in central and provincal government; national parliament created; Amritsar massacre
1920–1922	First civil disobedience movement under Gandhi
1927	Simon commission
1929	British reiteration of dominion status
1930	January 26—Congress members take pledge of independence (date later celebrated in independent India as Republic Day)
	March—Gandhi's march to the sea protesting salt tax
	Nehru assumes Congress party presidency
	Iqbal propounds separate Muslim state
1930–1931	First round table conference in London: federation advanced
1930–1934	Second civil disobedience movement
1931	Second round table conference
1932	Third round table conference
1934	Jinnah elected permanent president of Muslim League
1935	India Act: all-India federation, constitution, bicameral federal legislature, provincial assemblies
1937	Provincial elections; Congress party gains
1939	British government reiterates dominion status
	November—Congress party resignations from posts

	December 22—Muslim League celebrates "Deliverance Day"
1940	Muslim League adopts partition concept
	Congress party proclaims third civil disobedience campaign
1942	Cripps mission: federation idea kept
1945	Simla conference; elections
1946	British mission to draw plans for self-government
1947	February—P. M. Attlee announces withdrawal from India by June, 1948
	June 3—Viceroy Mountbatten announces partition
	August 15—independence and partition

Growth of Indian Political Rights (1861–1945)

Date	Center		Provincial	
	Executive Council	Legislative Council	Executive Council	Legislative Council
1861	Enlarged from 5 to 6 members	6–12 members more; 3 Indians added (1862)	Restored in Bombay and Madras	Created for other provinces as need arose Indians similarly nominated by groups
1892	—	Enlarged to 18, including nominated Indians from certain groups		
1909	1 Indian appointed	18 enlarged to 60, including 5 appointed nonofficial Indians and 27 elected Indians from groups	Indians appointed	50 members elected on communal bases in 4 provinces
1919	Enlarged to 7 members, including 3 Indians	Bicameral national parliament created: Council of State (60) Legislative Assembly of 146; plus Chamber of Princes	8 governors' provinces with executive councils	8 provincial unicameral legislatures; dyarchy
1935	—	Bicameral: Council of State (260) and Federal Assembly (375); dyarchy		
War II	Enlarged to 12 members, with 7 Indians; then all Indians			Bicameral legislatures in 6 of 11 provinces; fully ministerial responsibility

Chapter 7

Independent India

Politics

On August 15, 1947, the Union of India became a dominion within the British Commonwealth. Nehru emerged as prime minister and Lord Mountbatten, the last viceroy, was designated governor general. In Karachi, Pakistan similarly was proclaimed a dominion, with Jinnah as governor general and Liaquat Ali Khan as prime minister. The realization of independence on the Indian subcontinent brought acute problems resulting from partition. Uncounted millions of Hindus and Muslims, fleeing from real or fancied fears, moved each way into the territory of the other state, and evacuation teams were dispatched to the newly created boundaries to supervise operations. Food was scarce in border areas. Refugees swelled city populations, whose low-income groups or destitute migrants contributed to unemployment problems. Years after partition, many streets in the capitals of Delhi and Karachi were still lined with flimsy shelters for the refugees, and many of them slept on sidewalks. Carrying what little they could, those who desired to move endeavored to establish themselves in a new life in a new country.

Yet more stayed home, to cast their lot in the adopted country by choice. In India, Muslims remained a minority of one-tenth; in Pakistan, Hindus constituted 15 per cent of the population. Equitable treatment of these minorities was an issue, particularly in the split Bengal area. Forced out of businesses in East Pakistan, many Hindus emigrated to already crowded Calcutta. Muslims from Calcutta flocked into East

Pakistan. With the press inflaming the refugee issue, anti-Muslim riots periodically broke out in Calcutta, and anti-Hindu riots in Dacca, the capital of East Pakistan. To ameliorate the situation, in April of 1950 Prime Ministers Nehru and Liaquat Ali Khan signed the Delhi Pact, affirming in explicit terms the rights of minorities in their respective states. The agreement assured each of "complete equality of citizenship irrespective of religion...." But the problem of minority rights persisted, and into the 1970's ugly incidents prevailed in both countries with respect to those who followed the differing faith.

Equitable distribution of assets was also at stake. The community property settlement in the political divorce proved to be cumbersome. The Union of India, as the successor government to British India, was in physical possession of the cash balances of the previously undivided India. By agreement, almost $170 million was to be transferred to Pakistan as its share. But with the quarrel over Kashmir erupting subsequent to independence, many Indians, including high officials, opposed the payment, since they reasoned that Pakistan would use the money to prosecute a war against India. Just before his death, Gandhi went into a fast for the solution of this issue and for better relations toward Muslims in India. Payment of the Pakistani share of the assets was soon arranged.

Economic problems augmented administrative ones. Prior to partition, a standstill agreement, effective until February of 1948, was signed to provide for free trade between India and Pakistan and to arrange for the mutual free movement of goods, persons, capital, and money remittances. The agreement soon broke down. In November, 1947, Pakistan imposed an export levy of fifteen rupees on each bale of jute, an action which dealt a decisive blow to Calcutta jute mills that processed the raw jute raised in East Pakistan. In retaliation, the Indians imposed an export duty on finished jute that was in excess of Pakistan's export duty. Pakistan replied with imposts on cotton, raw hides, skins, and cottonseeds; Indians countered with export duties on machine-made cloth, oilseeds, and manganese, and raised the price of coal needed by Pakistan. In September, 1949, another economic crisis built up when most sterling bloc countries, including India, devalued their currency, while Pakistan did not. Regarding the move as hostile, India noted that non-devaluation would raise its $75 million debt, incurred through an adverse trade balance, to Pakistan by 44 per cent. In turn, India, on a "very rough guess" claimed that Pakistan owed it some 3 billion rupees, payable in Indian currency. India severed trade relations, but Pakistan's economy was temporarily shored up by the Korean war, when world requirements rocketed needs and prices for Pakistani raw materials, as cotton, jute, and wool. In 1951, a trade agreement was concluded between the neighbors, though trade and commerical questions were not regularized until 1960.

The distribution between the two states of waters from the Indus river, its tributaries, and the Punjab canals was another subject of embittered dispute. With rainfall scanty in West Pakistan, its agriculture depended on irrigation waters from the Indus and its five streams (with an annual flow twice that of the Nile and ten times that of the Colorado) of the Jhelum, Chenab, Ravi, Beas, and Sutlej. During the British period, dams or barrages were built, and the Punjab developed into one of the most prosperous provinces of British India. Upon partition, India came to control the upper courses of the rivers that supplied much of the water but for which Pakistan had need. Since most of the rivers flowed through Indian territory before they reached Pakistan, India could divert the water before it reached the canals in Pakistan.

In 1947, the Partition Committee and the Punjab Boundary Commission recommended the distribution of water through the canals to remain the same as in the undivided Punjab. The recommendation was not implemented, and Pakistan claimed that India was building dams on the rivers to divert the necessary water. It requested that the canal waters dispute be referred to the International Court of Justice at The Hague. India replied that negotiations should continue between the two countries. After a five-year impasse, the two states referred the problem to the International Bank for Reconstruction and Development, known popularly as the World Bank, where it remained under study for another eight years. In September, 1960, the Indus Water Treaty was signed by Nehru and President Ayub Khan of Pakistan. The treaty established an Indus Basin Development Fund to administer some $900 million of projects in the area over a ten-year period. The funds were to be underwritten by a governmental consortium. The agreement gave the water rights of the three eastern rivers to India and of the three western rivers to Pakistan. Pakistan was to construct irrigation canals from the west rivers to replace eastern losses, but India was to pay for their construction. With settlement achieved on the issue, the Punjab canal-waters problem indicated that India and Pakistan could reach agreement on basic issues—in this instance, on a necessary economic regional matter.

The disposition of princely states was another legacy of partition. The Indian Independence Act of 1947 had applied directly to former India and not to the princely states, whose status was different and governed by treaties, though British paramountcy was held to have lapsed on Indian independence day. The Act provided for accession to either dominion to be determined, in effect, by considerations of religion and of geographic propinquity. Most of the states acceded to India, but the disposition of three of them came to be problematical. Junagadh, a small coastal state in Kathiawar, contiguous to India, had a Muslim ruler but a non-Muslim populace. In September, 1947, the ruler signed an accession agreement with Pakistan, but India objected, and two months later, with the outbreak of disorders in the state, its troops took over the capital city of the same name to save it from "administrative breakdown." In a plebiscite held later, its non-Muslim majority voted to accede to India, a procedure that was confirmed by integration into one of the Indian states.

A similar situation existed in Hyderabad, second largest of the Indian princely states. Its Muslim ruler or nizam also ruled over a non-Muslim populace. An unenlightened, conservative man, the nizam tried to act independently of the British, the Indians, and the Pakistanis. He demanded equality with the British, and he wanted to remain aloof from either new state. India, completely surrounding his territory, desired it; distant from Pakistan, accession there was impracticable. The situation festered until September, 1948, when Indian troops entered Hyderabad city from five different points in a "police action" to restore law and order. In a hundred-hour campaign, they took over the princely state, which was added to the Indian political and administrative roster.

As the third test case, Kashmir proved to be the most controversial and the most durable issue. Technically known as

Jammu and Kashmir state, it was the largest of the Indian princely states, but, in a reverse switch on Junagadh and Hyderabad, it had a Hindu ruler presiding over a predominantly Muslim population. Upon independence, the Hindu ruler, an autocratic bumbling maharajah, disliking both India and Pakistan, made no decision on accession. Hindu, Muslim, and Sikh refugees poured into his kingdom. In October, 1947, into the political chaos came as well armed Muslim tribesmen from Pakistan. These troops occupied the northern third of the state, where they proclaimed Azad (Free) Kashmir. Taking fright, the Hindu ruler executed an instrument of accession to India, with the support of Sheik Abdullah, a Muslim, but one who was sympathetic to the Indian cause at the time. By air lift, the Indians dispatched troops and arrived at the Kashmiri capital of Srinagar. Abdullah became the prime minister, the maharajah faded away, but Pakistan refused to recognize the act of accession. It supported Free Kashmir, while the Indians backed Abdullah.

As governor general of India, Mountbatten accepted the Kashmir accession and stated the desirability of a plebiscite to confirm the action. Nehru agreed with this stand but stipulated that the Muslim invaders were to leave first. Prime Minister Liaquat Ali Khan also concurred with the concept of a plebiscite but demanded, in turn, that the Indians had to retire first and that a coalition government was to replace that of Abdullah's. Nehru did not accept these Pakistani prerequisites. India took the matter to the Security Council of the United Nations, where, on the last day of 1947, it charged Pakistan with aggression. Presenting its side of the case, Pakistan replied forcefully, and a three-months debate ensued. In April, 1948, a Security Council resolution recommended the withdrawal of both Indian troops and Muslim tribesmen and created a United Nations Commission on India and Pakistan (UNCIP) to proceed to Kashmir to extend good offices between the two disputants. Despite a succession of mediators, the United Nations did not solve the problem, and by April, 1962, Kashmir had appeared on the Security Council agenda for the hundredth time. Another partition had descended on the subcontinent with the state frozen in halves at the cease-fire line.

Meanwhile, that part of Kashmir occupied by Indians was

moving into the Indian political orbit. In October, 1950, the General Council of Jammu and Kashmir National Conference, which dated from pre-partition days as a voice of the nationalists, adopted a resolution to call a constituent assembly. This was effected and Abdullah's party won. In October, 1952, the assembly convened and modeled a constitution after that of India's. Two years later, it ratified the state's accession to India, which in turn formalized the accession in 1957. Three years later, India's Supreme Court assumed jurisdiction over Jammu and Kashmir state, apparently sealing the integration. In the interim, fearing Abdullah's desire for an independent state, his subordinates and Indians in 1953 ousted and jailed him. Five years later, he was released, then jailed again, where he remained until 1964 when Nehru, shortly before his death, released the Kashmir leader to discuss once again the status of Kashmir with him and, through him as a representative, with Pakistan. Into the 1970's the issue remained unresolved and border disputes in Kashmir remained endemic.

As India assimilated princely states in the first years of its national life, it also defined the nature of its own government. Called prior to independence, in December, 1946, a constituent assembly met and worked for the next three years to draw up a constitution. The document became effective on January 26, 1950, when the Republic of India was proclaimed. A bulky work, perhaps the longest of its kind, the Indian constitution, as it was originally released, consisted of 251 pages, 395 sections, and 8 schedules. It was drafted by a committee of distinguished Indians under the chairmanship of an untouchable, Dr. Ambedkar. Secular and noncommunal in nature, it did not establish a Hindu state nor did it provide for separate electorates for minorities, except in temporary ten-year concessions to Anglo-Indians, untouchables, and certain tribes.

The constitution termed India a sovereign democratic republic. Its bill of rights pronounced the equality of opportunity in public employment and the rights to free speech and assembly, subject to "reasonable restrictions." It abolished untouchability and it proscribed religious instruction in institutions supported wholly by state funds. It required the state, within ten years after its inception, to provide free compulsory education for all children under the age of fourteen, a provision later found impossible to implement. After fifteen years, Hindi was to replace English as the official language, which turned out to be another constitutional provision difficult to effect. Though a secular state, the government prohibited the slaughter of cows and cattle. As to citizenship qualifications, any person domiciled in India when the constitution went into effect was considered a citizen if he or either parent had been born in India or had been resident for five or more years prior to the promulgation of the constitution. Other articles provided for the acquisition of citizenship by immigrants from Pakistan, by Indians who had migrated to Pakistan and had then returned, and by Indians overseas. In economic policy, the constitution vaguely advanced an economic system that did not result in the concentration of wealth and means of production to the common detriment. In foreign affairs, India was to promote peace, security, respect for treaties and arbitration procedures, and honorable relations with all. Partly because of Nehru's personal and ideological commitment to the West, prestige factors, and economic preferences, India remained a full member of the Commonwealth. It accepted the queen as the symbol of the Commonwealth's independent member nations, though the queen was not to be the head of the Indian state.

Conforming to an Anglo-Saxon tradition in its main outlines, the constitution defined the national organs of India. It established an independent judiciary and a bicameral central legislature. The upper house, known as the *Rajya Sabha*, or the Council of States, had 250 members, of whom 12 were nominated by the president to represent groups and the rest were elected for six-year terms by elected members of the legislative assemblies of the respective states. The lower house, the *Lok Sabha*, or House of the People, had 500 members, with 20 representatives from union territories and the others elected for five years by universal adult suffrage. A president as head of state was elected indirectly for five years by an electoral college composed of members of both houses of parliament and the elected members of the lower houses of the various states. The vice president was elected indirectly for a similar term by members of both houses, and he presided over the upper house. Actual power resided in the prime minister, responsible to the legislature. A council of ministers advised both him and the president. Ministers had to be elected to parliament, and if one were not a member of a house for a minimum of six consecutive months, he ceased to hold a portfolio.

At the state level, twenty-seven political entities were established in four categories. In the first were nine former provinces of British India, in the next two were eighteen former princely states, and in the last category were territories and other areas, as Sikkim and the Andaman and Nicobar islands. The relationship between the union and the states was outlined in three extended lists. Certain rights were reserved to the center, as defense, foreign affairs, war and peace, communications, commerce, justice, income taxes, excise and customs. The state list concerned local government functions, as prisons, education, fisheries, and police. A concurrent list concerned criminal law, civil and criminal procedures, inland shipping and navigation, trade, and price controls. Federal in theory, but with more powers resident in the central government, the Indian political structure operated in a centralized manner. States rights were subordinated to central powers. The national government could interfere in state affairs if state governments were not properly carrying out functions, and the president of the republic in grave emergencies could issue proclamations, which then superseded state powers.

In November, 1956, the States Reorganization Act abolished the four categories and rearranged state boundaries to coincide more closely with major linguistic groupings. In this process of administrative tidying up, the number of states and state legislatures was halved, for the reorganization resulted at the time in fourteen states (and six union territories). But despite the philosophy of linguistic arrangements, the large state of Bombay was not divided, though it had two major linguistic groupings, Marathi and Gujarati. After several years of unrest over this issue, in May, 1960, Bombay was split into two entities with the creation of Maharashtra and Gujarat states. The latter, home of Gandhi, built a new capital at Gandhinagar, some 40 miles north of Ahmadabad, a major Indian textile center.

A festering linguistic and minority issue concerned the Naga tribes, who lived in Assam on the Burmese frontier. How to incorporate effectively the 400,000 Nagas into the Indian nation proved to be ticklish. After the war, some Naga leaders demanded an independent state for their people. In 1954, one of them, named Phizo, launched a guerrilla resistance movement against Delhi that involved at least ten thousand followers over the years. In mid-1960, the central government started procedures to transform the territory into the sixteenth state with its own governor, legislature, and council of ministers, but it was to be placed directly under the prime minister rather than the home ministry. In 1962, a bill was introduced in the Lok Sabha to establish a new Naga state on the above lines, but the actual creation of the state was delayed until the following year. Other states, also in the northeast, followed in 1972: Manipur, Tripura, and Meghalaya. The Sikhs continued to agitate for political recognition, and the Congress Party, succumbing to sectional pressures, agreed in 1966 to divide Punjab into two states, Punjab with a Sikh majority and Haryana with a Hindu one. Both states shared the common capital of Chandigarh. Nearby Himachal Pradesh was promoted from territorial status to statehood in 1971. The concept of state borders as based on linguistic divisions was debatable. In mid-1961, Nehru admitted that it had been a mistake. Pessimists projected a balkanization of India along regional, tribal, ethnic, and linguistic lines.

Despite potential centrifugal pulls, after the inauguration of the constitution, India, as the world's largest political democracy, held its first national and state elections in a period that lasted from October of 1951 to February of 1952. Of the 176 million eligible voters, some 106 million valid votes were polled for candidates for the Lok Sabha and 102.5 million for state legislative offices. With eight principal and forty local parties contesting seats, the Congress Party polled 45 per cent of the national popular vote, to gain 363 of the 489 Lok Sabha seats. It gained control of all but one of the state assemblies. The second national and state elections transpired over a three-week period in February and March, 1957. Of the 193.1 million eligible voters, 120.7 million valid votes were cast. As the biggest single election in the world, it involved the distribution of 200,000 polling stations and almost 3 million ballot boxes. At stake were 494 seats in the lower house at Delhi, and 3,102 in the state assemblies. Each voter cast two votes, one for the Lok Sabha and one for a candidate in the state legislature. To prevent fraudulent practices, each voter was marked with indelible ink on the index finger. Since many of the electorate were illiterate, symbols, rather than names, indicated party choice. With five major parties contesting seats, the Congress increased in national popular vote to 48 per cent, but it lost one state, Kerala, to the Communists. In the third national election of February, 1962, of the 210 million eligible voters that included 100 million women, some 54 per cent went to the polls. The Congress won 45 per cent of national votes and 360 of the 507 Lok Sabha seats, and emerged dominant in twelve state assemblies. In the fourth national elections of February, 1967, the seats of the Congress in the Lok Sabha were pared to a bare majority, while the party lost its lead in eight of the sixteen state assemblies (Nagaland had as yet no assembly).

As the major political organization in independent India, the Congress traditionally garnered the overwhelming number of national and state elective positions. With an estimated over-all membership of 5 million, the Congress effected its program through its top policy-making body, the All-India Congress Committee, with its Working Committee, which met in annual congresses. Substantially formulating governmental policy in the overwhelmingly one-party state, the Congress platform counseled social and economic changes through evolution rather than through force. Retaining its unquestioned predominance at the center and in most of the states, the party has controlled the machinery of government. It capitalized on its prestige as the party of national independence, though its leadership and organization has changed. Of, but also above, party affiliation, Nehru, as Gandhi did, played the leading figure in the early years of independent India. His role was secure, though from time to time in the first decade it was threatened by disgruntled groups within the party. In 1950, a conservative wing advanced for party presidency a conservative, but Nehru threatened to resign. Always an effective tactic, it swung the Congress back to endorse his domestic and foreign policies, for the Congress could not renounce or surrogate Nehru's leadership in his lifetime.

Over the years, Nehru's position was enhanced in the government as well as in the party. In addition to the post of prime minister, he held concurrently, from time to time, additional posts as chairman of the planning commission, foreign minister, and defense minister. Centralizing power and refusing to delegate authority, Nehru and his personality ruled both party and government until his death. After his death, the Congress advanced Lal Bahadur Shastri for the position. Shastri, a former Home Minister from the north but with strong backing in south India, a past secretary general of the party, and a born compromiser, stepped into the political vacuum. He served as prime minister for a year and a half. Subsequent to his demise in the post, Mrs. Indira Gandhi, Nehru's only daughter, filled the position. A multitude of problems faced the leadership of the Congress party, which split in late 1969. Mrs. Gandhi called for special elections in March, 1971, in which her faction won 351 of 517 Lok Sabha seats.

Minor Indian political parties existed in varying form on communal or ideological grounds. The Mahasabha, a past leading Hindu communal party under militant V. D. Savarkar, a Brahman Maharashtran, was anti-British and anti-Muslim. Savarkar and Gandhi differed on nonviolence, which the former termed "absolutely sinful." He opposed the concept of Pakistan as well as Gandhi's good will toward Muslims. During the Second World War, when many top Indian leaders of other parties were in prison, the Mahasabha grew powerful. Gandhi's assassin, Vinayak Godse, had been an earlier member of the party, and public hostility to the party was aroused by the act. Savarkar himself was tried for complicity in the assassination, but he was released, whereupon he retired to his Bombay home. While some party members appeared in cabinet posts, the Mahasabha in post-partition India declined in importance.

Lesser Hindu communal parties included the R.S.S. (the Rashtriya Swayamsevak Sangh or National Volunteer Association), similar in nature to the Mahasabha. Founded in 1925, it was a fascistic-type organ, and it was held responsible for much violence in the Punjab upon partition. After Gandhi's death, feeling ran high against this party as well, and the R.S.S. was outlawed and its leaders placed under arrest. While there was no formal connection between the two, the Mahasabha claimed to be a political entity and the R.S.S. a cultural organ. Another party was the Bharatiya Jan Sangh (the Indian People's Party). It was founded in 1952 by Dr. Shyam Prasad Mookerjee, who resigned from both the Congress and the Mahasabha. It gained considerable ground over the decade, to provide the principal opposition to the Congress in the 1962 state elections in Madhya Pradesh. Other minor parties included the All-India Forward Bloc in the tradition of Bose and the Muslim League in a decimated form. The revivalist Sikh party, or Shiromani Akali Dal, demanded a separate nation of Sikhistan. Its leader, Master Tara Singh, a former schoolmaster, was jailed by the government for much violence during partition. He sporadically fasted on the issue of a separate state, which was finally realized by splitting Punjab.

Representing interests of the untouchables was the All-India Scheduled Castes Federation under Dr. Ambedkar. To advance conservative private interests, in 1959 the Swantantra or Freedom party was founded by octogenarian Chakravarti Rajagopalachari, a former Congress president and governor general of India after Mountbattan. He reflected the disapproval in business circles of the Congress program for organizing cooperative farms, a collective economy, and a trend toward increased state enterprise and controls in Indian economic development. In its first contested elections, those of 1962, it emerged as the third largest party in India. It won 18 out of 507 Lok Sabha seats, and it provided the chief opposition to the Congress in four state legislatures. It emerged after the 1967 elections as the second strongest party in the land, but subsequently lost strength.

On the other side of the ideological political spectrum, opposing the Swatantra platform of private enterprise and agreeing more with the Congress program of government controls over the economy, were spokesmen of the Socialist movement. Dating to prewar days, after the second civil disobedience movement, in 1934, the left wing of the Congress organized itself into a Socialist Party under the leadership of Jayaprakash (JP) Narayan, who had picked up Marxist ideas in American universities. Working within the Congress, he and his colleagues became disenchanted with the parent party because of its failure to take an aggressive position advocating social reform. They protested against failure of the Congress to provide the masses with food and housing, and to check black-marketing. After independence, in March, 1948, the wing opted out of the party to form an independent Socialist Party of India.

In 1952, the Socialist Party merged with another one of similar ideology, the Praja Party (the Peasants, Workers, and People's Party). This had been formed the year before in a similar break-off from the Congress, under Acharya J. B. Kripalani, a Gandhian stalwart, who had been dissatisfied with the Congress measures for peasantry and labor. Kripalani advocated land redistribution and cooperative farming, but he opposed industrial nationalization. After the merger, the Praja Socialist Party operated as a coalition for four years, and in 1956 it split up again into the Praja Socialist Party and the Socialist Party. For his part, Narayan left formal politics and in the mid-1970's fashioned a peaceful protest, nonparty, anticorruption movement.

Farther to the left was the Indian Communist Party. Cooperating with the government during the war after the Japanese advance in Southeast Asia in 1942, the Communists grew in strength. At the same time, they alienated themselves from other Indians because of their apparent anti-nationalist stand. After partition, which they favored, Communist activities entered a phase of violence that lasted four years. A revolutionary line resulted in part from decisions taken in a Communist-sponsored Asian Youth Conference held in Calcutta in February, 1948, as well as in the second Communist party congress held shortly thereafter. At this time the incumbent secretary general of the party, P. C. Joshi, was removed in favor of B. T. Ranadive, who had advocated the active approach. Peasant uprisings were fomented, and in Hyderabad in the Telengana district, with tactics patterned after Chinese Communist guerrilla warfare models, a soviet was established.

The government stamped out the Communist revolt in Telegana, and in October of 1951, just prior to the first national elections, the Communist party announced from "somewhere in India" that the violent program had failed. The so-called right wing of the party adopted a policy of trying to come to power through elections. This split in the Communist party reflected a growing and deeper split between the partisans of the Moscow line for peaceful coexistence and the partisans of the Peking line that still advocated revolution. The divided lines were reflected in a change of leadership. Ranadive was removed from office and S. A. Dange was made acting head. Contesting state and national legislative seats as strongest party in opposition to the Congress, Communist candidates won 180 (out of 587) contested of the former and 27 of the latter. In the 1957 elections, the party held its own at the national level, but it won Kerala state. In the 1962 elections, as still the second largest opposition party, it gained 29 out of 507 Lok Sabha seats and 166 in state assemblies. In the 1967 elections, it lost ground nationally but gained again Kerala state.

As an unusual instance of Communists freely voted into power at the state level, the Kerala Communist state government lasted twenty-seven months, from April of 1957, to July of 1959. In the 1957 elections, after the regrouping of southern Indian state boundaries, the Communists won 60 of the 126 state legislative seats, but five fellow-traveling independents gave the party a majority of four. Various factors operated to favor the Communists. With the new realignment of state boundaries, the reorganization transferred many Congress votes from Kerala to the neighboring state of Madras. Moreover, a weak Congress organization existed in Kerala, and it provided no solutions to the basic problems of food and employment. Though Kerala was the most literate of Indian states, many of the educated were numbered among the unemployed, estimated at one million.

Communist leader E. M. S. Namboodiripad, a Brahman and former Congress party member, who, after joining the party in 1940 gave up all his inherited lands to it, assumed the post of state minister. The Communist program called for the elimination of foreign estates and industries, the promise to labor of a 25 per cent increase in wages and bonuses of at least 12½ per cent, the distribution of government land to the landless, the establishment of "people's committees" to rival the authority of local courts, and the control of private schools. The last-named policy contributed directly to Communist downfall, for the Communists endeavored to muzzle the many private schools, Christian and Hindu, with the right to name teachers, interfere in school management and curriculum, and regulate payment of salaries. By mid-1959, violence developed, and with the breakdown of law and order Nehru advised the president to take over administration. Kerala became temporarily a president's province. New elections were held in February of 1960, when a coalition of the Congress, Praja Socialist Party and the Muslim League won 94 out of the 126 seats. But the troika did not work well together, and after vicissitudes, a state Congress ministry emerged in 1962.

Though the Communists had registered gains in Kerala and held their own in the Lok Sabha, they faced problems. After the party's founding in the mid-1920's, the Communists were subject to twists and turns of Comintern policy. Upon Indian independence, they faced counter-measures by Nehru, who, while endeavoring the coexist with Communism abroad, realized its domestic dangers. Internal party divisions reflected external problems. With the development of ideological schisms in the international Communist movement, the Indian Communist Party, as others, was rent into factions: the pro-Soviet Communist Party of India (CPI), the internationally non-aligned Communist Party of India (Marxist), and the pro-Chinese Communist Party of India (Marxist-Leninist) or the so-called Naxalites, who advocated violent revolution.

In mid-1975, the Indian political scene took a drastic turn. Mrs. Gandhi, faced with continuing divisions in her party and from without and herself now charged with corrupt electoral practices by an Allahabad court, declared a state of emergency. Assuming full dictatorial powers, she arrested several thousand people, including all major opposition leaders, imposed rigid press censorship, and suspended constitutional rights. She validated her acts "to save democracy" and hoped the emergency would be temporary. Under these measures, the country embarked upon a new reoriented course.

Economics and Society

In economic matters, after initial uncertainty the government drew up comprehensive plans as over-all blueprints for the nation's development. Nothing of note was accomplished in the first three years of independence until 1950, when initial planning concepts were adopted. That year, the Colombo

Plan for Cooperative Economic Development in South and Southeast Asia was jointly devised by various Commonwealth governments at a conference in the capital city of Ceylon. It outlined a six-year regional plan to cost over $5 billion, from which development outlay some two-thirds was to go to India and one-seventh to Pakistan. Later expanding in time and in scope to include almost all non-Communist countries in Asia and interested western powers as well, about two dozen countries eventually became involved. The formulation of the Colombo Plan gave impetus in India in 1950 to establish the Planning Commission. It was charged with the duties of preparing India's proposals for the Colombo Plan and implementing the constitutional aims to extend social justice up to the capacity of the country's resources. Headed by Nehru, the Planning Commission involved seven cabinet ministers and a staff of 250. Two years later, it was augmented by the creation of a still larger National Development Council. Nehru presided as chairman and all members of the Planning Commission and chief ministers of central and state government were included.

Large-scale Indian efforts were necessary to relieve large-scale economic problems. The country was one of the most disease-ridden and poverty-stricken states in Asia. The overwhelming majority of its people lived in rural areas with an annual per capita much below $100 and a life expectancy of twenty-six years. Population increased faster than resources, and it was estimated that India by the year 2000 would have one-third of the world's population. The government experimented with birth control projects, but, though India had no religious scruples against family planning, the social and agrarian nature of Indian life placed a premium on children.

Land reform schemes had an essential place in the planned economic revolution. The national government formulated the over-all policies of agrarian reform, but the states implemented, legislated, and administered them. Though four-fifths of the people earned their livelihood directly from land, its distribution was woefully inequitable. Prior to 1947, only 4 per cent of the rural population owned half the country's agricultural holdings, while three-fourths of the population owned only 16 per cent. The size of the farms was generally small and uneconomic in nature, for the small holdings were usually less than five acres in size. Sometimes they consisted of scattered strips impossible to cultivate on modern lines. Often the peasant had little or no money to purchase better seeds or needed implements. To help ameliorate conditions, the Indian government sought to effect improvements. It eradicated intermediaries, as the historic *zamindari*, that existed between the peasant and the state. It reduced rents, fixed ceilings on the extent of permissible land holdings, redistributed and consolidated scattered holdings, and promoted cooperative farming and management systems in the villages. By 1956, the program to abolish intermediaries was largely completed. Payment for the requisitioned land was initially assumed by Delhi at a cost of some $750 million, and the land was redistributed to farmers at reasonable costs. All states initiated action to regulate tenancy rents, but they fixed varied ceilings on agrarian holdings.

The succession of five-year plans have been basic to India's economic development. In July, 1951, the first one was inaugurated. It cost some $4 billion. Three-fourths of the funds came from internal Indian and Colombo Plan sources and the remaining fourth emanated from external sources, chiefly the United States, which extended $500 million. The goals of the plan broadly concerned themselves with improving the agricultural, industrial, and social welfare sectors of the state. The plan aimed to raise the national income by 11 per cent, to increase the food supply, to expand enrollment in primary schools, and to build industrial plants. The results at the end of the plan in mid-1956 were encouraging. Food imports were reduced, national income rose by 18 per cent, and industrial production increased. With good weather contributing to favorable agricultural conditions, millions of new acres were added to land under cultivation and harvests were unusually good. Food grain production went up by 20 per cent.

In industrial planning, India's objective was a mixed economy, one in which basic industries would be owned and developed by the state and other sectors of the economy by private initiative. In the public sector were placed steel plants, machine-making industries, petroleum, chemicals, electronics, locomotives, airplanes, and shipbuilding. The private sector assumed projects in textiles, cement, autos, engineering works, and pharmaceuticals. The state had to take the lead in industrial efforts because capital was scarce and factories were few.

Upon independence, industry accounted for only 6 per cent of the national income and employed less than 2 per cent of the labor force.

The second five-year plan, submitted to parliament in May, 1956, called for an outlay of approximately $10 billion. One-third was allocated to the private and two-thirds to the public or governmental sector. The contrast between the first and second plans lay in the greatly increased expenditure contemplated for industrial expansion and in more financing from private sources. With one-tenth of total funds to come from abroad, including $225 million from the United States, the plan's objectives were again to raise income over 25 per cent, expand steel and coal outputs, increase food grain production, and double electric power. More industries came under state control and operation. But as implementation of the plan proceeded, problems of financing became acute. The heavier and costly industrial emphasis caused a sharp reduction in India's foreign credit balance. Higher costs on imported commodities and inflationary prices on projected imports forced the government to embark on drastic financial measures. Adverse harvests cut down food production. The plan had to be modified within a year or two of its inception and goals were cut back.

Despite setbacks, the third five-year plan, introduced in March, 1961, budgeted about $22 billion for all sectors of the economy. Three-fourths of the funding was provided internally and the rest came from external sources. An international consortium of ten countries and the World Bank formed an "Aid India Club" to raise annual loans to help implement the plan. Total pledged foreign aid amounted to almost $5.5 billion, including $2.3 billion from the United States. According to the plan, per capita income by 1966 was to reach $81, self-sufficiency in food grains was to be realized, and 14 million new jobs created. After several interim annual plans, the fourth five-year plan, 1969–1974, called for expenditures of some $35 billion. India's fifth five-year plan, with projected expenditures of $70 billion, commenced in 1974, but problems increased as achievements were recorded. The costs of defending Indian border areas cut into the budget, and it was difficult to find the equivalent of 15 per cent of the gross national product (the total worth of country's goods and wages) which had to be reinvested to keep the economy going. India registered improvements in economics, but a discouraging feature was that the take-off point, at which the economy could sustain itself, receded into the background.

The plans covered a wide variety of projects, but one with great daring, utility, and imagination was the construction of the Bhakra dam, located on the Sutlej river 150 miles from Delhi. As Nehru's "new temple of faith," the dam, finished in the mid-1960's, was a multi-purpose one, designed and constructed by American technicians. Conceived as early as 1908, the dam enjoyed a favorable location where the rushing river widened out into the plains. As the second highest dam in the world, Bhakra, 740 feet high, was to impound 7.5 million acre-feet of water, or enough to meet all of India's domestic supply needs for one year. It was to irrigate 10 million acres of land, of which 6.5 million had never before been irrigated, and it was to generate one million kilowatts of electricity, or as much as all India had in 1950.

Another bold program was the nation-wide village community development project. On October 2, 1952, the anniversary of Gandhi's birthday, the campaign was initiated. With substantial help from the United States government and the Ford Foundation, the initial phase launched 55 projects covering 16,000 villages with 11 million people. Each community project consisted of three "blocks," covering 150 square miles, 100 villages, and an average population of 66,000. It was frankly admitted that a single village was too small a unit to plan for sound economic and social development. Through cooperative endeavor, progress would be better achieved. Under the program, villagers participated in projects relating to modern agriculture, public health, cottage industries, sanitation, animal husbandry, building of roads and schools, community centers, hospitals, demonstration farms and digging new wells. By 1962, the program had reached three-fifths of rural India, but with its growth came a concomitant growth of bureaucracy in managing the extensive project. From Delhi, the Union Ministry of Community Development and Cooperation branched out through lower echelons of state, district, and block development officers, extension officers, and village level officials. Project officers abounded, and paper work threatened to smother practical accomplishments.

A second agrarian program, unofficial in nature but peculiar to India, was the *bhoodan*, or voluntary land gift movement, initiated by Vinoba Bhave, a ninety-pound ascetic. A Maharashtran Brahman, he early became attracted to Gandhi's program, and in 1920, with the start of the first civil disobedience movement, Gandhi chose him to be the first practitioner of passive resistance. Not until 1951, however, did he make national and international headlines when he began his movement. That year, walking through strife-torn Telengana in Hyderabad, noting its aggravated and pronounced problems of agricultural poverty and Communist activity, he hit upon the idea of land redistribution as the answer to economic and political ills. The main point of his program was to put land ownership into the hands of tenant farmers working on the estates. He embarked on a campaign with this aim and endeavored to persuade landholders and absentee landlords, particularly those with large holdings, to donate their land for redistribution to the landless. Bhave considered the land gift as part of a general religious crusade a well, and he applied this argument of moral uplift to potential donors.

In the first few years, the campaign had a measure of success, and spread to other states. By 1955, Bhave had received land gifts of about 4 million acres. But there were some catches in the program. It appealed to the wealthy and landed classes rather than to the poor, who were only to receive charity. Much of the donated land turned out to be inarable, of marginal nature, or of questionable title. Proceeding further, as a second stage Bhave envisioned *gramdan*, or a village gift movement, in which all who owned land were to donate holdings to a pool from where redistribution would take place. By the end of 1960, 4,000 Indian villages had donated themselves to the movement. Not stopping there, the idealist conceived of a third and international stage in which he advanced the feasibility of land-plenty countries, as Australia, giving acreage to land-scarce states, as Japan.

The Indian government took strides in commerce, transport, and communications. Half of the total annual Indian foreign trade of $3 billion was conducted with the United States and the United Kingdom. Before and during the Second World War, India enjoyed export surpluses of its three main crops, tea, jute, and cotton. The situation changed somewhat after independence, with less world demand for and rising prices of these commodities. But alternate exports, as hides, skins, manganese, pepper, and mica, found increased shares in world markets. In transport, because of its 3,000-mile-long coastline, Indian shipping emphasized more coastal than international trade. Of great importance to the country was the railway system, the single largest employer in the country. It employed over a million workers and paid an annual $350 million in wages. About 4 million passengers traveled daily on Indian railroads. India's industrial shops manufactured 20,000 freight cars annually, signaling equipment, and many of the locomotives. Air travel dated to the 1920's, when a Department of Civil Aviation was formed and flying clubs were founded. In 1932, two Indian air companies were established, and in 1939, a route was formulized between Delhi and Karachi. In 1953, the government nationalized the two air transport companies, which were the domestic Indian Airlines, and the Air India International. From the four international airports of Madras, Delhi, Calcutta, and Bombay, Air India served some twenty foreign countries, including Russia.

In heavy industry, official plans called for diversification and self-sufficiency. During colonial rule, the British had emphasized a plantation economy, jute production, and coal extraction, while Indians established cotton textile companies and iron and steel mills. Alleging a lack of economic balance after independence, the Indian government, desirous of achieving a balance of heavy, medium, and light industries, re-examined the industrial structure of the nation. To increase domestic sugar refining capacities, the Indian government got five leading foreign sugar machinery manufacturers, in affiliation with local manufacturers, to produce almost ten complete sugar mill plants a year. British manufacturers permitted their Indian counterparts to produce jute mill machinery of latest design in India. A half-dozen first-class Indian engineering firms turned out textile machinery. Light industry was decentralized, with state governments, rather than Delhi, taking primary concern. Each state established small industries institutes and industrial extension centers to render assistance to specified industries.

The steel industry, which had a long history in India, registered gains. Dating to 1830, attempts to manufacture iron and steel by modern methods had taken place, but efforts failed in those early years. In 1874, the Barakar Iron Works commenced operations, and by 1900 had produced 35,000 tons. In 1907, the Tata Iron and Steel Company was formed. Two other important manufacturers included the Indian Iron and Steel Company, founded in 1908, and the Mysore State Iron Works, started in 1923. In 1939, total steel production in India reached 800,000 tons; in 1958, it was 1.3 million tons; in 1961, production registered 3.5 million tons of steel ingots. The five-year plans emphasized state development of additional steel plants, with help from a variety of sources. West German funds and technical aid helped build a mill at Rourkela in Orissa, a British cooperative venture financed the Durgapur project in West Bengal, and the Soviet Union helped to finance Bhilai in Madhya Pradesh. By 1963, all three reached their initial million-ton outputs. After the United States withdrew its offer of aid to help finance the Bokara mill, the Soviet Union extended credits for the realization of this project.

Whether light or heavy industry, private enterprise, both foreign and native, played a role as outlined by the government in achieving a socialist pattern of society. In 1955, some $1.1 billion worth of private foreign investments, including $100 million from the United States, were concentrated in India. In 1956, the government drew up a policy to regulate and define the roles of private and public investments. Seventeen basic industries were reserved for state ownership and operation, mixed operations were allowed in others, and consumer industries were relegated mainly to the private sector.

With industrial growth came development of labor unions. Most of these were politically oriented. The largest union was affiliated with the Congress, while others were tied to the Communist and Socialist parties. Rivalry existed among them. Many unions were minuscule in form, for any seven employees could form one. Some Indian government leaders were former veterans of labor movements; Gandhi himself had organized the Ahmedabad Textile Workers Union, one of the best in the country. But as civil servants responsible to the government and the country as a whole, in office they became less sympathetic to labor. On its part, the attitude of private enterprise toward labor was often one of exploitation, and, with a surplus labor supply, sweatshop conditions could exist.

India kept abreast in programs of atoms-for-peace. In 1948, the Atomic Energy Commission was established. Its first project was concentrated at Trombay near Bombay. Built at a cost of $20 million, with Canadian help under the Colombo Plan and a staff of 2500, in mid-1956, the plant commenced operations. By 1965, it was scheduled to produce electricity from atomic energy. Three additional atomic plants to generate power were projected: one at Tarapur, United States aided, 80 miles north of Bombay, with two reactors to produce 400,-000 kilowatts by 1966; one in Rajasthan, Canadian aided, to produce 200,000 kilowatts by 1968; and a third near Madras. Indian uranium reserves were estimated at 30,000 or more tons.

The planned social revolution in India was as important as the political and economic changes. No foreign regime in India had ever tried to destroy, nor could they have destroyed, the ancient Hindu pattern of society, which provided stability, continuity, and unity in Indian history. But Hinduism was subject to change and to evolution, and at an ever-increasing tempo. British reforms stimulated changes, and, in an independent India, the caste system was exposed to further pressures. The continued spread of education and the media of modern and mass communication and transport weakened old traditions. To run for office, candidates of high-caste backgrounds had to seek votes from low-caste groups. The constitution advanced the equality of women, dedicated the government to social justice and equality, and abolished untouchability.

The problem of the untouchables aroused the greatest attention in India and evoked the most comment outside it. In 1961, some 70 million could have been classified in this category. Untouchables also had been variously termed exterior castes, harijans, and so-called scheduled castes, because the constitution of 1950 had required them to be listed in separate state schedules. They formed part of a larger group of India's population termed the Backward Classes, who numbered more than 150 million. Backward Classes included such designated peoples as Scheduled Tribes, Denotified Tribes, and other "socially and educationally backward classes," a phrase that was never satisfactorily defined. In 1955, the Untouchabilities Offenses Act came into effect, to forbid discrimination in the use of wells and in access to shops, restaurants, hotels, and places of entertainment.

A further series of reforms was enacted in a Hindu Marriage Act, Hindu Minority and Guardianship Act, Hindu Succession Act, and Hindu Adoptions and Maintenance Act. The traditional privileges, differences, and distinctions based on custom and caste were removed. Marriage was recognized as contractual, and it was permitted between parties of differing castes. Divorces were sanctioned for women as well as for men. In inheritance, the law was amended so that daughters were given rights equal to those of sons. To what extent acts such as these were effective was debatable, for legislation was not necessarily equated with immediate changes in social attitudes. The answer as to their effectivity and their utility depended on the person queried, for the responses could, and did, vary. Evaluation in pragmatic terms of such basic laws in a country of almost half a billion inhabitants was problematical.

A contributing factor to social change was the expansion of educational facilities. According to the 1950 constitution, education was to be primarily a state concern, but more and more Delhi took it over because of the vast scope of the problem. In 1961, India reported almost 50 million in the primary and secondary schools, with another million registered in colleges and universities. Language barriers were monumental in trying to give equal educational opportunities to students enrolled throughout India. It proved to be impossible to provide jobs for all graduates, and the problem of the unemployed intellectual was acute. The intelligentsia often demanded white collar jobs and tended to despise manual labor and technical or engineering positions. Nehru urged educated young Indians to return to their villages, to dirty their hands, and to work with the villagers in digging wells and in building roads. Many were reluctant to do this. Most of India, at least 77 per cent, were illiterates, and the figure was doubtless higher since so many dropped out of school but were yet claimed as literates. Many of the children had no more than three years of schooling and after dropping out they lapsed into illiteracy. And most of Indian population was youthful. Three-quarters were under thirty-five, and half were in the age group of from five to twenty-four.

Some traditional aspects of Hinduism seemed to be going, but others, in spite of laws and regulations, seemed to remain. A certain secularization of religion in Hinduism could be argued. Its study seemed to grow, but its orthodox content seemed to decrease. Religion, subsumed under the subject of history in schools, became a standard course with standard texts. In becoming a part of school curriculum, religion remained no longer a preserve of the Brahmans or any priestly class. Indian epics were translated from the Sanskrit into regional languages; societies edited cheap translations of Hindu prayers, stories, and folklore. The government-controlled radio beamed classical Indian music and singing. Railroads granted concession rates for pilgrimages and festivals. Travel was great, since there was always a festival to attend in India.

Modern Indian literature borrowed from ancient themes but dressed them in modern guise. Imaginative writing in India had inspiration in the epics, but authors reworked them, much as Shakespeare borrowed and reshaped themes from Holinshed's *Chronicles* or Plutarch's *Lives*. Indian writers drew upon a national tradition, but the problem of linguistic medium remained, as whether to write in the vernacular, Sanskrit, Hindi, or English. For adequate sales, multilingual translations were necessary. The scool of modern writers included Santha Rama Rau, daughter of an Indian diplomat. Educated in England and at Wellesley College in New England, married to an American, the authoress interpreted India to western readers in a series of books and articles dating from the mid-1940's. More indigenous in nature was the author R. K. Narayan of Mysore, who portrayed his home city and surroundings in the fictional city of Malgudi, the setting of his novels. Writing in English, author of novels that included *The Financial Expert*, *The English Teacher*, and *The Bachelor of Arts*, Narayan wrote feelingly and descriptively of such familiar locations as the railway station, the "good" residential district of town, the bazaars, the temples, the mission college, and the Regal haircutting saloon. Quite realistically, his characters on the last page "vanished into life."

The Indian press flourished. The number of Indian newspapers totaled over 7,000, but many of them were of little note. The most influential dailies were published in the largest cities. Some were published in English, while others were composed in Indian languages. More dailies were printed in English, and press leadership remained with those issued in English. Circulation of newspapers remained small by western standards, few achieving more than 100,000 copies. Freedom of the press, constitutionally guaranteed, was a critical issue for the government. Editors, nourished in the nationalist struggles, felt free to attack leaders, including Nehru, of an independent India. A constitutional amendment was introduced in 1951 to amend the section on freedom of press so that nothing in the stated guarantees of freedom of speech and expression was to affect the operation of existing laws as they obtained in matters that included state security, foreign relations, public order, and contempt of court.

The Indian movie industry, said to be the second largest in the world, produced a plethora of films, many of which were inferior in technical matters and debased in stories. A few achieved international recognition, notably the trilogy by Satyajit Ray, called *Panther Panchali, Aparajito,* and *The World of Apu*. Radio broadcasting was important. There were over thirty radio stations in the country, with extensive news coverage, educational programs, and entertainment, all under government ownership. More than a million and a quarter sets were in operation. Television had not yet established itself.

Related to cultural and educational affairs was the language problem. Nationalism desired the replacement of English as the official language and as the medium of instruction in the schools, but the question remained as to what would replace it. North Indians wanted Hindi, while those from the Deccan and the south advanced their vernaculars. The constitution committed India to Hindi, a decision that was adopted by a single vote. It was declared to be the national language, and English, which enjoyed the status of an official language until 1965, was relegated to a position as an "associated" language. The matter of which script to utilize was also an issue and was related to the language problem. The modern Indian languages employed differing systems of writing, though all were indigenously derived. All were alphabetical but quite difficult to learn, with their numerous forms and shapes. The central government was concerned with the simplification of scripts to ease the problems of education and of modern printing.

Public health problems remained vast. Undernourishment was widespread and diets were insufficient. Few cities, much less towns and villages, had a protected and safe water supply or adequate sewage facilities. Doctors and nurses were few; midwives were in short supply. Along a broad front, the government supported schools that taught traditional systems of medicine as well as western techniques. Attacks on traditional diseases, with the help of foreign aid and of United Nations organs, drastically reduced the toll from malaria, cholera, and tuberculosis. Much was being accomplished and much remained to be done. Though India was socially backward still in many ways, the republic had set into motion a large-scale political, economic, and social revolution.

Foreign Affairs

In foreign affairs, India's preoccupations, not uniquely, were with national security and national well-being. These were to be achieved by peaceful means wherever appropriate, but the use of force was never officially precluded by the Indian government, any Gandhian image of nonviolence to the contrary. Nehru, as "Mister Foreign Affairs," embodied and personalized one of its most significant policies, that of nonalignment. He interpreted the term as nonalignment in relation to military blocs, rather than in relation to political, economic, or cultural affiliation. Similar in nature to the policy of nonintervention in early United States national life, the Indian government was more concerned with solutions to overwhelming domestic considerations.

India not only had pressing difficulties at home to face; it also had little real power to exercise in international affairs. Non-involvement was a logical result of that fact. Moreover, India feared that too close a tie with a major bloc would endanger its relations with another great power bloc, and Nehru at any rate did not believe in the value of power blocs. India needed aid from as many sources as possible, and India counted on Russia to support it on the Kashmir issue. The philosophy of India's foreign policy was spelled out most vividly in the Five Principles, or *Panchshila* (a term variously spelled), but first elaborated in a 1954 Indian-Communist Chinese treaty relating to Tibet. These principles included a mutual respect for the other's territorial integrity and sovereignty, nonaggression, noninterference in the other's internal affairs, equality and mutual benefit, and peaceful coexistence. India sincerely, if unwisely, counted on Panchshila to give it freedom from foreign entanglements so as to allow it to concentrate all of its energy on vital nation-building tasks. India felt it could not divert scarce resources to military when it had to strain every effort to mount the costly five-year plans.

Enunciation of idealistic principle was simpler than execution of realistic practice. In the elimination of French and Portuguese colonies from its borders, the Indian government felt constrained to use force against the latter. In 1952, France gave up Chandernagore, a suburb of Calcutta, one of its five possessions, after a referendum. Two years later, after an agreement with France, India took over the administration of the other four French colonies, including Pondicherry, some 200 square miles in area. In 1956, a treaty was signed in New Delhi by which France formally ceded the territories to India, though the treaty was not ratified by the French National Assembly until mid-1962. India and France remained on good terms, and France became a member of the "Aid India" club.

On the other hand, Portugal remained stubborn about its possessions of Goa, Diu, and Daman, 1615 square miles in area with about 700,000 in population. After independence, discussions between India and Portugal over the colonies grew acrimonious. In mid-1953, India withdrew its mission to Lisbon, and after another two years it severed diplomatic relations. Incidents and border clashes aggravated the dispute until December, 1961, when Indian troops occupied Goa, the chief and oldest Portuguese colony, in a twenty-six-hour campaign. Goa was placed under military rule for five months until it and the other former Portuguese colonies became federally administered territories. Both Mysore and Maharashtra states contended for Goa's eventual absorption into their respective jurisdictions, but Goans voted for continued central rule.

The Indian government was concerned as well with the security of the Himalayan border states. In 1949, succeeding to British political and strategic interests, India concluded a treaty with Sikkim, which became a protectorate by giving India the right to conduct defense matters and to station troops there. Sikkim had a Congress party that urged accession to India, though geographic and ethnic factors pulled it toward Tibet and beyond that to China. More remote than Sikkim, but in a similarly protected status, Bhutan in a 1950 treaty gave India the right to control defense matters and foreign affairs but not the right to station troops. An independent country, Nepal was caught in its own cold war between India and China. In 1953, Indian troops intervened to quell a peasant uprising, and Nehru declared that it was not possible for India to tolerate an invasion of Nepal from any source.

A third immediate consideration of India's foreign policies, besides those of the colonial enclaves, a closed issue, and of the border states, a potential problem, was India's position in the British Commonwealth of Nations. While the Indian National Congress more than once formally went on record to sever all political ties with Britain, upon independence in 1947 India became, and upon the creation of the republic in 1950 it remained, a member of the Commonwealth. In 1958, the British prime minister, Harold Macmillan, as the first one in that position, visited India. Three years later, Queen Elizabeth paid India (and Pakistan) a royal state visit. Nehru himself often commuted to London, the scene of the annual meetings of the Commonwealth prime ministers and other international conferences.

India took interest in the 3 million Indians in the component parts of the Commonwealth and empire. Many of the emigrants, initially going abroad chiefly as indentured labor in the nineteenth century for generally seven-year terms, upon the expiration of their contracts stayed on in their adopted countries. Their numbers were augmented by later arrivals, who pursued a new life in Ceylon, Burma, Malaya, the Pacific and Caribbean islands, and in Africa. Indians clashed with spokesmen of the Union of South Africa, where Gandhi had earlier lived, on the policy of *apartheid*, or segregation, that affected Indians as well as Africans. They condemned strongly that policy of racial discrimination, and they helped to create a situation by which South Africa had to withdraw from the Commonwealth on this issue.

In its relations with non-Communist Asian countries, India was oriented primarily toward Southeast Asia, a historic orientation. Recently emerging itself from colonial status, India pursued an anticolonial theme. The Second World War was scarcely over when the Congress adopted in September, 1945, a resolution asking for Indian freedom from "imperialist domination" and for independence of neighboring Burma, Malaya, Indochina, and Indonesia. In the conviction that Asian countries could cooperate in common international aims, Indian convoked in New Delhi prior to independence in the spring of 1946 the unofficial Asian Relations Conference, attended by delegates from twenty-eight countries, including autonomous states of the Soviet Union. At this first major Asian postwar conclave, topics of mutual interest were discussed, as national movements for freedom, agricultural resources, industrial development, and cultural problems. An Asian relations organization was established to provide for further liaison and meetings, but this never amounted to much. Some years later, India, Pakistan, and other Asian countries created an Asian-Arab political bloc, for a time a strong factor in the United Nations, but neither the conference nor the bloc created a third force in international affairs.

India convened a conference on Indonesia, sometimes called the second Asian Relations Conference, in January of 1949. This took place after the second Dutch "police action" that resulted in the capture of the central Javan city of Jogjakarta, then the capital of the beleaguered Republic of Indonesia, and the imprisonment of President Sukarno and other Indonesian leaders. The conference was attended by representatives from fifteen Afro-Asian countries and by observers from another four, but none were invited from the Soviet Union. Nehru condemned the Dutch attack as "naked and unabashed aggression." The conference adopted a series of resolutions that called for sanctions against the colonialists. The United Nations Security Council seconded the action, and, by the end of 1949, Indonesia had received its independence, in part because of pressures generated by a united Asian stand on the matter.

As one of the five Asian sponsoring powers, India convoked the Asian-African Conference at Bandung on Java in April, 1955. Twenty-nine Afro-Asian countries sent representatives. Nehru attended, as did Prime Minister and Foreign Minister Chou En-lai of Communist China. Discussions ranged over a selection of topics, including that of anti-colonialism, an issue that was becoming almost trite because of frequent reiteration over the years and yet compelling in attractiveness to many Asians. In a closing speech Nehru forcefully stated that Asia was no longer passive, it was no more submissive—it was dynamic, it was full of life. There were to be, he concluded, no dictation in the future, no "yes-men" in Asia. Within another six years after Bandung, however, the issues of western colonialism and imperialism seemed to be shopworn as far as India was concerned. When efforts were made at the 1961 Belgrade Conference of Nonaligned Nations to sound similar warnings, Nehru characterized them as worn out. The prime minister emphasized the problems of nuclear arms power and of space testing as more contemporaneously relevant.

Toward individual non-Communist Asian countries, India revealed a varied approach. In regard to Thailand and the Philippines, formal and correct but not cordial diplomatic relations were established. With Chiang Kai-shek's Republic of China on Formosa, only minor trade ties existed. Indian forces did not participate in the Korean War of 1950–1953, though they cooperated in the work of the truce and repatriation commissions. Personal ties of Nehru were closer with fellow neutralists as Prime Minister U Nu of Burma and President Sukarno of Indonesia. In regard to Indochina, Nehru stated in early 1950 that "we have not interfered in any way and we intend keeping apart." But a representative of the Indian government served as chairman of the three International Control Commissions established for Vietnam, Laos and Cambodia by the Geneva Conference of 1954 on Indochina. India again showed a proclivity toward mediating, rather than contributing military forces to, disputes. Little animosity was shown to and no reparations were claimed from Japan, which was admired as the first Asian country of modern times to stand up to a western power—Russia, in 1905. India declined to attend the 1951 Japanese Peace Conference in San Francisco. It claimed that Japan had been treated too harshly because the treaty had deprived Japan of territory and because the continued presence of American troops and the Security Treaty with the United States limited Japan's freedom to make its own defense arrangements.

Toward the Arab world sympathy was elicited for nationalist causes, but there was no policy of unity with Muslims or Arabs on religious grounds. Latin American problems did not figure prominently in Indian foreign policy considerations. Representatives from India participated in some "bloc" meetings with Africa, which showed, however, an increasing tendency to form sub-blocs among its own three dozen independent countries on that continent.

Indians did not view Communism or the Soviet Union with the preoccupation and alarm that existed in the United States, because they believed that the ideology had some features applicable to domestic situations. They felt that, when Russia went through its own revolution, the Soviet economic state was not greatly different from their own. Russian progress, the argument went, could be similarly matched by other economically underdeveloped countries. Indian relations with Russia were enhanced in the mid-1950's on foreign relations grounds when, after Pakistan accepted military aid from the United States, Russia tended to side with India. Nehru twice journeyed to Moscow, in 1955 and in 1961. In late 1955, Bulganin and Khrushchev visited India (and Burma and Afghanistan). They received a warm welcome, partly because this was the first visit by leaders of any major state to India. Five years later, Khrushchev again visited the country.

The first trip resulted in the successful negotiations for the first important Soviet economic aid project in India, that of the Bhilai steel mill. Between 1955 and 1973, the equivalent of over $1.4 billion in credits were extended to India, and in the early 1970's, the annual trade turnover reached about $500 million. In 1962, because of boundary disputes with Communist China, military as well as economic aid was conceived and India began to negotiate with Russia for MIG fighter planes. Prime Minister Shastri went to Moscow in the spring of 1965 to confirm Russo-Indian friendship, but winds of change were blowing, and Prime Minister Kosygin made plain some Russian reservations. Enmeshed in his own differences with Communist China and now extending aid to Pakistan as well, the

Russian leader left the impression that his country aimed to keep both India and Pakistan as friends. In August, 1971, a twenty-year friendship treaty was signed, and the next month Mrs. Gandhi visited Russia. Two years later, Soviet Communist party leader, Leonid Brezhnev, returned the visit.

Despite territorial problems between India and China, Indians seemed to consider the Chinese more Asian than Communist. When the Communists overran mainland China in 1949, India extended recognition to the new regime on the grounds that this was just due for the world's most populous nation, one of great size, and one in control of its territory. Recognition was granted despite past close ties, dating from 1925, that existed between the Chinese Nationalists and the Indian National Congress. In the course of prewar Chinese nationalist struggles against domestic rivals and the Japanese, the Congress supported Chiang Kai-shek. In 1939, Nehru visited Chiang at Chungking, the inland wartime capital of unoccupied China. In 1942, Chiang traveled in turn to Delhi to arouse, without success, more effective Indian participation in the war. But India and Nehru were more concerned in a strong, stable, and united China than in its ideology, and so diplomatic allegiance was switched in 1949. India pushed for the presence of the Chinese Communists in United Nations organs. It did not favor the General Assembly resolution branding China as an aggressor in the Korean War, and it advocated that the Chinese Communists be represented at the Japanese Peace Conference. Nehru visited Peking, and Chou En-lai several times visited India.

Despite Indian accommodations in policies toward Communist China, border problems loomed. When the Chinese Communists first invaded Tibet in 1950, India formally protested the action. The Chinese replied that, since Tibet was an integral part of Chinese territory, the matter was a domestic affair. But that same year India and China concluded a nonaggression pact. Again in 1954, they firmed a treaty of trade and commerce. Five years later, more problems arose in the course of a Tibetan revolt. The young Dalai Lama fled from Lhasa to India, but Nehru did not take any steps officially to recognize either him or his plight. In 1959, trouble also flared up when it became publicized that the Chinese Communists had occupied 5,000 square miles of what Indians claimed to be their territory in the Aksai Chin plateau of the Ladakh district of Kashmir state. The Chinese Communists had built a strategic road through the area to connect their border areas of Tibet and Sinkiang.

In 1962, renewed hostilities broke out in that area once again, and additionally in the North East Frontier Agency (NEFA), on the Assam border, east of Bhutan. This border was part of the over-all so-called MacMahon line, drawn up by the foreign secretary of the Government of India in the Simla Conference of 1914. The agreement was initialed by the British, Tibetan, and Chinese representatives of the Republic of China, but which never ratified it. Into this disputed area (from the Chinese point of view), the Chinese Communists suddenly crossed the Himalayan ranges, to threaten oil-rich Assam. After a campaign lasting only some weeks and without any losses to their side, they withdrew back over the mountains. The reasons advanced for their campaign might have been several: to test Indian border security, to win Asian respect or fear through a show of force, to divert Indian resources from economic to military matters, or to back their disputed territorial claims by force. At any rate, though the Chinese Communists had come to boundary agreements respecting the MacMahon line with Burma, Nepal, and Pakistan (and a separate one with Afghanistan), unlike the Indians they considered the question of the northeastern and northwestern Indian boundaries to be not properly adjudicated.

Toward the United States, relations prior to Indian independence were not auspicious. The Department of State seemed to go along with British switches in policy regarding partition rather than to show concern with solutions as Indians interpreted them. In February, 1947, Washington approved the Labour government's solution for a federal and undivided India. When in June the government came out for partition, the Department of State applauded the contrary action. After 1947, cold war considerations and the Korean War complicated relations, so that, by the 1950's, issues were plentiful between India and the United States. For one, the Indians thought that the United States was not quick enough to recognize colonial struggles in postwar Asia and Africa. Though they commended the American grant of independence to the Philippines, they claimed that the action was not enough, for it seemed to Indians that Americans supported the Dutch cause in Indonesia, the French in Indochina, the British in Malaya, and, more immediately, the Portuguese in Goa, which Secretary of State John Foster Dulles in President Eisenhower's administration had termed a Portuguese province.

Again, the two governments differed on Communist China's admission to United Nations organs. As noted previously, India did not attend and it did not sign the United States sponsored Japanese peace treaty, for it thought, among other objections, that the treaty was too harsh (though Burma also declined to attend the meeting or to sign the same treaty but for the opposite reason; it thought the terms were not harsh enough). India disapproved of the creation of Israel, since it involved partition, a concept anathema to many Indians. But in 1950, India recognized Israel after three Muslim countries, Turkey, Indonesia, and Iran, had done so. On other issues, Indians thought that Americans overemphasized military solutions to area problems with the creation of the Southeast Asian Treaty Organization (SEATO), the Central Treaty Organization (CENTO), and various bilateral mutual defense treaties that the United States had concluded with Asian countries. Indians decried United States military aid to Pakistan, as they did its nuclear testing. In sum, issues were those in the political and military spheres, probably the most brittle kind.

Despite mutual differences, the United States extended much economic aid to India. It began in 1947, and by 1974 over $9 billion had been committed. The nature of official American aid was many-sided. In technical assistance, the United States sent experts to India or trained Indian technicians in their own country, in the United States, or in a third country. The United States exported commodity items (as steel, locomotives, and freight cars) to support various projects in the five-year plans. Half the total amount of aid ($4.5 billion) was in the form of surplus food, a part of which was donated and the rest (some $3 billion) paid for in rupees that the United States placed back as counterpart funds into local development projects. In 1973, the United States cancelled $2 billion of this Indian debt. United States surpluses saved up to 30 million Indians annually, roughly equivalent to the population of Spain.

As other United States financial sources, Export-Import Bank loans extended to India facilitated purchases in the United States of projects involving dollar costs. Development Loan Fund credits were used to purchase goods, usually in currency other than hard-to-get dollars, in the United States or in other countries. Augmenting economic programs were cultural ones. Educational exchanges were effected through the Fulbright and Smith-Mundt Acts. The United States Information Service disseminated information in English and in Indian languages through its libraries, publications, book translation programs, and radio broadcasts. After the Communist Chinese border intrusions of 1962, upon Indian request the United States commenced to extend military aid.

Because of the importance of India as a non-Communist though nonaligned state, Americans had early proposed long-range economic plans for the country. In 1952, Chester Bowles, Ambassador to India, suggested to the United States Congress a four-year billion dollar program, half in loans and half in grants. His proposal was not acted upon. In 1958, when India was encountering problems with the second five-year plan, the idea was revived by two senators. Sherman Cooper, Republican of Kentucky and a former ambassador to India, and John F. Kennedy, Democrat of Massachusetts and later President, placed before the Senate a resolution recognizing a special American interest in India's economic development. They recommended that the United States "join with other nations in providing support of the type, magnitude, and duration, adequate to assist India to complete successfully its current program for economic development." The Senate accepted the resolution as an amendment to the Mutual Security Act of 1958, but it was deleted when the bill was in conference with the House of Representatives.

The next year, the two senators again introduced a similar resolution to the effect that "the United States Government should invite other friendly and democratic nations to join in a mission to consult with India on the detailed possibilities for joint action to assure the fulfillment of India's second five-year plan and the effective design of the third plan." Joining them were two representatives, including Bowles, now a congressman, Democrat of Connecticut, who introduced a similar resolution in the House. Neither proposal was acted upon at the time, but the concurrent initiative taken in both houses indicated a strong bipartisan congressional interest in India's economic stake. Despite initial failures at attempting long-range programs to India, a change of Congressional mind occurred when a two-year commitment for 1961 to 1963 of some $1 billion was extended through an international consortium to help finance India's third five-year plan. Moreover, in 1960, a four-year surplus food agreement, the first of its kind, which set a precedent for similar long-term food agreements, was signed with India to cover the use of 17 million tons of grain valued at $1.2 billion. This was the largest trade agreement in world history to that time. Washington continued to extend emergency food programs, but it hinted that American agricultural resources were not limitless.

In Washington, the Indian government was represented by efficient and able ambassadors, including Nehru's sister, Madam Vijaya Lakshmi Pandit. In turn, American ambassadors in Delhi were also of generally high quality. Chester Bowles, ambassador in the early 1950's and again in the mid-1960's, practically became an Indian. On his first tour, his young daughter rode a bicycle to school, and at the age of seventeen she wrote a book recounting her Indian experiences. Ambassador Ellsworth Bunker, a career foreign service officer, projected the image to Indians of a kind, courteous, and helpful elder brother. John Galbraith, the Harvard University economist of *Affluent Society* fame, was numbered in ambassadorial ranks. State visits augmented diplomatic ties. In December of 1959, President Eisenhower included India in his tour of South Asia, where he registered a great emotional impact on Indians. A decade later, President Nixon included India on a global trip. After independence, Nehru visited the United States thrice—in 1949; in 1956, when he visited Eisenhower on his Gettysburg farm; and in 1961, when he met President Kennedy in Newport, Rhode Island. Prime Minister Indira Gandhi in 1966 journeyed to Washington where President Lyndon Johnson sought congressional support for a $1 billion emergency famine relief program and $300 million to establish an Indian-American foundation to "promote progress in all fields of learning" in India. She again visited Washington in late 1971.

Nongovernmental American organs supplemented official programs. Private foundations, as the Ford and Rockefeller Foundations, engaged in projects amounting to millions of dollars. The former assisted in the village community development projects; the latter tended to emphasize medical and public health programs. United States universities participated in exchange programs in which agricultural education played a leading role. Helping out in this field were the state universities of Illinois, Kansas, Missouri, Ohio, and Tennessee. Private religious and benevolent organizations contributed financial aid as well; between 1947 and mid-1958 this totaled $6.5 million. The Quakers were particularly effective in the community development projects. The study of the United States and of American institutions expanded in Indian universities, and American universities and colleges, numbering into the dozens, offered more and more courses relating to South Asia. The total volume of instruction and research on South Asia in the United States surpassed that in any other country, outside of the subcontinent itself. For those who sought in either country an understanding of Indian-American relations, a plethora of information was available.

Chronology

1946	Asian Relations Conference
1947, Aug. 15	Union of India created
1949	Sikkim treaty; Conference on Indonesia
1950	Bhutan treaty
Jan. 26	Constitution of Republic of India promulgated
April	Delhi Pact: India and Pakistan affirm minority rights
1951, Oct.–Feb. 1952	First national elections
	First five-year plan inaugurated
1954	India-China treaty relating to Tibet; Five Principles enunciated
1955	Bandung Conference
1956	States Reorganization Act
	Second five-year plan inaugurated
1957, Feb.–March	Second national elections

1959	Chinese occupy northwest territory claimed by India
1960	Regularization of trade between India and Pakistan
	Indus Water Treaty
	India-held Kashmir integrated as Indian state
1961	Third five-year plan instituted
1962, Feb.	Third national election
	Border hostilities with China in northwest and northeast
1967, Feb.	Fourth national election
1969	Fourth five-year plan; Congress Party splits
1971, March	Fifth national election (special)
Aug.	Twenty-year Russian friendship treaty signed
1975, May	Sikkim incorporated as Indian state
June	Mrs. Gandhi declares state of emergency

Republic of India

I. Political Divisions, 1947–1956

Part *A* States	Part *B* States	Part *C* States
Assam	Hyderabad	Ajmer
Bihar	Jammu and Kashmir	Bhopal
Bombay	Madhya Bharat	Bilaspur
Madhya Pradesh	Mysore	Coorg
Madras	Pepsu	Delhi
Orissa	Rajasthan	Himachal Pradesh
Punjab	Saurashtra	Kutch
Uttar Pradesh	Travancore-Cochin	Manipur
West Bengal		Tripura
		Vindhya Pradesh

Part *D* Territories and Other Areas

Andaman and Nicobar Islands
Sikkim

II. States Created Since 1956

Andhra Pradesh (1956)
Assam (1956)
Bihar (1956)
Gujarat (1960)
Haryana (1966)
Himachal Pradesh (1971)
Jammu and Kashmir (1956)
Karnataka (Mysore, 1956)
Kerala (1956)
Madhya Pradesh (1956)
Maharashtra (1960)
Manipur (1972)
Meghalaya (1972)
Nagaland (1963)
Orissa (1956)
Punjab (1956)
Rajasthan (1956)
Sikkim (1975)
Tamil Nadu (Madras, 1956)
Tripura (1972)
Uttar Pradesh (1956)
West Bengal (1956)

Chapter 8

Border Lands

Pakistan and Bangladesh

Emerging as a new country, Pakistan had manifold problems. During the first decade of its existence, it was harassed by political unrest, downfall of governments, and serious emergencies. Muslims, previously united in pre-independent India, became subject to divisive forces, including that of geography. Pakistan, as the largest Muslim nation in the world, was split into eastern and western wings. East Pakistan, smaller in size but more populous than its western counterpart, felt neglected, a thousand miles away and separated by Indian territory. Regional leaders, notably H. S. Suhrawardy, who became a prime minister, demanded parity and equality of treatment; failing this, later spokesmen opted for independence. The western half was politically favored, since it initially started with some eight political subdivisions as matched against one province for all of East Pakistan, and the composition of the national assembly reflected this arrangement.

Moreover, differences in languages, in economics, and dissatisfaction with the western-dominated Muslim League led to sporadic rioting in the eastern provincial capital city of Dacca and other centers. To advance their cause, in 1954, eastern political leaders formed a United Front coalition. Framing a twenty-one-point program to further Bengali nationalism, the party handily won elections for local assembly seats over the oppositionist League, but the governor general stepped in to administer the province before real party gains could be registered. The next year, the One Unit Bill was passed that amalgamated the political parts of West Pakistan into one province, to establish both wings on a theoretically political par.

The lack of commanding leadership compounded the national issue of centrifugal regional relations. As the first governor general of Pakistan, Jinnah, the Great Leader, the outstanding name in Pakistani politics, carried everything on his shoulders for over a year. After his death in September of 1948, leadership passed to a capable but less dominating personality, Prime Minister Liaquat Ali Khan, who was assassinated by a Pathan fanatic in 1951. With the deaths of these two men, no outstanding name emerged for several years. After Jinnah, Pakistan experienced a succession of three more governors general until 1956, when the then promulgated constitution of the Islamic Republic of Pakistan abolished the position and substituted for it the office of president. And subsequent to Liaquat Ali Khan's initial tenure as prime minister, six men filled that office until 1958, when General Mohammed Ayub Khan, after a coup, wiped it out upon assuming the presidency. With the general's sudden accession to power that year, after a decade of kaleidoscopic leadership, Pakistani politics revolved around one dominant central figure holding one top office.

Long-drawn-out Pakistani efforts at constitution making, as well as in defining Islam's place in the new state, helped to cloud the political scene. Acting as interim parliaments at the national and provincial levels were organs elected in pre-independent India. As first governor general, Jinnah convened the eighty-member constituent assembly, which also possessed concurrent legislative powers, to draw up a constitution. Compared with Indian progress at the same time, Pakistan registered a slower pace in formulating the document. In 1949, the Pakistan assembly passed an Objectives Resolution that declared Pakistan to be an Islamic state. The assembly then also considered a Basic Principles Interim Report, which advocated Urdu as the national language, though the East Pakistanis, who preferred Bengali, eventually realized the inclusion of their tongue.

Linguistic differences were augmented by religious controversies. In drawing up the interim report, orthodox Muslims and modernist schools split on the nature of the new state. A 1952 amended version leaned toward an orthodox view, for the latter document recommended that all acts were to be consistent with the Koran and with Islamic law and that a board of Muslim experts was to be established to review all bills. In 1954, just when a constitution was on the verge of being realized, the governor general abruptly dissolved the assembly to prevent enactment of the document, which called for restrictions on his office. The next year, after a change in governors general, a second constituent assembly was convened, and, after deliberations of a year, it proclaimed the Islamic Republic of Pakistan in 1956.

In effect only two and a half years, the 1956 constitution provided for a president as chief of state, to be chosen by popularly elected national and provincial assemblies, and a prime minister as head of government, to be appointed by the president and responsible to the assembly. A cabinet was decreed and a unicameral assembly was formed, with 310 members, one-half from each wing, elected by direct popular vote. The document outlined lists of federal, provincial, and concurrent powers. It set up an independent judiciary, and it expressed Pakistani desire to remain in the British Commonwealth. Islamic features were present, but not so prominently as the orthodox had desired. Only the president was to be a Muslim; other offices were open to any citizen. And while no law repugnant to Islam could be enacted, a commission, not necessarily composed of orthodox Muslims, was to review constitutional provisions. Citizens were assured fundamental rights, as freedom of speech, association, and religion and equality before the law.

General Iskander Mirza was named provisional president until elections could be called, but, because of continuing political uncertainties, religious differences, and official personality clashes, elections were never held. Crises snowballed until late 1958, when strong man Ayub Khan took over the government. On October 7th, with Khan's consent, Mirza dissolved the central and two provincial governments, abrogated the constitution, abolished political parties, and declared martial law. As commander in chief of the army, Khan was named Chief Martial Law Administrator. In the ensuing weeks, many were arrested, party leaders were jailed, and ex-cabinet officials were hustled off to prison. But the coexistence of two strong men in two top posts proved to be untenable, and, on October 27th, Ayub Khan took over the presidency, packed the Mirzas off to London by plane, and abolished the prime ministerial position. The new president formed an eleven-man cabinet with three generals, and proceeded to put Pakistan on a new footing.

Sanctioned by martial law, he initiated many administrative reforms in the early months of his regime. Graft and corruption were cleaned up. It suddenly became easier for people to get in touch with officials, long lunch hours were proscribed, and information was released on politicians' wealth and on private business affairs. Charges of accepting bribes or other official misconduct were liable to imprisonment sentences of up to fourteen years. On the advice of West German financial experts, the government curbed inflation, reduced spending, tightened controls on trade, encouraged foreign investments, increased exports, and reduced imports.

As another fresh start, Ayub Khan moved the capital from hot, crowded Karachi, with its dominant business and commercial interests, temporarily to his home town of Rawalpindi, in the northwest, while the new capital of Islamabad, 4 miles away, was planned by Greek architects. The official declaration of the interim capital and the initial move were made in 1959 on the first anniversary of Ayub Khan's assumption of power on October 27th. The next year, on the eve of the second anniversary of the coup, the $40 million master plan for Islamabad was revealed. Developed in a favored location in the Murree Hills on a plateau some 2,000 feet high, surrounded by springs, lakes, and trees, Islamabad promised to symbolize the new Pakistani spirit under new leadership.

Another reform was Ayub Khan's concept and implementation of the basic democracies, which embodied the philosophy of implementing democratic procedures from the grass-roots level upward. According to the president, the heart of the matter was to assure the most effective representative government in a country like Pakistan, which lacked some prerequisites for democracy, such as political sophistication, a high literacy rate, and good communications systems, all of which obtained in the more advanced western democracies. He advanced the concept of guided democracy, which called for elections from below but direction from above. In formulating this approach Ayub Khan rationalized that citizens were best qualified to vote only in small circles for officials with whom they were most familiar. The president also maintained that local organs could provide a fresh supply of leadership, and that they could channel communications between the central government and the populace.

Announced in mid-1959, promulgated on the now familiar date of October 27th that year and subsequently implemented, five levels of authority were established from the union councils in rural areas or town committees in urban centers to the national organs. East and West Pakistan were each divided into 40,000 constituencies, each averaging a population of one thousand, and each electing one representative. All citizens, male and female, of at least twenty-one years and of good character, were entitled to vote for the 80,000 Basic Democrats on the union councils or the town committees. Each council or committee consisted of fifteen members, ten elected members from ten such constituencies and five appointed by the central government. The council or committee chairman was elected from one of the ten elected members, and his position was to be ensured through representation on the four higher echelons. The councils and committees concerned themselves with a wide array of administrative functions, as formulating local budgets, raising funds, and overseeing executive, judicial, and social matters.

Next up the ladder came the subdistrict or subdivisional councils, with jurisdiction over areas to coincide with already existing police stations. Restricted largely to coordinating functions, half of its membership consisted of chairmen of union councils or town committees, while the other half were nominated official or unofficial members. Similar in constitution was the third tier of district councils, with half of their members elected from councils and committees and the other half nominated. District councils, presiding over an administrative unit dating to British times, concerned themselves with a variety of important functions, as furthering education, building primary schools, erecting libraries and reading rooms, promoting cultural and athletic activities, maintaining public roads and bridges, ensuring water supplies, and initiating village cooperative projects and cottage industries. The fourth level consisted of divisional councils, also based on pre-existing British administrative units, composed half of appointive and half of elective membership, of which one-fourth were chairmen of union councils or town committees.

At the apex of the structure, and largely restricted to advising the government on broad economic plans, were the two provincial development advisory boards, chaired by the governors of the two wings and composed of membership half appointed at large by the government and half appointed from lower administrative units, with at least one-third of these as chairmen of councils of committees. Though higher echelons could veto actions of lower tiers, the chairmen of union councils and of town committees were represented on all levels, which gave to the people, even through a largely indirect electoral system, some sense of participation in decision making. In December, 1959, elections, the first in Pakistan, were held to implement the structure of the basic democracies. Some 98 per cent of the eligible voters participated in the campaign for the 79,850 elected members on the union councils or town committees. In a second and indirect election of February, 1960, the Basic Democrats confirmed Ayub Khan as president, and gave to him the mandate to effect another constitution.

Sworn into office at Rawalpindi, President Ayub Khan formed a constituent commission to make general recommendations for a new constitution. After two years of endeavor, in March of 1962 they announced the terms of the new constitution, which were implemented three months later. More secular in nature than its predecessor, the second document called for a Republic of Pakistan under a strong president, elected indirectly. In part confirming what had already been the practice, its provisions stipulated that the president was to be a Muslim and that he was to be elected by the union councils and town committees. Limited to two five-year terms, the president could be prolonged in office for a third term by legislative act. The office of vice president was not provided for, but the speaker of the National Assembly was to function in the absence or indisposition of the president.

A unicameral national assembly of 156 was established of which six had to be women, and of which total, half were elected by the basic democracies from each east and west wing. To coincide with the first presidential term, which was to end in 1965, the first legislative term was initially limited to three years, but five-year terms were provided for subsequent assemblies. The national legislature had the right to deal with forty-seven exclusive subjects, including foreign affairs and defense. It was to meet at Dacca, rather than in the new political and administrative capital of Islamabad, to counteract East Pakistani feelings of less favored treatment. Bengali and Urdu were proclaimed national languages, though English was continued as the official one for a decade, after which a commission was to consider its replacement. Only licensed political parties were allowed.

In provincial administration, the two-province structure was confirmed, each with a governor appointed by the president, who also approved the cabinets of each governor. Two provincial assemblies, with five-year terms, were created, both with 155 elected members (including five women) plus the provincial governor, to be elected by the basic democracies. In April of 1962, the 80,000 Basic Democrats elected the first national assembly of 156; in the following month the 40,000 in each wing elected the 155 members to the two provincial assemblies. Pakistan's version of constitutional democracy got off to a start. It was chiefly indirect in nature, centralized in structure, and revolved around the president as a strong figure. In November, 1964, voters in a second national election elected another round of 80,000 Basic Democrats. These put Ayub Khan, whose opposition for presidential office was Jinnah's sister, back into office two months later for another five-year term.

In economic affairs, upon partition Pakistan as a new state had few industries, a heavy concentration of labor in agriculture, and a shortage of technicians. It was worse off than India in these respects. In the first several years of national life, emphasis was placed on the consolidation, planning, and execution of policy. The first major official industrial policy statement in 1948 emphasized the concept, as India had, of an equitable distribution of wealth, with the government to own and to operate key economic sectors. For a time the Korean War created demands for the basic Pakistan exports of cotton, jute, and tea. Temporary prosperity resulted, but from the resultant buildup of export crop inventories, world price reductions for them, and subsequent domestic food crop failures, a surplus of exports turned into a surplus of imports.

As the economic bubble was bursting, the government announced its first over-all plan, to cost $1.1 billion and to cover the years mid-1951 through mid-1957. As part of the over-all Colombo Plan to spur long-range development programs of participating countries, this six-year plan was devised to increase foreign exchange earnings and government revenues as well as to raise standards of living. The plan was hardly under way when, in 1953, it was reviewed and revised in light of foreign exchange difficulties. In 1955, a new $2.3 billion five-year plan was prepared, though its details were not finalized until the following year.

The first five-year plan, 1955 to 1960, emphasized agriculture and paid particular attention to East Pakistan, an underdeveloped area. Some of the manifold aims of the plan were to create 2 million new jobs, to increase food grain production by 13 per cent, to extend village aid to 26,000 villages, to irrigate 3 million acres of new lands, to produce an additional 580,000 kilowatts of electric power, to build 3,000 new post offices, to provide for 35,000 new telephones, and to increase foreign exchange earnings by $102 million. Some outside aid was contributed to the plan, but adverse factors bogged it down. Pakistan business men felt cramped by numerous government regulations. Since their government stressed social justice and an equitable division of national wealth, many of them failed to expand their business enterprises. Moreover, agricultural problems as soil erosion, silting, water-logging, and high salinity held back irrigation schemes, particularly in arid areas of West Pakistan. Political instablility also hampered sound economic planning. With exports of agricultural raw materials commanding low and fixed prices in exchange for imports of manufactured goods with high prices, Pakistan recorded an adverse balance of trade. Stipulated plan targets were not met, and population rise outpaced economic growth.

In drawing up the second five-year plan, 1960 to 1965, the government consulted outside sources, including West German financial experts and Harvard University economists. In early 1960, these advised the government to relax controls, improve incentives, remove food price controls, and pay more attention to the private industrial sector. Costing about $4 billion, the plan, with roughly half of the funds to be realized from abroad, called for an increase in the national income of 20 per cent, self-sufficiency in food, more employment opportunities, and an increase in the range and quality of social service as well as in large-scale industrial production. The international consortium that had extended aid to India's development plans similarly extended aid to Pakistan. A total of almost $2 billion, half from the United States, was realized from this external joint source. Though the impact of the first plan on the economy was slight, the second accelerated economic development, and there was a fairly rapid increase in both national and per capita incomes. The gross national product rose from $5.8 billion in 1955 to $8.5 billion in 1965. Though population increased in that decade from about 80 million to some 110 million, per capita income grew from $66 to $75.

Buoyed by more realistic approaches and multilateral outside help, through the National Economic Council, Pakistan projected a $10.4 billion third five-year plan to cover the years 1965 to 1970, which coincided with Ayub Khan's second term of presidental office. With a quarter of the total funding to come from external sources, as compared to almost half in the second plan, half of the total outlay of the third plan was allocated to each wing in Pakistan and three-fifths designated to the public sector and the rest to the private sector. The plan included aims to increase the gross national product by 37 per cent, to reduce the existing level of disparity in income per head between East ($66 in 1965) and West ($86) Pakistan, to provide at least 5.5 million new job appointments, and to arrest population growth by taking decisive steps toward birth control. The suggested development expenditure was expected to lead to an annual rate of growth of 6.5 per cent as compared with 5.2 per cent during the second period. The plan sought to achieve an annual agricultural growth rate of more than 5 per cent, among the highest in the world. The success of the third plan was pivotal, since it constituted the first stage of a twenty-year perspective plan when, by 1985, Pakistan expected to have a population of 190 million. In 1970 a fourth five-year plan commenced.

Since about 90 per cent of Pakistan's population depended on agriculture as the source of wealth, and since the export of agricultural products constituted a similar percentage by value of Pakistan's foreign exchange, agrarian development was considered vital. In 1959, the government initiated a program of land reform that restricted land ownership per capita to 500 acres of irrigated land or 1,000 acres of dry land. As a result, about 3.5 million acres of farmland were sold to poor peasants on easy terms. Like its Indian counterpart, a Village Agricultural and Industrial Development (AID) program was initiated as a type of self-help community development project to affect some 12,000 villages with a population of 11 million scattered throughout the country. In 1959, AID was renamed the National Development Organization, but it bogged down by preoccupation with statistics, graphs, and charts. It lost its importance after the formation of the Basic Democracies which became the primary instruments for social and economic reform.

Industry, almost nonexistent at partition, registered gains with government encouragement. Pakistan became self-sufficient in cotton and woolen textiles, jute goods, and electric wire and cable production. Its firms manufactured such consumer goods as aluminum and brass utensils, bicycle tires and tubes, and shoe leather. Pakistan encouraged domestic and foreign private investments through such organs as the Pakistan Industrial Development Corporation and the Investment Promotion Bureau. Foreign sources were tapped to help discover additional power reserves, in which the country was limited. Half of Pakistan's coal needs was imported, and only low-grade iron ore existed in the Punjab. Natural gas discoveries led to development of that fuel source from fields in West and East Pakistan. To help alleviate shortages, multi-purpose power projects were developed, as those at Warsak, constructed with Canadian help under the Colombo Plan, and at Karnaphuli in East Pakistan, the largest single project in the country. In transport, the government owned and operated the two separate railway systems. Inland waterways were utilized, particularly in the delta lands of the eastern half, but the road network was of lesser importance. In ocean shipping, Karachi served as the main port for the west and Chittagong similarly serviced the east. External and internal air networks were developed, and Pakistan International Airways utilized Karachi and Dacca as bases for international operations.

Pakistan planned for the nuclear age. The Pakistan Atomic

Energy Commission coordinated efforts and enrolled the services of some 250 nuclear engineers and scientists and embarked on an educational program to recruit more. An atomic energy center existed at Lahore, a regional center primarily designed for training personnel in the use of radioisotopes and radiation sources and for research in basic nuclear sciences. Atomic energy agricultural research centers at Tandojam (West Pakistan) and at Dacca provided facilities for the application of nuclear energy in the field of agriculture. Medical radioisotope centers opened in Karachi, Lahore, and Dacca for the diagnosis and treatment of complicated diseases. Preliminary field operations in West Pakistan led to the discovery of uranium ore and other radioactive minerals, and more projects relating to peaceful uses of the atom were under construction in the mid-1960's.

Pakistan's social policy pledged itself to the creation of a welfare state, which was to secure the well-being of the people, irrespective of caste, creed or race, by raising the standard of living of the common man. It established a system of social security, provided for medical benefits, and aimed at free and compulsory primary education, for the literacy rate ranged about 15 per cent. School facilities for over 6 million were constructed, and over 100,000 Pakistanis attended institutions of higher learning. Pakistan's system of education embraced Islamic studies, supported mainly by private funds, that concentrated on the Koran and Islamic tradition and law. The emancipation of women was encouraged, pologamy was discouraged, and women entered into public careers. The press published within circumscribed limits, for the government was empowered by law to assume management of newspapers considered to be offensive. Public health problems were pressing and medical staffing inadequate. In 1959, there was only one doctor for every 8300 persons and one nurse for every 38,000. Despite overwhelming odds, President Ayub Khan, like Indian leaders, was active in trying to improve the standards of his fellow nationals.

In foreign affairs, Pakistan concerned itself primarily with India. At the heart of differences was the unsettled matter of Kashmir, a sensitive and expensive concern of both countries. Between 1947 and 1955, with three-fifths of the annual central revenues budgeted for defense, Pakistan spent $2 billion in that sector, much of it aimed at maintaining its position in Kashmir. Upon Ayub Khan's accession to power, he appeared to advance a conciliatory policy toward India. Though Nehru characterized the rise to power in 1958 as a "naked military dictatorship," the Pakistan president ignored the remark. Instead, as the first Pakistani head of state to do so, he attended a reception tendered by the Indian ambassador. Other conciliatory gestures were extended and acted upon—a trade agreement doubling the amount of trade with India was signed, some border disputes were settled, and the Indus Water Development Treaty with Nehru was firmed. In 1963–1964, bilateral talks on Kashmir proceeded, but these bogged down and the issue continued to hang fire. Other border disputes broke out, including one in the Rann of Cutch, a desolate area of sand in dry seasons and marshes in wet months, located in the Kathiawar peninsula.

Toward neighboring Muslim countries relations were generally friendly, but boundary and minority disputes continued with Afghanistan, the only country to vote against Pakistan's entry into the United Nations. Afghanistan took the stand that the 1893 Durand Line, which demarcated the border between it and British India in favor of the latter, could better be moved farther to the east. It also advanced the notion of an independent state of Pushtunistan, to be peopled by Pushtu tribes. This was to be carved wholly out of northwest Pakistan, though many of the tribes lived across the border and though a plebiscite in that area in June of 1947, prior to partition, indicated that the Pushtus in what is now Pakistan wanted to affiliate with the new country. In 1955 and again in 1961, diplomatic relations were severed between the two countries, and the surface transit trade of land-locked Afghanistan through Pakistan was blocked. The two countries concluded transit arrangements that included a projected short-run railroad, Afghanistan's first, across the border, but recurring border problems tended to sour relations.

On the other hand, toward Iran, with much common history, Pakistan maintained close diplomatic and cultural ties. Toward secular Turkey, a friendly but correct line was advanced. In 1964, upon the initiative of the Pakistani president, an overall organ called the Regional Cooperation for Development was firmed among Pakistan, Iran, and Turkey to accelerate the pace of national development and contribute to area peace and stability. As a Muslim nation, Pakistan sought out friendship with most of the other Muslim countries. As early as 1952, a conference of Muslim theologues from the Islamic world convened at Karachi, where the prime minister pledged his country's cooperation in pan-Muslim movements. Shortly thereafter, Pakistan proposed a conference at Karachi of prime ministers of Muslim countries for mutual consultations. Ayub Khan in office traveled extensively throughout Arab and Muslim lands, and the Arab League opened an office in the capital. Though tending to be more secular in character than many of his countrymen, the president founded an Institute of Islamic Research in Karachi to present Islam as a "national, dynamic way of life."

Among Communist countries, Pakistan formalized diplomatic relations with Russia, but it received no aid until 1961. Dissatisfied with the meager results of eight western oil companies in prospecting for further oil reserves, Pakistan signed an agreement with the Soviets, who provided for a $30 million credit to finance costs of Soviet oil-prospecting equipment and material and pay for salaries of Soviet technicians in training Pakistanis. The twelve-year loan carried an annual interest rate of 2.5 per cent, and repayment was stipulated in Pakistani rupees. In 1964, another credit of $10 million was extended for the purchase of heavy-duty Soviet tractors. Russia tended to support India's side in the Kashmir dispute in the '50's, but in the internationally fluid South Asian situation in the '60's, Pakistan-Russian relations improved. Cultural and scientific delegations exchanged visits, air service between Moscow and Karachi was inaugurated, and Pakistani students pursued Russian subjects—a previously suspect academic undertaking. In 1965, Ayub Khan flew to Moscow, where agreements on more trade, economic cooperation, and cultural exchanges resulted, though no announcements specifically referred to the Kashmir question. But, in January of 1966, Moscow extended good offices in the Kashmir dispute by convening the two belligerents at the Tashkent conference, which helped to clear up mutual antagonisms for a time.

In early 1950, Pakistan became the third non-Communist country, after Burma and India, to recognize the Chinese Communist regime in Peking. The next year ambassadors were exchanged. Subsequently, because of Chinese desire to buy cotton and Pakistani willingness to sell it, a significant growth of trade between the two countries resulted. Further enhancing relations was the fact that China possessed in its western regions a sizable Muslim population. Peking attempted to foster closer relations by encouraging contacts between various Muslim organizations in the two countries. Though Pakistan's decision in 1954 to join the Southeast Asia Treaty Organization was denounced by Peking, they evidenced little fear of or hostility toward Communist China.

Few issues existed between Pakistan and China. In the Kashmir issue, which preoccupied Pakistanis above all else, Peking stressed the need to reach a settlement through negotiations and a self-determination plebiscite, a stand which contrasted with Moscow's initial support of the Indians. In the Himalayan border disputes, Pakistan, though also claiming Kashmir, was not outspoken in denouncing Chinese aggression in the Indian-held portion. On the contrary, it came to a border agreement with China. As early as March, 1961, it proposed one with China, which, after taking almost a year to formulate a reply, began negotiations in February of 1962. A settlement was signed in March of 1963. The border treaty provided that Pakistan was to receive 1350 of 3400 square miles of disputed area in the Pakistani-held portion of Kashmir. China received the greater share of territory, but Pakistan received 750 square miles more than it was actually occupying at the time.

The border agreement was followed by an air transport agreement, and in mid-1964 Pakistan International Airways, using American-built jets, commenced flights from Dacca to Canton and Shanghai. Prime Minister Chou En-lai visited Pakistan several times in 1964, as he had earlier in 1956. Liu Shao-ch'i, president of the People's Republic of China, toured Pakistan in 1966. As indexes of diplomatic rapprochement between the two countries, the usual cultural, scientific, and political delegations exchanged visits. In 1964, Communist China extended a $60 million interest-free loan, its first, to Pakistan, and the next year, Ayub Khan went to Peking on his initial Chinese trip.

While enhancing Chinese ties, Pakistan continued close relations with the United States. Yet, its swing toward the western alignment had been only gradual. As early as 1950, Prime Minister Liaquat Ali Khan accepted an invitation to visit Russia, but instead he went off to visit the United States. Pakistani leaders appeared open-minded on cold war issues, and only in the early 1950's, when it appeared that Russia was siding with India in the Kashmir dispute, did Pakistan swing noticeably to the West. The western alignment culminated in defense pacts in 1954 and 1955. A mutual defense assistance pact was signed with the United States, Pakistan joined the eight-nation SEATO, and it adhered to CENTO. Nehru characterized these Pakistani pacts as aimed against India and as steps toward war.

The United States poured in military aid (figures were not published) as well as economic aid to Pakistan. Between 1951 and mid-1964, almost $3 billion of the latter had been extended. The types of American economic aid were of the usual varied pattern: dollar grants, counterpart funds, technical assistance, commodity programs, and food-surplus agreements. Despite this aid, Pakistanis were often disconcerted by concurrent American economic aid to India, and they became even more disenchanted with the commencement of American military aid to India after the 1962 Chinese Communist border aggressions. Pakistanis argued that the extension of either economic or military aid would abet India's efforts at expanding domestic military programs, which, they claimed, were aimed primarily against them. Pakistanis argued that up to 80 per cent of India's troops were lined up on mutual borders, which necessitated in turn, the argument ran, large Pakistani forces to contain the Indians. Some United States senators from time to time voiced criticisms of the allegedly large numbers of military troops in Pakistan, the expense of maintaining them, and their utility, but Ayub Khan pointed out that his army of 200,000, air force of 15,000, and navy of 5,000 to 6,000 vessels were not unduly inflated in protecting security interests in both East and West Pakistan. In the course of the three weeks' undeclared war with India in September of 1965, over Kashmir, when troops of both countries invaded the territory of the other, the United States suspended all aid programs to Pakistan (as to India). Economic aid resumed the next year, but not military until 1975.

Despite surges of neutralist sentiment in Pakistan, state visits were exchanged. In 1957, Prime Minister Suhrawardy traveled to the United States to seek American support in the Kashmir dispute. Ayub Khan thrice visited the United States. In late 1959, President Eisenhower reciprocated, and President Nixon called a decade later. But by the early 1970's the domestic and international climate had changed. At home, unrest developed over the indirect election process, and Ayub relinquished the presidency to General Yahya Khan. Direct elections were held late the following year for a constituent assembly and five provincial assemblies (Sind, Northwest Frontier, Punjab, and Baluchistan in the west, plus East Pakistan). In the west, the People's Party, led by Zulfikal Ali Bhutto, emerged triumphant, while the Awami League swept the boards in the east.

After inconclusive talks with Bhutto, on March 26, 1971, Sheik Mujibur Rahman, leader of the League, proclaimed an independent Bangladesh. He was immediately arrested and deported to the west. Civil war by now had erupted between Bengali nationalists and the Pakistani army. In the course of the year, over ten million refugees fled into eastern India. The Indian government assisted the East Pakistan guerrilla fighters. Brush fires escalated into a fortnight's full-scale war between India and Pakistan. India, recognizing Bangladesh, occupied the eastern sector for some weeks. Bhutto, now Pakistan's new president, released the Sheik, who returned to Dacca in early January, 1972, to proclaim himself prime minister.

The political balance of the subcontinent altered radically. Many countries recognized the new state. The United States, with historic Pakistani treaties, acted more slowly, but promised a $400 million aid program in the first year. The Chinese Communists, also weighing Pakistani ties, refused to establish diplomatic relations and kept Bangladesh out of the United Nations. In March, 1973, national elections were held in Bangladesh, and the Awami League predictably swept into victory. Pakistan reconciled itself slowly and bitterly to Bangladesh reality. Pakistan in April, 1973, adopted the country's third constitution, which called for a president, prime minister, and bicameral federal legislature. In February, 1974, Pakistan recognized Bangladesh, where, within the year, Sheik Mujibur abolished parliamentary rule and assumed the presidency. In August, 1975 he was killed in a military coup which established a new regime under President Khondakar Mushtaque Ahmed, a former minister of commerce, who was forced to resign by a group of generals in November, 1975. Chief Justice A. M. Sayen of the Supreme Court then became president under a newly proclaimed constitutional amendment, but Bangladesh politics was bogging down in military and civilian factions.

Sri Lanka

Ceylon's history was related to that of the subcontinent, but it proved a variation of the pattern. The earliest tribes, or Veddas, were displaced by the Sinhalese, who began to arrive in numbers from south India in the sixth century B.C. and were subsequently converted to Buddhism. In the eleventh century A.D., Hindus known as Ceylon Tamils arrived, while the later Indian Tamils, brought by the British, came in the nineteenth century to work on agricultural estates. With Sinhalese composing the majority of the population and Tamils collectively a substantial minority, communal problems between the two groups became aggravated in an independent Ceylon. European powers arrived in the sixteenth century. After three hundred years of rule by the Portuguese and Dutch over some parts of the islands, as a result of the Napoleonic wars Ceylon passed to the English, who united the island by 1833. Governed as a crown colony, it was not incorporated, as Burma had been, with India.

Under British administration, prosperity came to Ceylon and agriculture was extensively developed. Tea, rubber, spices, and coconut derivatives became major export commodities. Population rapidly increased. In 1857, it was 1.7 million; in 1927, it was 5.1 million; after the Second World War it had again doubled. Western schools, some of them missionary-sponsored, were introduced. English became the chief linguistic medium. The literacy rate rose to 65 per cent—a high percentage for Asia. Life expectancy was sixty years, and Ceylonese enjoyed the highest standard of living in South Asia. In the course of the first half of the twentieth century, the British made some progress in sharing the government with indigenous peoples. Various missions were sent out from London, and two constitutions were effected. In 1931, the first one bestowed universal adult suffrage, though the British kept most of the powers in their own hands. In the course of the

Second World War, a commission visited the island to propose measures for constitutional changes. In May of 1946, a draft constitution was presented to Parliament, which passed in late 1947 the Ceylon Independence Bill. On February 4, 1948, Ceylon entered the family of nations in a relatively smooth transition from colony to state.

Ceylon remained in the Commonwealth as a self-governing dominion, with the English monarch as a symbol of the free association of equals. Though sporadic talk was raised of its becoming a republic, as India and Pakistan had done, Ceylon into the 1970's maintained its initial structure. The state was headed by a governor general, appointed by the crown. Possessing some effective powers, he appointed half the members of the upper house of parliament, some of the lower house, cabinet members, the prime minister, and the judges. He served as the commander-in-chief of the armed forces, and he was exempt from questioning in any court of law. The parliament was bicameral. The upper house was a continuing Senate of thirty members, of which one-third retired every year and of which half were appointed and half were elected by the lower house. The lower body initially was composed of 101 members, 95 popularly elected for five-year terms and six appointed by the governor general. In 1960, the total was raised to 151 and all were made elective.

More so than India or Pakistan, Ceylon in its first years of independence remained closely tied to Great Britain. Fear of huge neighboring India, and the large Indian minority in the island, heightened ties with Britain. Ceylon's economy was closely integrated with that of Britain's, and estate products, of which the British owned most of the tea and half of the coconut trees, found their main market in the United Kingdom. Many Britons were employed in government posts, and defense arrangements with the British, lasting to 1962, included the use of bases and of the magnificent harbor of Trincomalee in the northeast.

The first major postwar political party was also pro-British. Founded in 1946 prior to independence, the United National Party, a coalition of various groups and aligning the island with the West, governed Ceylon until 1956. The first three prime ministers were from this anti-Communist party. However, rising tides of nationalism and anticolonialism soon manifested themselves. In the elections of 1956, the victor was the Sri Lanka (Ceylon) Freedom Party, led by Oxford-educated Solomon West Ridgeway Dias Bandaranaike. The new government pledged itself to social and economic reforms, and it was strongly tinged with a neutralist approach to the cold war. In spite of his English training, the new prime minister, an Anglican-turned-Buddhist, wished to transform his country into a republic, to cancel the British defense arrangements, to adopt Sinhalese as the national language, and to nationalize essential industries and services.

Tamils reacted to some of these proposals, and violence rose between the two groups. In defense in 1957 Tamils formed the Federal Party to press their cause. They proclaimed mass civil resistance campaigns, they pushed for Tamil as a second official language, and they proposed a federation to give them a greater degree of autonomy. Vicious riots broke out as communal feeling ran rampant. As a climax to the chaos, the prime minister was assassinated in 1959 by a Buddhist extremist. After two other men temporarily filled the position, when the Freedom Party won the April, 1960, elections, his widow, Mrs. Sirimavo Bandaranaike, became the world's first woman prime minister. Strong-minded in her own right, she continued to clash not only with the Tamils, but also with the right wing, the press, domestic and foreign private enterprises, and other religious groups.

Her administration was confronted with problems of rampant inflation, unemployment, strikes, rising governmental expenditures, and unrest in rural areas, the prime minister's primary source of political support. Ceylonese, about 85 per cent literate, for years yearned for higher living standards. Education from kindergarten to university was free, medical treatment cost nothing, and train and bus travel was subsidized. Nearly 18 per cent of the annual national budget of some $460 million went to lower consumer rice prices, of which commodity half was imported. Importing much food, Ceylon endeavored to sustain itself on a tea, rubber, and coconut economy that grew at a rate of 0.8 per cent annually while population spurted at 2.6 per cent. The welfare bill, price supports for farm produce, and salaries for top-heavy government administrative bureaus left little money for capital investment and the hope of creating a diversified industrial economy that might raise the annual per capita income of $123.

With her parliamentary margin down to three seats, and convinced that neither she nor her Freedom Party alone could solve Ceylon's problems, she sought help from Marxist-oriented political groups and the Ceylonese Communist party (founded in July of 1943), prior to the general elections of March, 1965. The electoral verdict rejected the alliance and the ultra-left program of nationalization and of state control of almost all the means of production. But it did not express much enthusiasm for the returning moderate United National Party, the chief opposition party, which formed a new cabinet under Dudley Senanayake, who had before been in office as prime minister. The party had to depend on outside support and on shifting political allegiances of temporarily aligned groups.

The main problem for Ceylon's new government, as for all the previous ones, was to put the economy in order. Ceylon discovered that it could not sustain itself for long on the traditional plantation economy because its population expanded too rapidly for its own welfare. Since the island produced only 40 per cent of its own food, it was obliged to import not only rice but also other necessities of life. With only one-fourth of the land in cultivation, some additional acreage was found to alleviate the problem, but most of this was located in the arid north. Industrialization was limited in scope, and there was little iron and no coal or petroleum. The most remunerative factories were those limited to small-scale production, as food processing, plywood, cement, ceramics, and paper.

In its first six-year $262 million plan (1947 to 1953), agricultural development was emphasized. The second six-year $531 million plan (1954 to 1960) was broader in scope to include industry and social welfare services. But after S.W.R.D. Bandaranaike came to power, he expressed dissatisfaction with the plan. Through the National Planning Council his government announced, instead, the inception of a ten-year program, 1959 to 1968, of economic development, which gave great weight to industry and to state ownership of basic industries. The plan envisaged an investment of $2.6 billion during the period, it aimed to increase the national income by 88 per cent, and it sought to create 1.3 million new jobs capable of taking in not only those currently unemployed but also all fresh entrants into the labor force. Mrs. Bandaranaike carried on the nationalization policies, and put other segments of the economy under government control and direction. Senanayake reversed the trend. The 1970 elections again swept into power the Sri Lanka Freedom Party as dominant faction in a united front. Mrs. Bandaranaike assumed the premiership, and her administration reoriented the country once again. In 1971, a serious leftist uprising, led by youths who believed the administration not tough enough, threatened to disrupt national life, but Russian aid, paradoxically, helped to quell the dissidents. Another five-year plan was begun. On May 22, 1972, in a new constitution to replace the pre-independence document, Ceylon adopted the name Sri Lanka and became a free and independent republic, relinquishing its dominion status.

In world affairs, Ceylon posited friendship toward all and alignment with none. In 1950, the capital city bestowed its name to the Colombo Plan. In 1954, Colombo was again the site of a preparatory meeting of five powers (India, Pakistan, Burma, Indonesia, and Ceylon), who called the Afro-Asian Conference at Bandung. Relations with India were of paramount importance. The problem of people of Indian orgin in Ceylon, who numbered about a million and who had constituted a major stumbling block in Indo-Ceylonese relations since the two countries became independent, reached solution with the signing of an agreement in October, 1964, between Mrs. Bandaranaike and Prime Minister Shastri. Its terms stipulated that 525,000 of the stateless Indians in Ceylon were to be repatriated over the next fifteen years to India, while 300,000 Indians were to be granted Ceylonese citizenship. In May, 1973, Mrs. Gandhi visited Sri Lanka to allay again Ceylonese fears of Indian "expansionism."

In 1955, when Soviet Russia relaxed its veto, Ceylon entered the United Nations. Two years later, it exchanged diplomatic missions with Russia and that same year it commenced to sell tea to the Russians. Trade agreements were subsequently signed. In March, 1958, the Soviets extended a five-year $28.4 million loan with a 2.5 per cent rate of interest to build sixteen industrial projects, later reduced to six because of alleged Ceylonese inefficiencies.

With Communist China, it also maintained trade ties dating

to 1951. As a non-member of the United Nations at the time, it refused to abide by a General Assembly resolution of February that year recommending trade embargoes of goods to North Korea or to Communist China. In 1952, it signed a five-year rice for rubber barter trade agreement with China to sell 50,000 tons of rubber a year in exchange for 270,000 tons of rice. Later agreements projected similar exchanges through 1968. Aid programs augmented trade patterns. In 1957, Communist China gave a $15.7 million five-year grant to improve rubber production. The next year it extended a $10.5 million loan, with a 2.5 rate of interest, to recoup flood damage losses. In 1962 she convoked a six-power conference to negotiate the Sino-Indian dispute, without success. In 1970, after her return to power, her government recognized North Korea, East Germany, North Vietnam and the Viet Cong regime in South Vietnam. In 1972, Communist China extended another loan of $39 million.

The United States maintained diplomatic representation in Colombo since independence. Among its ambassadors was numbered Miss Frances Willis, one of the few women career foreign service officers in the Department of State, who served during the prime ministership of Mrs. Bandaranaike. The United States channeled economic aid to the island to the sum of almost $90 million through mid-1962. The following year, it halted its aid program because of the government's policy of nationalizing the petroleum industry, which included the marketing outlets of two American oil companies, Caltex and Standard Oil of New Jersey, as well as of Shell, owned by British and Dutch interests. The companies claimed $13.6 million as compensation, but Mrs. Bandaranaike's administration offered $9.9 million. After agreement was reached between the more moderate and pro-western government of Senanayake and the affected parties, the two United States companies reportedly settled for $2.1 million each, and Shell for $6.3 million. In early 1966 negotiations resulted in Colombo for the resumption of American aid programs, which subsequently averaged $20 million annually. Ceylon looked to both West and East for sources of aid. The pendulum swung in varying directions at varying times, but geographically small Ceylon concerned itself with politically powerful interests in South Asia.

Not directly related to or administered by Ceylon, but yet

an area of past colonial British interest, were the neighboring Maldive Islands, a group of atolls some 400 miles to the southwest in the Indian Ocean. As a colony administered by the British, in July, 1965, it too was granted independence after some delays. Having promised Maldivians their independence two years previously, the British stayed on to iron out disputes that included the nature of the future British defense posture in the archipelago. The agreement, signed between the Maldivian prime minister and the British High Commissioner in Ceylon, provided for the retention by Britain of the Royal Air Force base and other facilities at Gan, on one of the southern atolls. The independent Maldives entered the United Nations and participated in international life. As the British pulled out of South Asian installations, including those in Ceylon, their military commitments were constantly constricted, partly through choice, to fewer areas and scattered archipelagoes in the Indian Ocean.

Afghanistan

Even more so than Ceylon, Afghanistan had to consider strong surrounding states. Wedged in by Pakistan, India, Russia, and China, it played the classic role of the buffer state, preserving its independence in part because of the interplay of competing western and Asian powers. In 1932, a constitution was formulated by a new ruling house, which had come to power three years previously. The king appointed the cabinet and the upper house or Senate of 45 members for life, but the lower house or National Assembly of 170 was elected. Political parties were proscribed, and Islam was declared the state religion. As a carry-over from ancient times, a council of tribal chieftains continued to exist, and it was consulted by the king in great assemblies when important but ad hoc issues arose. In November, 1933, the young king Mohammad Zahir Shah ascended the throne, but he remained in the background through the years. A first cousin and brother-in-law, Sardar Mohammad Daud, served for a decade (1953 to 1963) as prime minister, until the king, displaying independent action, replaced his relative with Mohammad Yusuf, the first commoner prime minister. The new premier, with a doctor's degree in physics from a German university, exemplified the new intelligentsia rising in the country. After serving for two years, he resigned, to be succeeded by four more prime ministers.

In late 1964, a new constitution was promulgated. It reiterated the structure of a constitutional monarch with a lower house of 215 members elected for four-year terms by universal suffrage and an upper house of 84 members—one-third directly elected, one-third elected by provincial councils, and one-third appointed by the king from among "well-informed and experienced persons." The ministers could be questioned in the parliament and overthrown by parliamentary vote. The document guaranteed basic human rights, a free press, an independent judiciary, and the right to form political parties. No member of the royal family could exercise political power except the king. What was being offered was a peaceful revolution, but the process was slow and involved. Elections were held in 1965, but serious problems faced Afghan leaders. Illiteracy prevailed, an independent press hardly existed, political parties were banned, potential centers of countervailing power barely existed, women played a subordinate role, and private enterprise was negligible in a situation where government agencies absorbed virtually all Kabul University graduates. Problems simmered along until a coup d'etat, headed by former prime minister Daud in mid-1973 while the King was absent on a European trip, abolished the monarchy, proclaimed a republic, and Daud became its president.

Economically, the country was poor, the poverty great, and the literacy rate optimistically placed at 8 per cent. Chief exports were karakul (Persian lamb) sheep skins, wool carpets, timber products, fruits, nuts, and vegetables. Afghanistan's major imports were textiles, machinery, vehicles, building materials, petroleum products, sugar, and tea. Two-fifths of its trade by volume was with the Soviet Union, with which it shared a common boundary, the Oxus river for a great part. There the Afghans developed a sea port as an alternative to Karachi, and the Russians built a modern road, with the highest tunnel in the world, to connect it with Kabul. More difficult surface routes through neighboring Iran gave access to the Persian Gulf. The single largest economic undertaking, with the United States and other countries participating, was the Helmand Valley reclamation and settlement project in the southwestern part of the country. Started in 1946 by the government on the country's largest internal river, the program called for a network of dams, water storage reservoirs, and irrigation ditches to water 400,000 to 600,000 acres of land. These and other national development schemes were blueprinted in three five-year plans, commencing in 1956.

In world affairs, Afghan monarchs and prime ministers were aware of their country's strategic location. They advanced a policy of neutrality or nonalignment in cold war politics and accepted aid from Communist and non-Communist sources. Ever willing to accommodate itself, commencing in 1921 the Soviet Union concluded a treaty of friendship, exchanged diplomatic relations, opened Soviet consulates, and sent Soviet technicians to help construct the country's economy. Rough estimates of postwar Soviet aid by 1973 ranged up to 1.5 billion, half of it economic and the other half military. In December of 1955, Bulganin and Khrushchev journeyed to Kabul, and the latter returned in March, 1960. In turn, King Zahir Shah consulted the Kremlin in mid-1962 (he had been to Moscow earlier in 1943). With Communist China, diplomatic relations were established in 1955, a treaty of friendship and mutual nonaggression was signed in 1960, and a boundary treaty was firmed in Peking in November, 1963, to negotiate peacefully some 80 miles of common borders. By the early 1970's, China had committed about $72 million in aid. The Afghan king visited Peking and President Liu Shao-ch'i journeyed to Kabul.

With the United States, diplomatic relations had existed since 1936, but American aid came into postwar Afghanistan at a rate much reduced from estimated Soviet figures. Between 1953 and mid-1973, United States aid neared $450 million, and all but a few million of it was economic, registered through the standard programs of surplus agricultural commodities, technical assistance, Export-Import Bank loans, and agricultural and education exchanges. In June, 1958, Prime Minister Daud visited the United States, and the king and queen came in September, 1963. Top official Americans traveling to Kabul included Vice President Richard Nixon in

December, 1953, and President Eisenhower, who stopped off for a five-hour state visit on December 9, 1959, and allegedly suffered a slight heart attack in the high-altitude flight over the towering Afghan mountain ranges. Though geography favored the Soviets, the more remote United States evidenced keen interest in the Afghan political scene.

Himalayan States

The Himalayan border states of Nepal, Bhutan, and Sikkim concerned themselves primarily with Indo-Chinese matters. Strategically sprawled along the borders of those largest Asian states, they executed policies of neutrality or accommodation in their own adaptations of the Asian cold war. In Nepal in 1951, the king, displacing the century-old de facto rule of the Rana family, restored sovereignty to the throne, appointed a cabinet, and, in the ensuing year, an advisory assembly. But the workings of the political establishment were not smooth. There were eight governments in as many years, until the promulgation in 1959 of Nepal's first constitution, granted by King Mahendra, who had acceded to the throne four years earlier. The seventy-seven article constitution created a constitutional monarchy with a bicameral assembly, an independent judiciary, a privy council, and a cabinet. In the elections of February–April that year, the Nepali Congress Party, founded in 1949, and influenced by the Indian National Congress party, won seventy-four out of the total of one hundred nine elected seats in the lower house.

Within two years, the new political machinery proved to be cumbersome and ineffectual. In December, 1960, the king abrogated the constitution, ousted the prime minister from office, and forced party leaders into exile. Taking over with a firm hand, in 1962 Mahendra introduced, as had Ayub Khan, a panchayat system of government but of four tiers, from the villages (3,543) and cities (15) through the districts (75) and zones (14) to the national panchayat or assembly. A second constitution that year confirmed the governmental structure and elections got under way. In April, 1963, the national panchayat of 125 members, of which six were nominated by the king and the rest elected by the zonal panchayats and class organizations, was inaugurated in a political system that precluded political parties, which the constitution forbade. The national organ sat in continuous session, with one-third of the members retiring every two years. Executive power rested with the king, who appointed a Council of Ministers. After Mahendra's death in 1972, his son Birendra carried on the system.

As comprehensive economic blueprints, Nepal formulated a five-year plan (1956 to 1961), followed, after a year's interim, by a three-year program (1962 to 1965) of development that stressed land reform, more efficient and modern tax collections, irrigation projects, and the development of industry. Another five-year plan to cost $263 million was projected for 1965 to 1970.

In foreign affairs, Nepal's relations with India, which established diplomatic liaison upon independence, were close but not necessarily friendly. With the United States in 1947 came recognition and a treaty of friendship, but not until 1959 was an American ambassador made resident at Katmandu. American aid, all economic, through mid-1971 totaled $110 million, and some of it was channeled through projects involving Indian participation, as in road-building projects and surplus food sales. In 1960 and 1967 King Mahendra visited the United States, but no top-ranking American official journeyed to Nepal.

With Russia, diplomatic relations were established in 1956; in mid-1958 Mahendra visited Moscow; the next year realized a Soviet aid agreement of $5 million. Communist China loomed more prominently in Nepali aid programs. In 1956, after China recognized Nepal, it extended a $12.6 million grant for the first five-year plan; four years later it followed up with an unrestricted grant of $21 million. In 1961, it signed a highway agreement extending another $10 million to complete a road from Tibet to Katmandu, where it was to link up with a road from the south financed by the United States and India. In October, 1961, a border agreement was signed which defined, according to the watershed principle, the 650-mile Tibet-Nepal border. Endeavoring to steer a neutral course, the Nepalese accepted aid from, traveled to, and coexisted with, both India and China.

Bhutan placed itself firmly in the Indian fold through a 1949 treaty that made it a semi-protectorate by giving India the right to control its external affairs. A king ruled over the country and a prime minister presided over the elementary structure of government that included an assembly of 140 to 200 members. No constitution existed. The Bhutanese National Congress, as the sole political party, operated from Indian territory. Bhutan utilized Indian currency and the Hindi language, sent its youth to India for higher education, closed the Tibetan trade routes which numbered some fourteen passes, and embarked on a $34 million road-building project to link the country with India. Five-year plans (1961–1965, 1966–1971) were underwritten wholly by India. The shortage of educational facilities and of skilled personnel constituted a serious impediment to Bhutan's economic and social progress. There were, in the mid-1960's, only 53 primary and secondary schools; the professional group included only two doctors, two engineers, and one lawyer. In 1962, as part of its modernization program, Bhutan joined the Colombo Plan and made strong pleas for assistance from non-Communist states. Communist China more than once offered aid, but the Bhutanese rejected these offers as well as Chinese claims on 300 square miles of their territory.

Like Bhutan, Sikkim accommodated itself to India. In a 1950 treaty, it gave to the Indians the right to control external affairs, communications, and defense, and to station troops in the country. The chief minister, or *dewan* (a title changed in 1963 to principal executive officer), represented India. A constitutional monarchy with a Buddhist maharajah, it possessed some autonomy in internal affairs, with a cabinet of three and a state council of seventeen, of which twelve were elected and five nominated. Elections were held in 1953 and subsequent years for state council seats, but no constitution was promulgated. Dominant communal Nepali political interests were represented in the National Congress and State Congress parties, who protested rigged elections favoring the minority Bhutiya interests, from whom the king derived. In 1973, demonstrations demanded popular government to replace the monarchy, but the Indian government intervened. To serve as an economic guideline, an Indian-financed seven-year plan (1954 to 1961) was implemented, followed by a five-year plan (1961 to 1966). Close ties continued with India, and domestic dissidence in 1975 caused the legislature to abolish the royal ruling house and seek integration into India as another state. This was achieved that year.

Chronology

Pakistan and Bangladesh

1947, Aug. 15	Pakistan born
1948	Jinnah dies
1954–1955	Pakistan enters western-oriented pacts
1955	One Unit Bill
1955–1960	First five-year plan
1956	Constitution; presidents replace governors general; Islamic Republic of Pakistan proclaimed
1958	Ayub Khan assumes presidency and abolishes premiership and constitution
1959	"Basic Democracies" structure announced; first local elections; land reform act; Eisenhower visit
1960	First presidential elections
1960–1965	Second five-year plan
1961, 1962, 1965	Ayub Khan visits United States
1962	Second constitution announced for a Republic of Pakistan; unicameral national assembly; first national and provincial elections
1963	Pakistan-Communist China border treaty
1965	Second presidential elections; Ayub Khan visits Peking, Moscow
1965–1970	Third five-year plan
1969	Gen. Yahya Khan assumes presidency; abrogates second constitution
1970, Dec.	Elections
1970–1975	Fourth five-year plan
1971, March 26	Bangladesh independence proclaimed
Dec.	Ali Bhutto assumes Pakistani presidency
1972, Jan.	Sheik Mujibur Rahman becomes prime minister of Bangladesh
1973	Third Pakistani constitution adopted; Bangladesh elections
1974, Feb.	Pakistan recognizes Bangladesh
1975, Jan.	Sheik Mujibur abolishes parliamentary rule, assumes presidency
Aug.	Sheik Mujibur killed, new regime established
Nov.	Khondakar Mushtaque Ahmed assumes presidency
	Chief Justice A. M. Sayen replaces Mushtaque Ahmed as president

Sri Lanka

1947–1953	First six-year plan
1948, Feb. 4	Independence achieved
1948–1956	United National Party in power
1954–1960	Second six-year plan
1956–1959, 1960–1965	Sri Lanka Freedom Party in power
1959–1968	Ten-year plan
1963–1966	United States aid programs suspended
1965–1970	United National Party in power
1970	Sri Lanka Freedom Party regains power in united front
1971–1976	Five-year plan
1972, May 22	Ceylon becomes Sri Lanka, relinquishes dominion status to become a republic

Afghanistan

1932	First constitution
1933–1973	Reign of King Mohammed Zahir Shah
1956–1961	First five-year plan
1962–1967	Second five-year plan
1964	Second constitution
1965	Parliamentary elections
1968–1972	Third five-year plan
1973	Coup d'etat establishes republic and presidency

Nepal

1951	King displaces Rana family authority
1951–1955	Reign of King Tribhuvan
1955–1972	Reign of King Mahendra
1956–1961	Five-year plan
1959	First constitution; parliamentary elections
1960	Constitution abrogated
1962	Second constitution; indirect panchayat system of elections
1962–1965	Three-year plan
1965–1970	Five-year plan
1972	Birendra assumes throne

Bhutan

1949	Indian protectorate treaty
1952–1972	Reign of King Jigme Dorji Wangchuk
1961–1965	First five-year plan
1966–1971	Second five-year plan
1972	Accession of Jigme Singhi Wangchuk to throne

Sikkim

1914–1963	Reign of Sir Tashi Namgyal
1950	Indian protectorate treaty
1953	First elections for State Council seats
1954–1961	Seven-year plan
1961–1966	Five-year plan
1963	Accession of Palden Thondup Namgyal to throne
1975	Royal house abolished; integration into Indian political structure

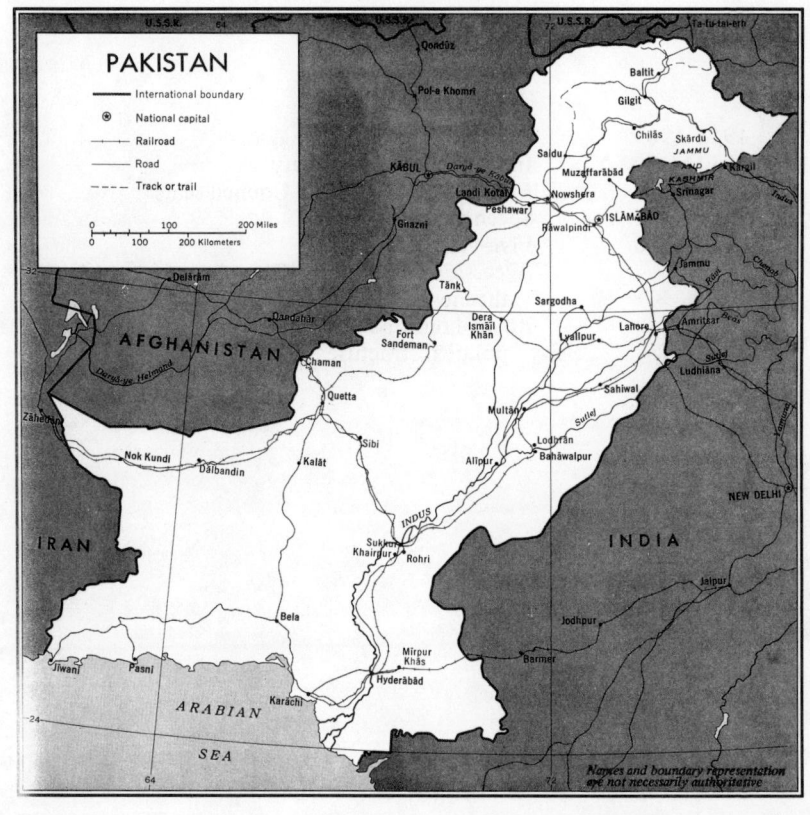

Bangladesh

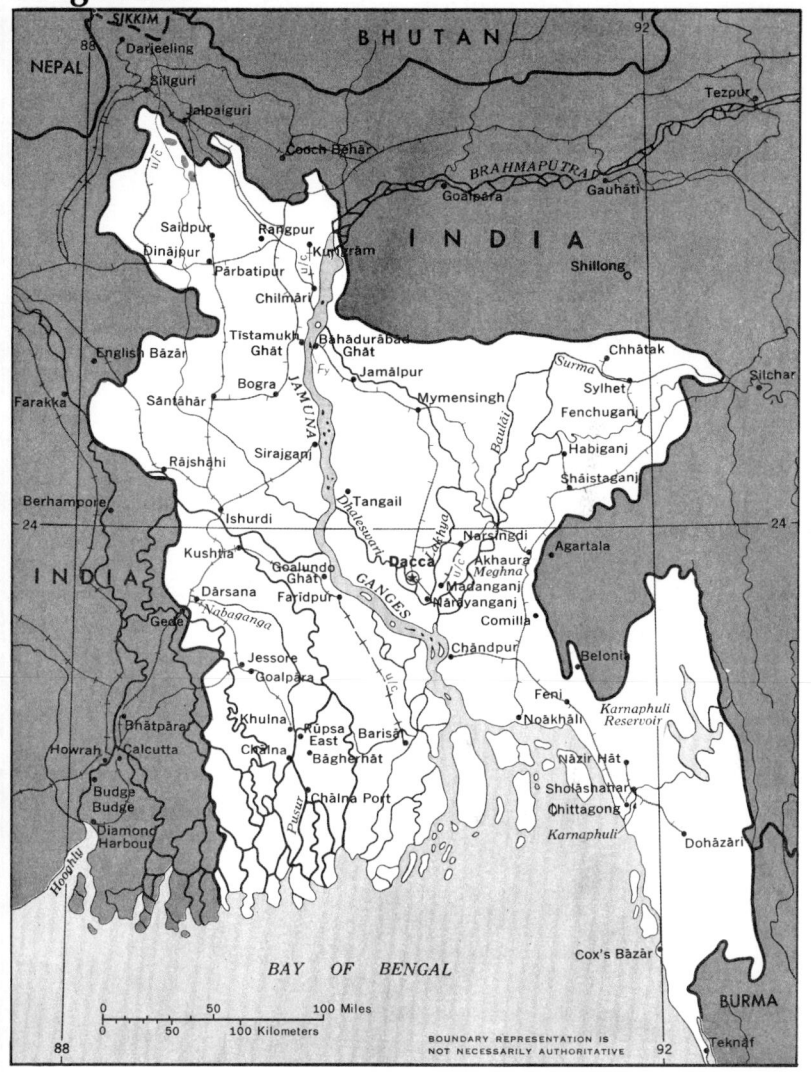

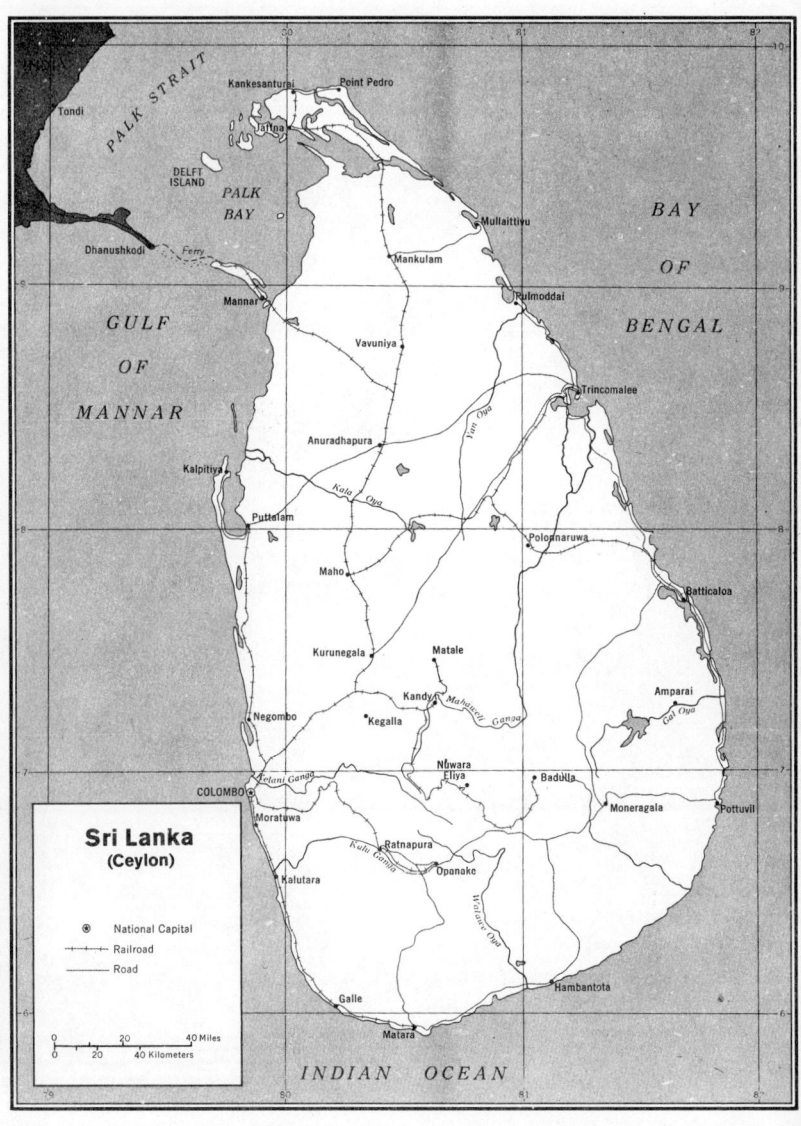

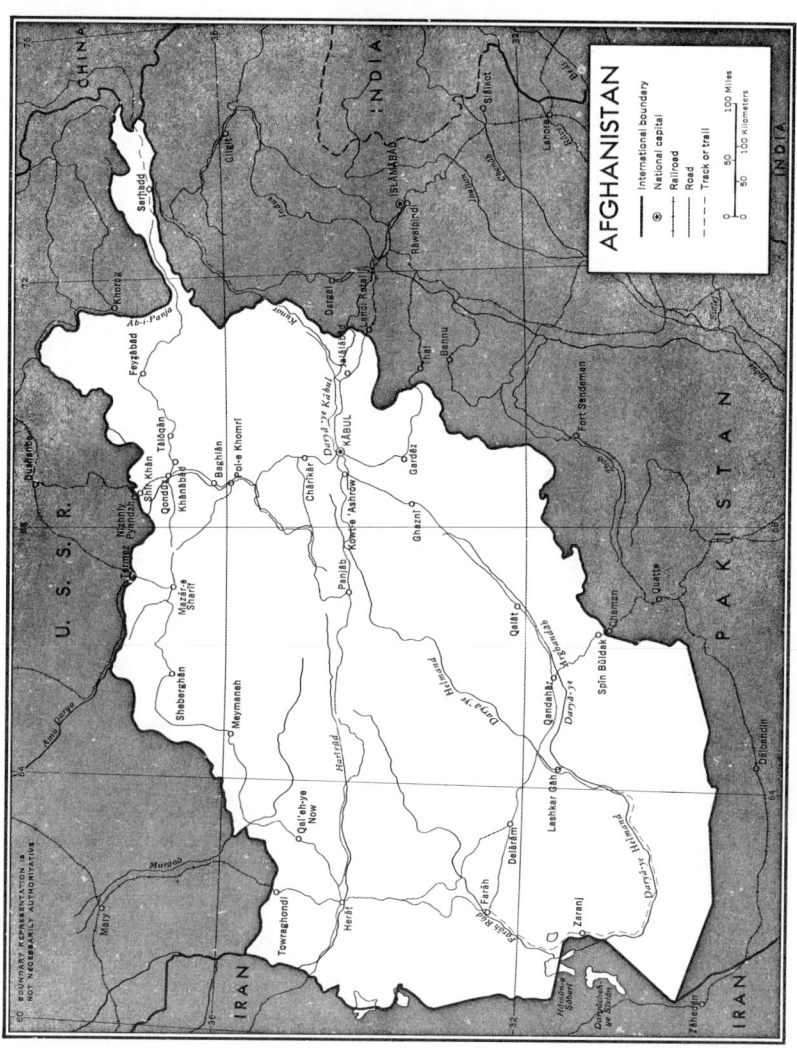

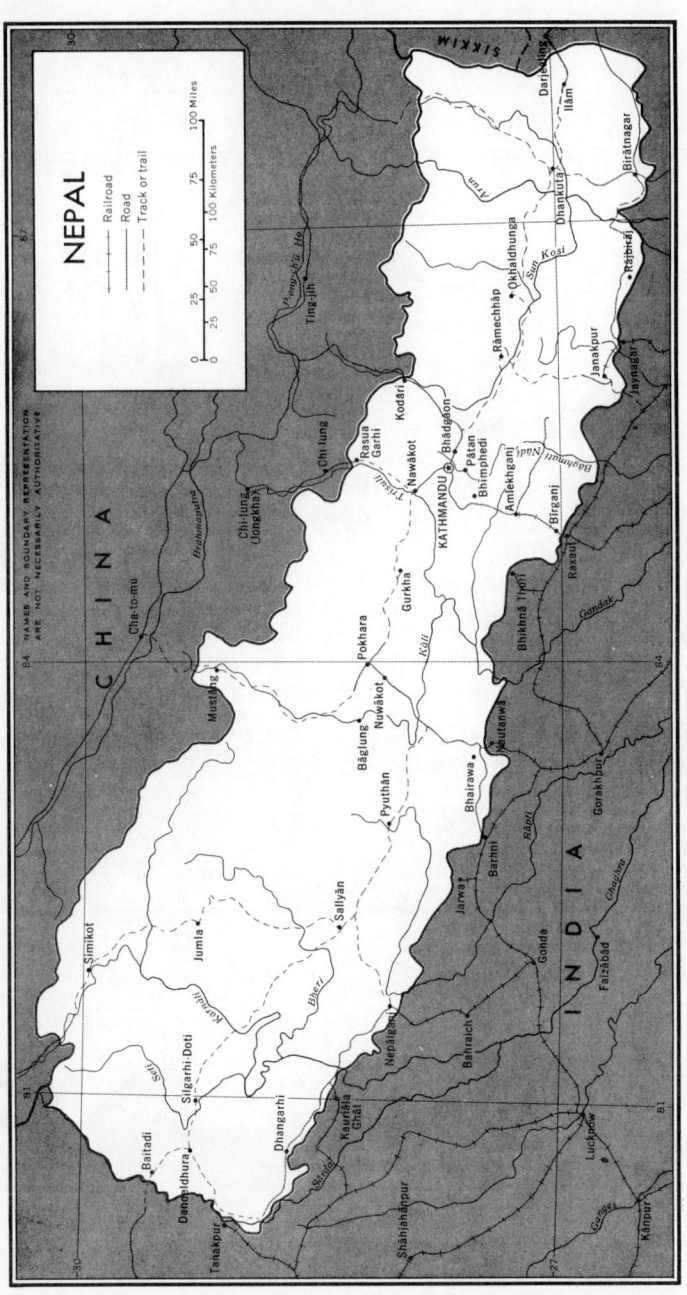

Bibliography

South Asia: General Reference

Brown, W. H. Norman, ed.: *India, Pakistan, Ceylon* (2nd ed., University of Pennsylvania Press, 1963).
———: *The United States and India, Pakistan, and Bangladesh* (3rd ed., Harvard University Press, 1972).
Case, Margaret H., comp.: *South Asian History 1750–1950: A Guide to Periodicals, Dissertations, and Newspapers* (Princeton, 1968).
Davis, Kingsley: *The Population of India and Pakistan* (Princeton, 1951).
de Bary, William and others, comps.: *Sources of Indian Tradition* (Columbia University Press, 1958; paperback, 1964).
Mahar, J. Michael: *India: A Critical Bibliography* (University of Arizona, 1964).
Philips, C. H., ed.: *Historians of India, Pakistan and Ceylon* (London, 1961).
Rose, Saul: *Socialism in Southern Asia* (New York, 1959).
Spate, O. H. K.: *India and Pakistan, A General and Regional Geography* (London, 1957).
Spear, Percival: *India, Pakistan, and the West* (4th ed., New York, 1967).
Talbot, Philipps, ed.: *South Asia in the World Today* (Chicago, 1950).
Tinker, Hugh: *India and Pakistan* (rev. ed., New York, 1967).

Sri Lanka

Bailey, Sydney D.: *Ceylon* (New York, 1952).
International Bank for Reconstruction and Development: *The Economic Development of Ceylon* (Baltimore, 1953).
Kotelawala, Sir John L.: *An Asian Prime Minister's Story* (London, 1956).
Tresidder, Argus J.: *Ceylon* (New York, 1961).
Wriggins, William H.: *Ceylon, Dilemmas of a New Nation* (Princeton, 1960).

Afghanistan

Gregorian, Vartan: *The Emergence of Modern Afghanistan: Politics of Reform and Modernization, 1880–1946* (Stanford, 1969).

Watkins, Mary B.: *Afghanistan: Land in Transition* (Princeton, 1963).

Wilber, Donald N.: *Afghanistan: Its People, Its Society, Its Culture* (New Haven, 1962).

Himalayan States

Chaudhuri, K. C.: *Anglo-Nepalese Relations from the Earliest Times of the British Rule in India till the Gurkha War* (Calcutta, 1960).

Jain, Girilal: *India Meets China in Nepal* (New York, 1959).

Karan, Pradynina N.: *Nepal, a Physical and Cultural Geography* (University of Kentucky, 1960).

Regmi, D. R.: *Modern Nepal, Rise and Growth in the Eighteenth Century* (Calcutta, 1961).

Pakistan

Andrus, J. Russell and A. F. Mohammed. *The Economy of Pakistan* (London, 1958).

Ayub Khan, Mohammed: *Friends, Not Masters: A Political Autobiography* (Oxford, 1967). Ex-president

Bhutto, Zulfikal Ali: *Foreign Policy of Pakistan* (Karachi, 1964). Foreign minister, later president.

Binder, Leonard: *Religion and Politics in Pakistan* (Berkeley, 1961).

Bolitho, Hector: *Jinnah, Creator of Pakistan* (London, 1954).

Callard, Keith: *Pakistan's Foreign Policy* (New York, 1957).

———: *Political Forces in Pakistan* (New York, 1959).

Ikram, S. M. and Percival Spear, eds. *The Cultural Heritage of Pakistan* (Karachi, 1955).

Iqbal, Muhammad: *The Reconstruction of Religious Thought in Islam* (Lahore, 1944).

Jennings, Sir William I., ed.: *Constitutional Problems in Pakistan* (Cambridge University, 1957).

Khan, Liaquat Ali: *Pakistan, Heart of Asia* (Harvard University Press, 1951). A prime minister.

Khan, Sir Muhammad Z.: *Pakistan's Foreign Relations* (Karachi, 1951). A foreign minister.

Maron, Stanley, ed.: *Pakistan, Society and Culture* (New Haven, 1957).

Qureshi, Ishtiaq H.: *The Pakistani Way of Life* (New York, 1956).

Symonds, Richard: *The Making of Pakistan* (London, 1950).

Wilber, Donald N. and others: *Pakistan* (New Haven, 1956).

Indian History: General

Brown, D. MacKenzie: *The White Umbrella: Indian Political Thought from Manu to Gandhi* (University of California Press, 1953).

Dodwell, H. H.: *The Cambridge Shorter History of India* (New York, 1934).

Majumdar, R. C. and others: *An Advanced History of India* (3rd ed., London, 1967).

Moreland, W. H. and A. C. Chatterjee: *A Short History of India* (4th ed., London, 1957).

Nehru, Jawaharlal: *Discovery of India* (New York, 1946).

Panikkar, K. M.: *A Survey of Indian History* (London, 1947).

Philips, C. H.: *India* (London, 1949).

Rawlinson, H. G.: *India, A Short Cultural History* (New York, 1952).

Smith, Vincent A., ed.: *The Oxford History of India* (3rd ed., New York, 1958).

Spear, Percival: *India: A Modern History* (University of Michigan Press, 1961).

Wallbank, T. Walter: *A Short History of India and Pakistan* (New York, 1958, paperback).

Pre-Muslim India

Bagchi, P. C.: *India and China, a Thousand Years of Cultural Relations* (Bombay, 1950).

Basham, A. L.: *The Wonder That Was India* (3rd rev. ed., New York, 1968).

Drekmeier, Charles: *Kinship and Community in Early India* (Stanford University Press, 1962).

Mackay, E. H.: *Early Indus Civilizations* (London, 1948).

Majumdar, R. C. and A. D. Pusalkar, eds.: *The Vedic Age* (London, 1951).

Piggott, Stuart: *Prehistoric India to 1000 BC* (2nd ed., London, 1962, paperback).

Sen, Gertrude Emerson: *The Pageant of Indian History* (New York, 1949).

Smith, V. A.: *Asoka* (2nd ed., Oxford, 1920).

Tarn, W. W.: *The Greeks in Bactria and India* (2nd ed., Cambridge University, 1950).

Wheeler, R. E. Mortimer: *The Indus Civilization* (2nd ed., Cambridge University, 1960).

Muslim India and the Coming of the West

Edwardes, S. M. and H. L. O. Garrett: *Mughal Rule in India* (London, 1930).
Elliot, H. M., comp.: *The History of India as Told by Its Own Historians; The Muhammadan Period*; ed. by John Dowson (8 vols., London, 1867–1877).
Lane-Poole, Stanley: *Medieval India under Muhammadan Rule* (London, 1916; re-edited, 2 vols., Calcutta, 1951).
Locke, J. C.: *The First Englishmen in India* (London, 1930).
Moreland, W. H.: *From Akbar to Aurangzeb* (London, 1923).
———: *India at the Death of Akbar, an Economic Study* (London, 1920).
Oaten, E. F.: *European Travellers in India* (London, 1909).
Prasad, Ishwari: *History of Medieval India* (Allahabad, 1940).
Smith, V. A.: *Akbar, the Great Mogul Emperor* (Oxford, 1917).
Spear, Percival: *Twilight of the Mughals* (Cambridge, 1951).
Srivastava, A. L.: *The Sultanate of Delhi* (Agra, 1953).

British India: General

Coupland, Reginald: *Britain and India* (rev. ed., London, 1948).
———: *The Indian Problem* (New York, 1944).
Hunter, William W.: *A History of British India* (2 vols., London, 1899).
Keith, Arthur B.: *A Constitutional History of India, 1600–1935* (London, 1936).
———: *Speeches and Documents on Indian Policy, 1750–1921* (2 vols., London, 1922).
Kincaid, Dennis: *British Social Life in India, 1608–1937* (London, 1939).
Roberts, P. E.: *History of British India* (3rd ed., Oxford University Press, 1952).
Thompson, Edward and G. T. Garratt: *Rise and Fulfillment of British Rule in India* (London, 1934).

East India Company

Ballhatchet, Kenneth: *Social Policy and Social Change in Western India, 1817–1830* (London, 1957).
Furber, Holden: *John Company at Work* (Harvard University Press, 1948).
Griffiths, P. J.: *The British Impact on India* (London, 1952).
Huttenback, Robert A.: *British Relations with Sind, 1799–1843* (University of California Press, 1962).

Moon, Penderel: *Warren Hastings and British India* (London, 1947; reissue, New York, 1962).

Philips, C. H.: *The East India Company, 1784–1834* (2nd ed., Manchester, 1961).

Spear, Percival: *The Nabobs* (London, 1932; reissue, 1963).

Woodruff, Philip: *The Men Who Ruled India* (2 vols., London, 1954–1955).

Mutiny

Kaye, Sir John and G. B. Malleson: *History of the Indian Mutiny of 1857–1858* (6 vols., London, 1908–1909).

Majumdar, R. C.: *The Sepoy Mutiny and Revolt of 1857* (Calcutta, 1957).

Sen, Surendranath: *Eighteen Fifty Seven* (Delhi, 1957).

British India Under the Crown

Bhandarkar, D. R., ed.: *India* (Annals, Vol. CXLV, 1929).

Coatman, John: *India, the Road to Self-Government* (London, 1942).

Cross, C. M. P.: *The Development of Self-Government in India, 1858–1914* (London, 1922).

Fraser, Lovat: *India under Curzon and After* (London, 1911).

Kondapi, C.: *Indians Overseas, 1838–1949* (Bombay, 1951).

Lee-Warner, Sir William: *The Native States of India* (London, 1910).

Menon, V. P.: *The Transfer of Power in India* (Princeton, 1957).

Minto, Countess: *India, Minto and Morley, 1905–1910* (London, 1935).

Nurulah, Syed and J. P. Naik: *A History of Education in India During the British Period* (Bombay, 1951).

O'Malley, L. S. S., ed.: *Modern India and the West* (London, 1941).

Nationalism

Andres, C. F. and Giriji Mookerji: *The Rise and Growth of the Congress in India* (London, 1938).

Besant, Annie: *Speeches and Writings of Annie Besant* (Madras, 1921).

Bose, Subhas Chandra: *The Indian Struggle, 1920–1934* (London, 1935).

Duffett, W. E. and others: *India, Today, the Background of the Indian Nationalist Movement* (Toronto, 1941).

Fischer, Louis: *The Life of Mahatma Gandhi* (New York, 1950).

Gandhi: *Autobiography, the Story of My Experiments with Truth* (Washington, 1948).
Moraes, Frank: *Jawaharlal Nehru, a Biography* (New York, 1957).
Nehru, Jawaharlal: *Toward Freedom* (New York, 1941).
Panikkar, K. M. and A. Pershad: *The Voice of Freedom, the Speeches of Pandit Motilal Nehru* (New York, 1961).
Prasad, Rajendra: *Autobiography* (Bombay, 1957). First president of Republic.
Saiyid, M. H.: *Mohammad Ali Jinnah* (Lahore, 1945).
Wolpert, Stanley: *Tilak and Gokhale* (Berkeley, 1962).
Younghusband, Sir Francis: *Dawn in India, British Purpose and Indian Aspiration* (London, 1931).

Independent India

Bowles, Chester: *Ambassador's Report* (New York, 1954).
Harrison, Selig S.: *India, the Most Dangerous Decades* (Princeton, 1960).
Kogekar, S. V. and R. L. Park: *Reports on the Indian General Elections, 1951–1952* (Bombay, 1956).
Lamb, Beatrice: *India, a World in Transition* (New York, 1963).
Menon, V. P.: *The Story of the Integration of the Indian States* (New York, 1956).
Mountbatten, Lord: *Time Only to Look Forward* (London, 1949).
Nehru, Jawaharlal: *Independence and After* (Delhi, 1949).
Overstreet, G. D. and M. Windmiller: *Communism in India* (Berkeley, 1959).
Palmer, Norman D.: *The Indian Political System* (Boston, 1961).
Panikkar, K. M.: *In Two Chinas* (London, 1955).
Patel, Vallabhbhai: *Our Indian Problems* (New Delhi, 1949). A deputy prime minister.
Poplai, S. L., ed.: *National Politics and 1957 Elections in India* (Delhi, 1957).
Talbot, Phillips and S. L. Poplai. *India and America, a Study of Their Relations* (New York, 1958).
Weiner, Myron: *Party Politics in India, the Development of a Multi-Party System* (Princeton, 1957).
———: *The Politics of Scarcity* (University of Chicago Press, 1962).
Zinkin, Taya: *India Changes!* (New York, 1958).

Philosophy, Religion, Culture (General)

Clements, E.: *Introduction to the Study of Indian Music* (London, 1913).

Eliot, Sir Charles: *Hinduism and Buddhism, an Historical Sketch* (3 vols., New York, 1921; reprint 1954).

Ghurye, G. S.: *Indian Costume* (Bombay, 1951).

Kabir, Humayun: *The Indian Heritage* (New York, 1955).

Radhakrishnan, Sir Sarvepalli: *East and West in Religion* (London, 1933). Indian philosopher, vice president and president.

——— and Charles A. Moore, eds.: *A Source Book in Indian Philosophy* (Princeton, 1957).

Weber, Max: *The Religion of India, the Sociology of Hinduism and Buddhism*, trans. and ed. by Hans H. Gerth and Don Martindale (Glencoe, 1958).

Hinduism

Bhattacharya, Jogendranath: *Hindu Castes and Sects* (Calcutta, 1896).

Bloomfield, Maurice: *The Religion of the Veda, the Ancient Religion of India (from Rig-Veda to Upanishads)* (New York, 1908).

Buhler, G.: *The Laws of Manu* (Oxford, 1886).

Farquhar, J. N.: *A Primer of Hinduism* (2nd rev. ed., London, 1912).

Hutton, J. S.: *Caste in India* (3rd ed., Bombay, 1961).

Macnicol, Nichol: *Hindu Scriptures* (London, 1938).

Muller, F. Max: *Upanishads* (Oxford, 1879–1882; 2 vols. reprint, 1926).

Prabhavananda, Swami and Frederick Manchester: *The Upanishads* (New York, 1957, paperback).

Radhakrishnan, Sir Sarvepalli: *The Hindu View of Life* (10th ed., London, 1957).

Buddhism and Other Religions

Archer, J. C.: *The Sikha* (Princeton, 1946).

Conze, Edward: *Buddhism, Its Essence and Development* (New York, 1951).

———, trans.: *Buddhist Texts through the Ages* (New York, 1954).

Farquhar, J. N.: *Modern Religious Movements in India* (2nd ed., New York, 1931).

Jaini, Jagmandarlal: *Outlines of Jainism* (Cambridge University, 1940).

Rhys David, T. W.: *Buddhism: Its History and Literature* (3rd ed., London, 1918).

Smith, Wilfrid C.: *Modern Islam in India* (2nd ed., London, 1946).

Whitehead, Bishop Henry: *The Village Gods of South India* (2nd ed., New York, 1921).

Art

Coomaraswamy, Ananda K.: *The Dance of Shiva* (rev. ed., New York, 1957).

———: *History of Indian and Indonesian Art* (New York, 1927).

Rowland, Benjamin: *The Art and Architecture of India, Buddhist, Hindu, Jain* (Baltimore, 1954).

Smith, V. A.: *A History of Fine Art in India and Ceylon* (2nd ed., rev., New York, 1930).

Wilkinson, James V. S: *Mughal Painting* (London, 1948).

Literature

Edgerton, Franklin, trans: *Mahabharata* (2 vols., 3rd ed., Harvard, 1952).

Emeneau, M. B., trans.: *Kalidasa's Sakuntala* (Berkeley, 1962).

Iqbal, Sir Muhammad: *Poems from Iqbal*, trans. by V. G. Kiernan (London, 1955).

Keith, Arthur B.: *A History of Sanskrit Literature* (Oxford, 1928; reprint, 1953).

MacDonell, A. A.: *India's Past, a Survey of Her Literatures, Religions, Languages and Antiquities* (Delhi, 1956).

Menen, Aubrey: *The Ramayana* (New York, 1954). An informal translation.

Narayan, R. K.: *The Bachelor of Arts, a Novel* (East Lansing, 1954). See also his other novels.

Prabhavananda, Swami and Christopher Isherwood, trans.: *The Song of God, Bhagavad-Gita* (New York, 1954, paperback).

Tagore, Sir Rabindranath: *Collected Poems and Plays* (New York, 1956).

Economics

Anstey, Vera: *The Economic Development of India* (London, 1952).

Darling, M. L.: *The Punjab Peasant in Prosperity and Debt* (4th ed. London, 1947).

Gadgil, D. R.: *Industrial Evolution of India* (4th ed., London, 1944).

Misra, B. B.: *The Indian Middle Class* (New York, 1962).

Srinivas, M. N. and others: *India's Villages* (2nd rev. ed., New York, 1960).

South Asia: Political Leaders

I. India

Governors General

Lord Mountbatten, 1947–1948
C. R. Rajagopalachari,
  1948–1950

Presidents

B. R. Prasad, 1950–1962
Sarvepalli Radhakrishnan,
  1962–1967
Zakir Husain, 1967–1969
V. V. Giri, 1969–

Prime Ministers

Jawaharlal Nehru, 1947–1964
Lal Bahadur Shastri, 1964–1966
Mrs. Indira Ghandi, 1966–

II. Pakistan

Governors General
  (*Presidents,* 1956–   )

Jinnah, 1947–1948
Khwaja Nazimuddin, 1948–1951
Ghulam Mohammed,
  1951–1955
Maj. Gen. Iskander Mirza,
  1955–1958
Gen. Mohammed Ayub Khan,
  1958–1969
Gen. Yahya Khan, 1969–1971
Ali Bhutto, 1971–1973
Fazal Elahi Chaudhry, 1973–

Prime Ministers

Liaquat Ali Khan, 1947–1951
Nazimuddin, 1951–1953
Mohammad Ali, 1953–1955
Choudhry Mohammed Ali,
  1955–1956
H. S. Suhrawardy, 1956–1957
I. I. Chundrigar, 1957
Firoz Khan Noon, 1957–1958
Ali Bhutto, 1973–

III. Bangladesh

Presidents

Justice Abu Sayeed Chowdhury,
  1972–1974
Mohammad Ullah, 1974–1975
Sheik Mujibur Rahman, 1975
Khondakar Mushtaque Ahmed,
  1975
A. M. Sayem, 1975–

Prime Ministers

Ta-Juddin Ahmed, 1971–1972
Sheik Mujibur Rahman, 1972–
  1975

IV. Sri Lanka (Ceylon)

Governors General

Sir Henry Moore, 1948–1949
Lord Soulbury, 1949–1954
Sir Oliver Goonetilleke,
  1954–1962

Prime Ministers

Don Stephen Senanayake,
  1948–1952
Dudley Senanayake, 1952–1953
Sir John Kotelawala, 1953–1956

South Asia: Political Leaders (Cont.)

IV. Sri Lanka (Ceylon) (Cont.)

Governors General
William Gopallawa, 1962–1972

Presidents
William Gopallawa, 1972–

Prime Ministers
S.W. R. D. Bandaranaike, 1956–1959
Wijananda Dahanayake, 1959–1960
Dudley Senanayake, 1960
Mrs. Sirimavo Bandaranaike, 1960–1965
Dudley Senanayake, 1965–1970
Mrs. Sirimavo Bandaranaike, 1970–

V. Afghanistan

King
Mohammed Zahir Shah, 1933–1973

President
Sardar Mohammad Daud, 1973–

Prime Ministers (to 1973)
Sardar Mohammad Daud, 1953–1963
Mohammad Yusuf, 1963–1965
Mohammad Hashim Maiwandwal, 1965–1967
Nur Ahmad Etimade, 1967–1971
Abdul Zahir, 1971–1972
Mohammad Musa Shafiq, 1972–1973
Sardar Mohammad Daud, 1973–

VI. Nepal

Kings
Tribhuvan, 1951–1955
Mahendra, 1955–1972
Birendra, 1972–

VII. Bhutan

Kings
Jigme Dorji Wangchuk, 1952–1972
Jigme Singhi Wangchuk, 1972–

VIII. Sikkim

Kings
Sir Tashi Namgyal, 1914–1963
Palden Thondup Namgyal, 1963–1975

INDEX

Afghanistan (A), Bhutan (B), India (I), Nepal (N), Pakistan (P), Sikkim (S), Sri Lanka (SL)

Abdullah, Sheik, 173, 174
Abul Fazl, 92
Act of 1919, 146, 151
Act of 1935, 151, 156-157
Afghanistan, 56, 81, 82, 83, 88, 90, 91, 120, 131, 220
Aga Khan, 143, 153
Agni, 30
Agra, 92, 100, 125
Agrarian problems and reforms, (I) 10, 11, 132-133, 184-185; (P) 218 (SL) 228
Ahimsa, 34
Ahmadnagar, 87, 98
Ahmedabad Textile Workers Union, 190
Aibak, 82, 83
Air transport, (I) 189; (P) 218
Ajanta, 62
Akbar, 86, 89, 91-95
Aksai Chin, 202
Alauddin, 84
Alberuni, 82
Alexander the Great, 41-42
Ali, Mohammed and Shaukat, 143
Ali, Muhammad, 139
Aligarh, 139
All-India Forward Bloc, 180
All-India Independence League, 150
All-India Forward Bloc, 180
ation, 180
Amaravati, 52
Ambedkar, Dr. B. R., 156, 174, 180
American images of India, 6
American studies of India, 6
Amritsar, 99, 147
Ananda, 37

Andaman islands, 176
Andhras, 52, 55, 57
Angkor Thom, 72
Angkor Vat, 72
Anglo-Muhammedan College, 139
Anuradhapura, 18
Apsarases, 69
Arthasastra, 42, 44, 61, 68, 70
Arya Samaj, 138
Aryans, 12, 28-31
Asian Relations Conference (1946, 1949), 198
Asoka, 36, 37, 45, 46, 61
Asoka pillars 46
Assam, 120, 130
Atharva Veda, 31
Atlantic Charter, 159, 161
Atoms for peace programs, (I) 191; (P) 218-219
Attlee, Clement, 151, 163
Aurangzeb, 77, 89, 96-97, 98
Avatar, 67
Azad (Free) Kashmir, 173

Babur, 89-90
Bactria, 41, 55, 56, 57, 58, 63
Bahman, 87
Bahmani, 86-87
Balban, 83
Baluchistan, 26, 131
Bandaranaike, Mrs. Sirimavo, 227, 229,230
Bandaranaike, Solomon W. R. D., 227, 228
Banerjea, Surendranath, 141
Bandung Conference (1955), 199, 229
Bangladesh, 17, 224-225
Barakar Iron Works, 190

INDEX

Barhut, 46
Baroda, 119
Bashir, 224
Basic democracies (P), 212-214
Basic Principles Interim Report (P), 210
Beas river, 41, 171
Belgrade Conference of Nonaligned Nations (1961), 199
Benares, 36, 100
Bengal, 65, 86, 111-112, 114, 117, 124, 130, 136, 164
Bengal partition, 143, 144
Bengal Rent Act (1859), 133
Bentinck, Lord, 120
Berar, 87
Besant, Mrs. Annie, 138, 145
Bhagavad Gita, 32, 34, 67
Bhakra dam, 187
Bhakti, 67, 69, 99
Bharata, 3
Bharatiya Jan Sangh, 180
Bhave, Vinoba, 188
Bhilai steel mill, 190, 200
Bhoodan movement, 188
Bhutan, 131, 236
Bhutanese National Congress, 236
Bhutto, Zulfikal Ali, 224
Bidar, 87
Bihar, 114, 130
Bijapur, 87, 98, 107
Bimbisara, 39
Bindusara, 45
Birendra, 235
Blavatsky, Madame H. P., 138
Bokara steel mill, 190
Bombay, 111, 114, 117, 130, 140, 176
Bose, Subhas Chandra, 152, 157-158, 180
Brahma, 33, 67
Brahman (world soul), 67
Brahmanas, 31
Brahmans, 13, 30, 32, 33
Brahmaputra river, 8, 125
Brahmo Samaj, 124, 138
British Commonwealth, 175, 197
British Indian Association, 141
Buddha, 33, 35-36
Buddhism, 15, 35-39, 45-46
Buddhist art, 46, 53, 58, 62

Bulganin, 200, 233
Bunker, Ellsworth, 205
Burma, 120, 121, 126, 127, 130, 131, 156, 199

Cabral, Pedro, 106
Calcutta, 8, 112, 114, 117, 125, 144, 169
Calicut, 106
Carey, William, 123
Carnatic coast, 8
Caste system, 13, 33, 70
Central Provinces, 130
Central Treaty Organization (CENTO), 203, 223
Chalukyas, 66
Chamber of Princes, 146
Chandernagore, 196
Chandigarh, 177
Chandragupta I, 59
Chandragupta II, 60, 62
Chandragupta Maurya, 39, 42-45
Charter Act (1793), 117
Charter Act (1813), 117, 122
Chelmsford, Viceroy, 145
Chenab river, 171
Chera. See Kerala.
Chiang Kai-shek, 201
China, 72-73
Chittagong, 218
Chola, 53, 55, 66-67
Chou En-lai, 199, 201, 222
Christians, 15
Churchill, Prime Minister Winston, 6, 159, 161
Civil disobedience movements, 148, 154, 159
Climate, 9
Clive, Robert, 113-115
Cloud Messenger, 61
Cochin, 106, 107
Colombo, 18, 107
Colombo Plan, 183-184, 191, 216, 229, 236
Communal electorates, 142, 143, 146, 150, 153, 155-156, 157
Communism (I) 150-151, 181-183; (SL) 228
Communist China, (A) 233; (B) 236; (I) 201-202; (N) 235; (P) 221-223; (SL) 229-230

Community development projects, (I) 187; (P) 218)
Congress Party. See Indian National Congress Party.
Constitutions, (A) 231, 232; (I) 174-176; (N) 234; (P) 211, 214-215; (SL) 225-226
Conti, Nicolo, 88
Cooper, Sherman, 204
Cornwallis, Lord, 118-119, 124
Coromandel coast, 8
Council of India, 129, 142, 144
Council of State, 146
Cripps, 160, 163
Curzon, Lord, 132, 135, 143
Cyrus the Great, 40

Dacca, 17, 126, 170, 209, 215, 219
da Gama, Vasco, 106
Dalhousie, Earl, 121
Daman, 107, 108, 196
Dange, S. A., 150, 182, 183
Danish East India Company, 109-110
Darius I, 40
Das, Chitta Ranjan, 149
Dasehra, 32
Dasyu, 29
Daud, Sardar Mohammad, 231, 232, 233
de Albuquerque, Affonso, 106-107
de Almeida, Francisco, 106
de Barros, João, 108
de Camoëns, Luiz Vaz, 108
Deccan, 8
Delhi, 82, 83, 84, 85, 89, 100, 177, 119, 127, 144
Delhi Pact (1950), 170
Deliverance Day, 158
Demetrius, 55
Devi, 33
Dhamma, 46
Dharma, 33
Diaz, Bartholomeu, 106
Direct Action Day, 163
Diu, 107, 108, 196
Diwali, 32
Diwan, 93-94
Dravidians, 12
Dupleix, Joseph, 113
Durga, 33

Durgapur steel mill, 190
Dutch, 108-109
Dutch East India Company, 108-109
Dyarchy, 146, 156, 157
Dyaus, 30
Dyer, General Reginald, 147

East Pakistan, 17, 209
Eastern Ghats, 8
Economic development plans, (A) 233; (B) 236; (I) 185-187; (N) 235; (P) 216-217; (SL) 228-229
Education, (B) 236; (I) 122, 132, 192-193; (P) 219; (SL) 227
Eight Anthologies, 54
Eisenhower, President, 205, 224, 234
Elections, (A) 234; (I) 157, 162, 177-178; (N) 234; (P) 214-215; (S) 236; (SL) 227-228
Elephanta, 66
Elizabeth, Queen, 197
Ellora, 66
English East India Company, 15, 110, 111-112, 114, 116, 117-118, 122, 124-125, 127
Epic Age, 31
Executive Council, 130, 140, 144, 146, 159, 160

Fa Hsien, 60-61, 72
Fatehpur Sikri, 92
Federal Party, (SL) 227
Firoz Shah Tughluq, 84-85
First World War, 144-145, 148
Ford Foundation, 187, 206
Formosa, 199
Fort St. George (Madras), 111
Fort William (Calcutta), 112
Freedom Party, (SL) 227, 228
French, 109-110, 196

Galbraith, John, 205
Gan, 231
Gandhara, 40, 42, 55, 56, 57
Gandharvas, 69
Gandhi, 132, 137, 140, 147, 148-149, 152, 154, 158, 161, 170, 179
Gandhi, Indira, 179, 205, 229
Gandhinagar, 176

Ganges river, 8, 125
Gangtok, 20
Garuda, 56
Genghis Khan, 83
Geography, (A) 19; (B) 20; (I) 8-9; (N) 20; (P) 16; (S) 20; (SL) 18
George V, King, 144
Ghazni, 81
Ghur, 82
Gilgit valley, 131
Goa, 107, 108, 129, 169, 203
Godavari river, 52
Godse, Vinayak, 179
Gokhale, Gopal Krishna, 137, 144, 148
Golconda, 87, 109
Gondophernes, 57
Gopura, 29
Governor's provinces, 130
Gramdan movement, 188
Granth, 99
Greeks, 56
Guilds, 71
Gujarat, 55, 57, 63, 86, 109, 137, 176
Gujars, 63
Guptas, 59-62
Gurkhas, 120
Guru, 99
Gwalior, 119

Harappa, 27
Hariana, 177
Harijans, 148
Harsha Siladetya, 63-65
Hartals, 154
Hastings, Warren, 118
Health problems and policies, (I) 133, 195 (P) 219
Helmand valley, 233
Herodotus, 40
Hinayana Buddhism, 37
Hindi, 13, 86, 194
Hinduism, classical, 32-34
Hindustani, 13
Hippalus, 54
Holi, 71
Home Rule League 145, 147,
Hsüan Tsang, 64-65, 72
Humayun, 90, 91

Hume, Alan, 142
Huns, 56, 63
Hyderabad, 97, 100, 113, 119, 129, 172, 181

Ibn Batuta, 84
I Ching, 72
Ilbert Bill, 141-142
India Act (1784), 117
India Office, 129
Indian Association, 141
Indian budget and fiscal policies, 133-134
Indian Civil Service, 116, 118, 130-131
Indian Councils Act (1861), 140
Indian Councils Act (1892), 142
Indian international trade, 54-55, 59, 71-73, 100, 124-125, 188-189
Indian Iron and Steel Company, 190
Indian languages, 12-13, 194
Indian law, 134
Indian military structure, 69, 134-135, 162-163
Indian National Conference, 141, 142
Indian National Congress Party, 138, 140, 141, 142, 145, 147, 149, 151, 157, 161, 163, 177, 178
Indian peoples, 12
Indian science, 62
Indian traditional politics, 68-69
Indian traditional society, 69-70
Indo-Gangetic plain, 8
Indonesia, 198, 199
Indore, 119
Indus Basin Development Fund, 171-172
Indus river, 2-3, 8, 125, 171
Indus valley civilization, 27-28
Industry, (I) 189-190; (P) 218; (SL) 228
Indus Water Treaty (1960), 171-172, 220
Institute of Islamic Research (P), 221
Institutes of Akbar, 92
International Control Commissions (Indochina), 199
Investment, (I), 190; (P), 218

INDEX

Iqbal, Muhammad, 153
Islam, 13-14, 77-79
Islamabad, 16, 212, 215

Jahangir, 95
Jainism, 34-35
Jains, 14-15
Jamshedpur, 134
Japan, 199-200
Jatakas, 38, 55
Jati, 33
Jawhar, 81
Jews, 15
Jhelum river, 56, 171
Jihad, 78
Jinnah, Muhammad Ali, 132, 140, 153-154, 163, 169, 210
Jizya, 78
Johnson, Colonel Louis, 162
Johnson, President Lyndon, 205, 224
Jones, Sir William, 122
Joshi, P. C,, 181
Jumma river, 59
Junagadh, 172
Justice Party, 147

Kabir, 86, 99
Kabul, 19, 41, 131, 232, 233
Kadphises I, 58
Kadphises II, 58
Kalat, 131
Kali, 33
Kalidasa, 61
Kalinga, 45, 49, 55
Kalima, 78
Kanauj, 63-64, 77, 81
Kanchi, 66, 212, 218
Kanishka, 58
Kanva, 52
Kapilavastu, 35
Karachi, 16, 212
Karli, 52
Karma, 33
Karnaphuli, 218
Karnataka, 208
Kashmir, 16, 66, 86, 129, 172-174, 202, 219-220, 222
Katmandu, 19, 120
Kautilya, 42
Kennedy, Jacqueline, 224
Kennedy, John F., 204, 205, 224

Kerala, 53, 66, 178, 182-183
Khalji, 83
Khan, Ayub, 17, 171, 210, 211, 212, 214, 220, 221, 224
Khan, Liaquat Ali, 169, 170, 173, 210, 223
Khan Sir Syed Ahmad, 139
Khan, Yahya, 224
Khilafat movement, 145
Khrushchev, 200, 233
Khyber Pass, 131
Kistna river, 52, 53, 87
Kitchener, Lord, 135
Kripalani, Acharya J. B., 181
Kshatriyas, 13
Kumaragupta, 60, 62
Kural, 54
Kurram, 131
Kushan, 56, 57, 58-59

Labor unions (I), 190-191
Ladakh, 202
Lahore, 17, 82, 219
Lahore Declaration (1929), 151
Lapse, doctrine of, 121, 126, 130
Law of Manu, 31
Legislative Assembly, 146
Legislative Council, 130, 140, 142, 144, 146
Lhasa, 132
Literature, modern, (I) 193
Little Clay Cart, 61
Liu Shao-ch'i, 222, 233
Lodis, 85, 89
Lok Sabha (House of the People), 175
Lucknow Pact (1916), 145

Macauley, Thomas, 122
MacDonald, Prime Minister Ramsay, 155
MacMahon line, 202
Macmillan, Prime Minister Harold, 197
Madras, 111, 113, 114, 117, 130, 140. See also Tamil Nadu.
Madras Industry, 23
Madura, 54, 84
Magadha, 39, 42, 65
Mahabharata, 31, 32, 61, 68, 83
Mahalwari, 124

Maharashtra, 66, 97-98, 176, 196. See also Maratha.
Mahasabha, 150, 179
Mahayana Buddhism, 37
Mahendra, King, 45, 234, 235
Mahmud of Ghazni, 77, 81-82
Malabar coast, 8
Malacca, 107
Maldive Islands, 231
Malwa, 57, 58, 86
Mamallapuram, 66
Mansabdars, 93
Maratha, 97-98, 100, 114, 117, 118, 119, 136. See also Maharashtra.
Mary, Queen, 144
Mathura, 56, 58, 81
Mauryas, 39
Maya, 34, 67
Mayo, Katherine, 6
Meerut, 126
Meerut Conspiracy Case, 150
Megasthenes, 42, 43
Menander, 55-56
Mesolithic Age, 23
Mewar, 90
Milinda. See Menander.
Minto, Lord, 144
Mirza, General Iskander, 211, 212
Missions, 122-123
Mizo tribes, 177
Mohenjodaro, 27, 28
Moksha, 34
Mongols, 83, 84
Mons, 72
Monsoons, 9, 54
Montagu, Lord, 145
Mookerjee, Shyam Prasad, 180
Morley, Lord, 144
Morley-Minto reforms, 114
Mother India, 6
Mountbatten, Lord, 163-164, 169, 173
Mount Everest, 20
Muhammad, 77-78
Muhammad of Ghur, 82
Muhammad Tughluq, 84
Multan, 82
Munda, 26
Muslim-Hindu accommodation, 85-86, 136, 145

Muslim-Hindu differences, 80-81, 135-136, 158
Muslim League, 143, 150, 153, 158, 159, 161, 162, 163, 180
Mysore, 117, 118, 119, 120, 196 See also Karnataka.
Mysore State Iron Works, 190

Nagas, 69
Naga tribes, 176-177
Nagpur, 119
Nalanda, 65
Namboodiripad, E. M. S., 182, 183
Nanak, 14, 99
Nandas, 39
Narayan, Jayaprakesh (UP), 180, 181
Narayan, R. K., 193
Narbada river, 59
National Defense Council (I), 159
National Development Council (I), 184
National Development Organization (P), 218
National Planning Council (SL), 228
Natural resources, (I) 9-10; (P) 17, 218
Nearchos, 42
Negapatam, 107, 109
Nehru, Motilal, 149
Nehru, Jawaharlal, 132, 140, 152, 158, 163, 169, 170, 171, 173, 177, 178-179, 184, 195, 197, 199, 200, 201, 205, 220
Neolithic age, 26
Nepal, 120, 234-235
Nepali Congress Party, 234
Nicobar islands, 176
Nikitin, Athanasius, 87, 88
Nirvana, 36
Nixon, Richard, 205, 224, 233
Nonalignment policy (I), 195
North East Frontier Agency, 202
Northwest Frontier, 17
Northwest Frontier Province, 130, 164

Objectives Resolution (P), 210
One Unit Bill (P), 16, 210
Orissa, 114, 130
Oudh, 60, 114, 119
Oxus, 57, 232

INDEX

Paes, Domingo, 88
Pahlavas. See Parthians.
Pala, 65
Paleolithic Age, 23
Pallava, 53, 55, 66
Panchayats (N), 234-235
Panchshila (Five Principles), 196
Pandit, Madame Vijaya Lakshmi, 205
Pandya, 53, 54, 66
Paramountcy, doctrine of, 121, 130
Parsis, 14
Parthia, 55
Parthians, 56, 57, 58
Partition, 153, 164
Pataliputra, 49, 50
Pathans, 19
Persia, 40, 66
Peshawar, 58, 59
Peshwa, 98
Philippines, 199
Phillips, William, 162
Phizo, 177
Planning Commission (I), 184
Plassey, 113
Pliny, 43
Pondicherry, 110, 113, 129, 196
Poona, 98, 100, 119, 137, 142
Population problems and growth, 11, 133, 184
Porbandar, 148
Portuguese, 106-108, 196
Porus, 41, 42
Praja Party, 181
Praja Socialist Party, 181
Prakrit, 31
Press (I), 123, 140, 193-194
Princely states, 16, 129, 157, 172-173
Punakha, 20
Punjab, 8, 17, 40, 121, 130, 132, 164, 171
Punjabi Suba, 177
Puranas, 32, 61
Pushtu, 19, 220
Pushtunistan, 220
Pushymitra, 49, 52

Questions of Milinda, 56
Quetta, 131

Radhakrishnan Vice President, 205
Rahman, Sheik Mujibur, 224
Rajagopalachari, Chakravarti, 180
Raja Todar Mal, 92, 93
Rajputan, 63, 66
Rajputs 63, 80, 81, 83, 84, 90, 92, 96, 99
Rajya Sabha (Council of States), 175
Rama, 32, 33
Ramakrishna, 138
Ramanand, 86
Ramanuja, 67, 86
Ramayana, 31, 32
Ranadive, B. T., 181, 182, 183
Rana family, 20, 234
Rann of Cutch 220
Rashtrakutas 66
Rashtriya Swayamsevak Sangh (RSS), 179-180
Ravi river, 171
Rawalpindi, 16, 212
Ray, Satyajit, 194
Raziya, 83
Record of the Buddhist Countries, 60
Regional Cooperation for Development (P), 220-221
Regulating Act (1773), 117
Rig Veda, 31, 33, 55
Rockefeller Foundation, 206
Roosevelt, President Franklin D., 6, 159, 161
Round Table Conferences, 155-156
Rourkela steel mill, 190
Rowlatt bills, 147
Roy, M. N., 150-151
Roy, Ram Mohan, 123-124, 138
Rudra, 30
Ryotwari, 124

Saint Thomas, 57
Saisunagas, 39
Saka era, 58
Sakas, 56, 57, 58
Sakyamuni. See Buddha.
Sama Veda, 31
Samudragupta, 59-60
Sanchi stupa, 46, 53
Sankara, 67
Sanskrit, 30-31

INDEX

Santha Rama Rau, 7, 193
Satyagraha, 148
Savarkar, V. D., 179
Sayyid, 85
Scylax, 40
Scythians. See Sakas.
Second World War, 158, 160, 162-163
Secretary of State for India, 129, 156
Seleucus Nicator, 43, 45
Sena, 65, 80
Senanayake, Dudley, 228, 229, 230
Sepoy mutiny, 125-127
Sepoys, 113, 118, 122
Serampore, 110, 123
Servants of India Society, 137
Shah Jahan, 95-96
Shah, Mohammad Zahir, 231-233
Shakuntala, 61
Shariat, 78
Shastri, Lal Bahadur, 179, 200, 224, 229
Sher Khan (Sher Shah), 90-91
Shias, 78
Shiromani Akali Dal, 180
Siddhartha Gautama See Buddha.
Sikhs, 14, 99, 100, 117-118, 121
Sikkim, 120, 197, 236-237
Sikkim National Party, 236
Sikkim State Congress, 236
Simla Conference (1945), 162, (1914), 202
Simon Commission, 151; report, 155
Sind, 17, 26, 40, 42, 71, 79, 120, 130, 132
Singh, Master Tara, 180
Singh, Ranjit, 121
Sinhalese, 18, 225, 227
Sita, 32
Siva, 33, 67, 69
Sivaji, 98
Slave Dynasty, 83
Soan culture, 23
Socialist movement, 150, 180-181
Socialist Party (I), 180-181
Social reforms, (I), 191-193; (P) 219
Somnath, 81
Southeast Asia, 55, 71-72

Southeast Asia Treaty Organization (SEATO), 203, 222, 223
Soviet Union, (A) 233; (I) 200-201; (N) 235; (P) 221; (SL) 229
Sri Lanka, 18, 225-231
Srinagar, 173
States Reorganization Act (1956), 176
Stupa, 36, 38
Sudras, 13
Sufi, 78, 99
Suhrawardy, H. S., 209, 224
Sunga, 49, 52
Sunnis, 79
Surat, 100, 109, 110, 111, 144
Sutlej river, 121, 171, 187
Sutras, 31
Suttee, 41, 120
Swadeshi, 143, 148
Swaraj, 143, 148
Swaraj Party, 149-150
Swatantra Party, 180
Sylhet, 164

Tamil Nadu, 208
Tamils, 53-54, 66, 67
Tamils (in Sri Lanka), 18-19, 225, 227
Tandojam atomic center (P), 219
Tantrism, 37-38, 65
Tarapur atomic plant, 191
Tashkent Conference (1966), 221
Tata family, 134
Tata Iron and Steel Company, 190
Taxila, 41, 49, 57
Telegana, 181-182, 188
Thailand, 199
Theosophical Society, 138
Tibet, 64, 65, 131-132, 196, 201
Tilak Bal Gangadhar, 137, 142, 148
Timur, 84, 85
Tranquebar, 110
Trincomalee, 18
Tripitaka, 38
Trombay atomic plant, 191
Tughluqs, 84

Udaipur, 90
Ujjian, 57

Unionist Party, 147
United Nations Commission on India and Pakistan (UNCIP), 173
United National Party (SL), 226
United Provinces, 130
United States, (A) 233; (I) 161-162, 202-203, 203-205, 206; (N) 235; (P) 223-224; (SL) 230
Universities Act (1904), 143
Untouchabilities Offenses Act (1955), 192
Untouchables, 13, 61, 191-192
Upanishads, 31
Urdu, 13, 85-86, 215

Vaisyas, 13
Vardhamana Mahavira, 34-35
Varna, 33
Vedanta, 31
Vedas, 30, 33
Veddas, 18, 225
Vedic India, 30
Vellore, 126
Vernacular Press Act (1878), 141
Viceroy, 130, 157
Victoria, Queen, 127
Vijayanagar, 87-88
Village Agricultural and Industrial Development (P), 218
Vindhyas, 8, 65
Vishnu, 33, 67, 69
Vivekananda 138

Wahhabiism, 138-139
Warsak, 218
Wellesley, Lord, 119
West Pakistan, 16-17
Western Ghats, 8
Willis, Frances, 230

Xavier, Saint Francis, 107
Xerxes, 40

Yaksas, 69
Yavanas, 56
Yayur Veda, 31
Younghusband expedition, 132
Yüeh-chih. See Kushan.
Yusuf, Mohhamad, 231-232

Zamindars, 124, 185
Zoroaster, 14